Monica Dickens

Monica Dickens MBE (1915–1992) was the great-granddaughter of Charles Dickens. Expelled from St Paul's Girls' School, she was then sent to a finishing school in France, before returning home to life as a debutante: 'The deb scene and the dances were absolute agony. I would look at the waiters and the maids at balls and know for certain that they were having a better time than I was. So I wanted to belong with them, down there where there was a bit of life.' She then spent two years as a cook and general servant, which she wrote about in her first book, *One Pair of Hands* (1939). The book, published when she was twenty-four, was a bestseller and established her reputation as a writer. During the Second World War, Dickens trained as a nurse and again successfully recounted her experiences in *One Pair of Feet* (1942). This was followed by *My Turn to Make the Tea* (1951), which is based on her time working as a reporter on a regional newspaper. In her career she wrote over fifty books for both adults and children, including the *Follyfoot* series, and for twenty years wrote a much-loved column for *Woman's Own*. She was also involved with the NSPCC, the RSPCA and the Samaritans.

Also Published by
Virago Modern Classics

My Turn to Make the Tea

ONE PAIR OF FEET

Monica Dickens

Introduced by Lissa Evans

VIRAGO

This edition published by Virago Press in 2022
First published in Great Britain by Penguin Books in 1942

1 3 5 7 9 10 8 6 4 2

A CIP catalogue record for this book
is available from the British Library.

ISBN 978-0-349-01601-6

Typeset in Goudy by M Rules
Printed and bound in Great Britain by
Clays Ltd, Elcograf S.p.A

Papers used by Virago are from well-managed forests
and other responsible sources.

Virago Press
An imprint of
Little, Brown Book Group
Carmelite House
50 Victoria Embankment
London EC4Y 0DZ

An Hachette UK Company
www.hachette.co.uk

www.virago.co.uk

To Doady and Denys

INTRODUCTION

First things first: yes, she was related to that Dickens; Monica's grandfather was Charles's eighth child. As she writes in her autobiography, 'Some of the Dickens aunts were outraged that I had played fast and loose with the name. Just as parents think that sex stopped with their generation, Charles Dickens was expected to be the last family member to appear in print.'

The economy and wit of this passage – as well as the unexpected mention of sex – is a good introduction to the author's writing style. Her language is crisp and vivid. She never lingers on scenes, and rarely embellishes; as a reader, you may sometimes crave more detail, but you'll never be bored.

It was boredom that kick-started Monica's writing career. At twenty-one, as 'an aging and disgruntled ex-debutante' whose friends were busily getting married, she decided to get a job. With no qualifications and no skills apart from those gained during six lessons at Le Cordon Bleu in Sloane Street, she called herself a cook, and began a series of 'below-stairs' jobs that took her from bijou London flats to the servants' hall of a country house. After she'd been demonstrating her slovenly inefficiency in the role for two years, a publisher she met at a party suggested that she write a book about her experiences.

'Writing,' as she recorded later, 'is easier when you don't know how difficult it is. I wrote *One Pair of Hands* in three weeks, sitting in the corner of the drawing-room sofa, with people coming in and out, and arguing, and having tea, and playing the piano and making jokes.' 'Don't worry about how to write. Just write,' the publisher Michael Joseph had told her, and she did.

She followed *One Pair of Hands* with two further volumes of autobiographical novels: *One Pair of Feet*, based on her wartime nursing experiences, and *My Turn to Make the Tea*, in which she lightly fictionalised her job as a journalist on a provincial newspaper. I first read all three as a teenager, and more than forty years later could still precisely remember certain phrases and descriptions: the girl with the gift for inappropriate simile ('she's bleeding like a dustbin'); the pink-faced couple dancing ('cheek to cheek, like two blancmanges meeting'); and the terrible, terrible wartime food ('great bowls of beetroot' and 'the pink rubbery circles known as Luncheon Sausage').

Reading these books again has been a pleasure; they are vastly entertaining, shrewd, youthfully judgemental and not always kind, but the latter quality means that the moments of pathos and horror – the aftermath of a chemical factory explosion; the young woman forced to seek an abortion – are all the more unexpected and affecting. Monica's naked curiosity and general bolshiness are easy to identify with, and as a narrator she always tells us what we're longing to know – it's like listening to a friend's anecdote, and egging them on: 'And what happened next?'

One Pair of Feet was published eighty years ago, and the narrative begins right at the beginning of the Second World War, when it seemed that 'women, having been surplus for twenty years, were suddenly wanted in a hundred different places at once'. Monica, having decided against joining the services ('I didn't think my hips would stand the cut of the skirt') is inspired by the film *Vigil in the Night*, a wildly romantic melodrama set in a hospital, and plumps for nursing. Within minutes of starting, she discovers that the reality is nothing like the fiction: 'In 1940, a nurse was a cross between a nun and a slave, and a probationer was as low as the bedwheels off which on slow afternoons we scraped the built-up wax with a kitchen knife.'

This is a world of six-day weeks and thirteen-hour shifts, where junior nurses are forbidden ever to speak directly to a doctor and where starched cuffs must be worn outside the ward at all times, even if the nurse in question is running to find ice for a patient with a torrential nosebleed. Monica, while trying to be a good nurse, is unable to ignore the endless, petty rules and restrictions that turn a busy and difficult job into utter servitude. Even off duty, there is no privacy as the nurses' rooms are regularly inspected by the matron. 'You did not belong to yourself any more; you were a cog in community life. It was a wonder we did not have to throw all our clothes into a common wardrobe at night, and draw at random in the morning.' The enforced association leads to both deep friendships and instant enmities, and Monica's whipcrack descriptions of her new companions are one of the joys of the book, as are the recollections of a social life that largely involves dancing with drunken servicemen on remote air bases, followed by cycle rides through the blackout, arriving back just in time to begin another exhausting shift.

When *One Pair of Feet* was published, in 1942, nursing newspapers were outraged by it, mostly on the grounds that the book was funny: 'Miss Dickens is not acquainted with the sane and wholesomely humoured women and girls who do their work with balanced minds and intelligence.' Monica herself insisted that what she had written was the truth, 'with a few changes to satisfy the laws of conscience or libel', and it reads exactly as this.

My Turn to Make the Tea, the third in what might be thought of as a 'real-life trilogy', is less episodic than the others, and shaped rather more like a novel, though there is no doubt that it is based closely on the author's experience of writing for the *Herts Express*. Monica was, by this time, in her thirties, and living on her own in a rural cottage full of animals. Refreshingly, none of the three books dwell on her single status, or address what was, at that time, an unusual degree of independence for a woman; nevertheless, in the mixed environment of the newspaper office, her sex ensured that her status was very low, something that she stoically accepts: 'you also have to take your turn at filling inkwells, fetching copy paper, washing-up yesterday's cups in cold water, and making tea. If you are the only girl, it is nearly always your turn.'

I love local newspapers, both as a reminder of my own provincial childhood and as a mainstay of historical research. The fictional *Downingham Post* is utterly recognisable, with its determinedly unsensational headlines ('COUNCIL VETOES NEW SEWAGE PLAN FOR BUNGALOWS'), its carefully transcribed list of attendees at the Licensed Victuallers' Ball, and its detailed account of the sparsely attended Saturday football fixture between Plastic Novelties 1st XI and Bingley Engineering Reserves.

Every event, however small, needs to be reported if a sixteen-page weekly newspaper is to be filled, and Monica touchingly conveys the mixture of drudgery and pride that the junior reporter's job entails, wondering 'whether readers might detect the stuff of genius in the report of Miss Alice Tufton's wedding, over which I had tried so hard, but which had come out exactly like all the other wedding reports that ever had been and ever would be in the *Downingham Post*.'

But this is also a boarding-house book, in the classic British tradition, and the stories of the inhabitants of 5 Bury Road (Monica being one of them), and their landlady, the loathsome Mrs Goff ('not exactly fat, for her bulk was more sideways than from back to front, like a drawing in a child's picture book of the unpopular nanny run over by a tram') weave through the book, giving a satisfying shape to the narrative.

These three volumes reflect only a small part of Monica Dickens's life. She married late, moved to America, adopted two children, worked with the NSPCC and the Samaritans, and helped to found the first branch of the latter in the USA. Her many novels, for both adults and children, cover subjects as disparate as child neglect and late romance, coercive relationships and lifelong friendship. She gives the impression of somebody who never stopped moving, who relished all experience and who rarely went along with expectations. The world of her youth is very different from our world, but she writes with a directness that cuts zestfully through the decades.

Lissa Evans

CHAPTER ONE

One had got to be something; that was obvious. But what? It seemed that women, having been surplus for twenty years, were suddenly wanted in a hundred different places at once. You couldn't open a newspaper without being told that you were wanted in the Army, the Navy or the Air Force; factory wheels would stop turning unless you rushed into overalls at once; the AFS. could quench no fires without you, every hoarding beckoned you and even Marble Arch badgered you about ARP.

The Suffragettes could have saved themselves a lot of trouble if they had seen this coming. Men's jobs were open to women and trousers were selling like hot cakes in Kensington High Street.

I could not make up my mind what to be. A lot of fanatics rushed into the most uncongenial jobs they could find, stimulated by a glow of self-sacrifice that lasted until the novelty wore off or the cold weather set in, but it seemed to me that, provided that it was just as useful, it was no less patriotic to do something enjoyable. At first sight, the choice seemed so enormous that the trouble was to decide what not to be, but a closer inspection revealed so many snags that in the end the trouble was to find something to which I had a hope of sticking.

The Services? I didn't think my hips would stand the cut of the skirt and I wasn't too sure about my legs in wool stockings. Besides, I've never been much good at drilling and all that. My school reports used to say: 'Not amenable to discipline; too fond of organising,' which was only a kind way of saying: 'Bossy.' I might have been a success as a general, but not as a private.

The AFS? I did try that for a while, but at the beginning of the war there was not much doing and I got discouraged with sitting all day in the back room of a police station knitting and eating sticky buns with six assorted women and a man with a wooden leg. At the end of a week, we all knew each other's life histories, including that of the woodenleg's uncle, who lived at Selsey and had to be careful of his diet. Messenger Dickens had once been down to Roehampton to fetch the Commandant's handbag and a small tube of soda-mints from the shelf in her bathroom.

A bus conductress? The idea appealed, but what about the questions of flustered old ladies, up for a day's shopping and an egg mayonnaise tea on the fourth floor? Anyway, although money is lovely to handle, they say that everything you eat afterwards tastes of coppers.

The WVS? I once accompanied six evacuees down to Exeter. Never again. They punctuated their questions with a piercing 'Eh?' or 'What say?' One of them had impetigo, and when we arrived, they all wanted to go straight back to Dalston East.

I worked in a canteen for a while, but had to leave after a terrible row with Mrs Templeton-Douglas, who could never subtract one-and-ninepence from half-a-crown. I sold some of her jam tarts for a penny instead of twopence, thinking they were the throw-outs we had bought at the back door of the ABG.

The Land Army? One saw oneself picking apples in a shady hat, or silhouetted against the skyline with a couple of plough horses, but a second look showed one tugging mangel-wurzels out of the frozen ground at five o'clock on a bitter February morning.

Ministries and Bureaux? Apart from the question of my hips again (sitting is so spreading), they didn't seem to want me. Perhaps it was because I can only type with three fingers and it always keeps coming red.

The Censor's Office I knew was in Liverpool, and I'd been there once.

Nursing? The idea had always attracted me, even in peace-time, but I suppose every girl goes through that. It's one of those adolescent phases, like wanting to be a nun. It was reading *Farewell to Arms*, I think, that finally decided me, though what sort of hospital allowed such goings on, I can't imagine. However, that was the last war. Then I saw Madeleine Carroll in *Vigil in the Night*, and that settled it. I was going to be a nurse in a pure white halo cap, and glide swiftly about with oxygen cylinders and, if necessary, give my life for a patient and have my name on a bronze plaque in the hospital corridor. I wasn't going to be a VAD either, I was going to start training and be a real probationer. I had heard that VADs never get beyond the charing stage and that however long they work in hospital it doesn't count as any training if they want a nursing job after the war. We were being tactfully prepared at the moment for a long war, and I thought I might at least emerge from it with some letters after my name and an enamel badge on my bosom. Provided, of course, that I could pass the exams, but having had all my meals for a month with a trained nurse when my sister was having a baby, I didn't see that they could be so difficult, if conversation was any guide to intellect.

Once the idea had taken root in my brain, it flourished there. The more I thought about it, the more certain I was that this was the one thing I really wanted to do. Perhaps it had been my *métier* all along and it had taken a war to disclose it. I was not discouraged by people who told me that the first year, at least, would be

3

unrelieved drudgery. I had weathered two years of being a cook-general, and knew that there were no lower depths to be plumbed.

I wasn't particular what hospital I joined, provided it was somewhere that could take me straightaway. A decision loses its charm unless you can act on it immediately. It's like buying a new hat; you must wear it at once or not at all. I wrote to several hospitals and some answered and some didn't, and the nicest reply came from the matron of the Queen Adelaide Hospital in Redwood, a town about fifty miles north of London, famous for being the home of a certain sort of sausage pie, probably delicious locally, but disappointing in a cellophane wrapper on station buffets. A doctor I knew had been House Surgeon at this hospital and had recommended it if only for the fact that the bath water was always hot.

Miss Sarah P. Churchman (Matron SRNCNB) had asked me for references, so I dictated one or two to friends with solid-looking surnames, saying how reliable and intelligent I was, with a gentle sympathy of manner that would make Florence Nightingale look like an SS Guard at Dachau. Sarah P. wrote again, still pleasantly, asking me to go down for an interview. She sounded deep-bosomed and motherly, beloved of all nurses and patients and the confidante of doctors in their matrimonial troubles. I prayed that she would like me.

Once when I was loitering at the bookshops in the Charing Cross Road, I had bought a ninepenny book called *Sister Fairchild's Manual for Nurses*. I hadn't really wanted it, but I had been so long at the stall reading the old volumes of the *Strand*, that the proprietor, a man with sinister pock-markings, had begun to hover. I had bought the first book that came to hand to pacify him while I finished the last instalment of *Lady Bracken's Ball*. Remembering it now, I took it with me in the train to Redwood to find out what demeanour befitted a nurse.

4

That ninepence was well spent. It's a wonderful book, thick as a Bible and full of illustrations of nurses in high caps and birds'-nest hair doing strange things with kettles and primitive gas jets. I stopped looking out of the carriage window at the different effects that the inhabitants of Watford had made out of a sliver of back garden and settled down to 'The Ethics of Nursing. Qualities required of the New Probationer. She must be a woman of intelligence,' I read, 'healthy physique, perfect temper, obedience, punctuality, cleanly habits, able for hard and exhausting work both mental and physical.' I didn't see that I was any of these things, so I went on to 'Dress', which told me that rustling petticoats, squeaking shoes and jingling chatelaines were out of place and that outdoor wear should be neat, modest and not likely to excite comment. I was wearing a navy blue Burberry, low-heeled shoes and a hat that had once been quite a saucy sailor on the back of the head, but was now harmlessly turned up at the back and down at the front. I seemed to be all right there and went on to learn that one should never sit in the presence of superiors and that conversation with them should be limited to essentials, personal matters and opinions being kept in the background. I wondered *en passant*, what I should do if Sarah P. offered me a chair, leaned her deep bosom confidingly on the desk and said: 'Now tell me *all* about yourself!'

Then my eye was caught by: 'A Nurse's duties to herself', and I read with horror that: 'passing her life amid scenes of sorrow, suffering and the results of what she has been taught to consider sin, she tends to become morbid, introspective and cramped. She must, therefore, off duty, seize every chance of relaxation in any sphere unconnected with her work.' I shut the book hastily, before I could get melancholia, and divided my attention between the greening country and the morning paper.

I was nervous, no doubt about it. I did so want to be a nurse, and I was frightened of the alien atmosphere of hospital. The smell alone makes you feel an outsider and everyone is always so much too busy to be bothered with you.

The train swung round a curve and I saw the miscellaneous architecture of Redwood Court: crenellations, spires, bastions, curly white balconies and fake Tudor outbuildings, all jumbled together in a dip of the rolling park, like oddments in a schoolboy's pocket. Then a spur of trees rose between us and in a moment we were drawing into the station, for there are no suburbs on this side of the town.

Up till now, I had known Redwood simply as a place that one passed through on the way to somewhere else. One only stopped there to buy a paper, or a genuine Redwood pie, or because Aunt Ethel was car-sick, or perhaps to lunch at the Rowan Arms in case there might not be anywhere farther on. Now, as I came out of the station, asked my way, and struck off up the High Street, I viewed it with more attention. If I got my wish, this might be my world for the next three years – stifling thought. Every inch of this pavement, every shop, and perhaps even some of the faces thronging by me, might soon be only too familiar. I should know by heart each vase and cabinet in the window of this antique shop, every signed photograph of unknown artistes in the window of that hairdresser. My feet would wear a path round the counters of this Woolworth's, and how many cups of coffee might I not drink at the 'Blue Lady Café. Morning Coffee, Light Luncheons, Dainty Teas. Meet your friends'?

It was quite a long walk to the hospital and by the time I reached the gates I was determined to be accepted. I was not going to have come all this way and have had this uphill walk for nothing.

To visualise the geography of Redwood, you must imagine the hill on which the town is built as a rather squat pudding and the town as a sauce which has been poured over and run down the sides. A currant in the sauce has remained sitting right on top of

6

the pudding and this is the Queen Adelaide Hospital. The side from which I approached it is the business part of the town, where the shops and cinemas and traffic lights are. The sauce has run thickly here, and collected in lumps, but down the other side, it slips into the pattern of residential Redwood: Victorian at first with large sombre houses in shrubby gardens, then brighter and more modern, a whole network of little streets of semi-detached paradises that you can own if you will only join the such-and-such building society. Beyond this, the custard has dripped on to the green plate of Suffolk plain in scattered properties that are not quite country houses, yet not of the town. They are inhabited by people who have guaranteed subscriptions at libraries and get their groceries from Harrods and give tennis parties with one court and eight people, who have to spend the afternoon protesting that they would really much rather sit and watch.

Between the business and the residential, two other streams of life run down from the hospital: on one side the long straight rows of mouldering plaster houses, where dressmakers live and little drapers' shops sell everything on earth except what you want, and women with piled up hair let rooms. On the other side, an untidy slum rackets cheerfully down to the very park wall of Redwood Court, which consequently is crowned with spikes and broken glass. Halfway down the hill on this poorer side there exists, for no apparent reason, an arty colony, full of little converted slum houses with blue doors, and women with corduroy trousers and hairnets and big dogs on leads, and grubby men in sandals. How and why this odd little collection got here is a mystery, for Redwood is anything but artistic, but they all seem quite happy and do mimes and plays that nobody else will produce, in a rather smelly basement theatre.

Over all this then, broods the hospital, and the sight of it as I breasted the hill and crossed the road to the main gate did nothing to put me at my ease. Illness is ugly enough, Heaven knows,

7

without its headquarters emphasising it. Surrounded by iron railings, it stands back from the road in a gravel space, large and square and grey, with symmetrical oblong windows and a slate roof from which tall iron chimneys pour dark brown smoke. The human etcetera, like the glimmer of a nurse's cap at a window, or a man in a white coat crossing the gravel, or the geraniums in the window of the porter's lodge, seemed insignificant beside the shadowy massif. I went in at the gate, past an assortment of cars and an ambulance, drawn up with tails to the railings, and stood uncertain on the open space. Like most hospitals, it is impossible to find the way in. The main door is tight shut and says 'NO ENTRANCE', another says: 'ORTHOPAEDIC CLINIC, OUTPATIENTS ONLY', and another 'X-RAY. NO ADMITTANCE WITHOUT A GREEN CARD'. At last, in a corner I saw a notice that whispered: 'Enquiries and Visitors' and I made for it, flattening myself in the doorway to let a blanketed stretcher go by. I came to a sort of glass ticket office, which must have been built round the vast man who sat palpitating inside. His blood pressure seemed terrifying, but I supposed the hospital knew about that.

I had to show him the Matron's letter before he would believe that I had an appointment with her. He seemed sceptical, and I imagined that he too adored Sarah P. and had constituted himself her bulldog to keep off annoyance. Following the direction of his short pointing arm, I went down a corridor, turned a corner and was immediately lost. He had promised me I should see a flight of stairs with a green door at the top, but instead, there was an archway, with a choice of three passages beyond. I plunged down one of these at random, meaning to ask the way, but never actually summoning the courage. I wandered for ages up and down stairs and along stone corridors past doors behind which Heaven knew what was happening and which opened now and then to let a preoccupied, unapproachable figure dash in or out. Sexless hands on the walls pointed the way to wards with names

8

like 'Grace Annie Sprock' and 'Herbert Waterlow', but I was too worried to wonder who these people were. I was beginning to wish I had pretended to be a cripple and made the porter take me up in the lift, when, pushing through some swing doors, I suddenly found myself in a ward full of beds. A clamorous woman with great shoes bore down on me.

'I'm in charge here,' she cried. 'You can't come breaking into the ward like this. Who do you want to see? You can't see them now.'

I thought of bursting into tears and saying: 'I've come to see me Mum,' but as I looked up at her, my eye was caught by the fantastic, equine length of her false teeth and I could think of nothing else. I stared.

'You can come back on Wednesday,' she was saying. Today was only Monday, and I thought how awful if I really had wanted to see me Mum. Still gaping, I was being shooed backwards by her apron and great feet, until eventually, I bumped into the swing doors and recovered my speech.

'Please,' I stammered, 'I want to see the Matron. I can't find the way.'

'Good gracious!' Her eyebrows shot up and so did her top lip, revealing a sweep of shining orange gum. She turned and clicked her fingers at a scurrying girl. 'Nurse Rogers! Show this – er – show the way to Matron's office and come straight back. Quickly, Nurse. You've got plenty of work to do here without jaunting over half the hospital.'

Nurse Rogers ducked her head and scuttled through the doors without looking to see whether I was following. I kept her in sight with difficulty. As I turned into a passage, she would be just disappearing at the far end, and up the stairs; all I knew of her was her back draught. At last I found her waiting for me on one leg outside a door that was, as promised, green, and said 'PRIVATE' across the top.

9

'Here,' she panted, already poised for flight, ducked her head again and was off like a water-rat. I hoped that I should never be sent to that ward. I should never stand the pace.

When I had recovered my breath, I knocked on the green door and waited, wearing a polite face. No answer. I knocked again, still politely, and then a bit louder. Perhaps Sarah P. was deaf. These dear old bodies often are. At last, I opened the door just far enough to put my head into the room, leaving my body still politely outside. There was nobody there. It was a chintzy room with a lot of photographs and a vase of Michaelmas daisies in the grate. An ordinary drawing-room, except for the large flat-topped desk that faced the door. As there was no one in the passage, I ventured in, and wandered round looking at the photographs: groups of nurses mostly, dating from the Crimea, or visiting Royalty with wide hats and waistless coats and bouquets. I inspected the desk for anything scandalous like dope or a forged death certificate, but there was not even a hypodermic syringe. I wandered out again and leaned against the wall in the passage, wondering whether I had come at the wrong time or even on the wrong day. Supposing she had been expecting me before. She would never take me now; *Sister Fairchild* had harped a lot on punctuality. Still, having got so far, I was determined to see the Matron if it meant propping up the wall till night-time. I waited nearly an hour, patiently at first, then restless, then aggrieved and was just beginning to feel really sorry for myself when I was brought bolt upright by a clack-clacking on the linoleum at the end of the corridor.

The figure that approached was like a plucked boiling fowl. This couldn't be the Matron – not with that corrugated perm, those horn-rimmed spectacles and that scrawny neck poking out of the high collar of her black dress. Why, she was quite young – well, not old enough to be a Dear Old Body, anyway. True, she wore no apron and she was slowing down, but this couldn't be

Sarah P. Churchman. Where was the bosom, where the dewlaps and the benevolent, understanding smile? She paused with her hand on the door-knob, cleared her throat efficiently and said: 'Yes? What is it?'

I told her what, and she said: 'Come in. You're early,' and went into the room, her back managing to convey that I should have opened the door for her.

She looked sparer than ever seated behind the big desk. Her face was very lined and the thick, distorting lenses of her spectacles made expressionless marbles of her eyes. She had obviously led a life of great rigour and was determined not to allow anyone else the indulgences that she had missed. I felt very soft and stupid, and forgot all about the *Fairchild* code of manners. I didn't think she would take me. She seemed vaguely scornful and only acknowledged my answers to her questions by writing scratchily with the back of a relief nib. She didn't even say: 'I'll let you know,' or 'I'll write,' or any of the things with which people usually conclude an interview. She simply said: 'Very well, thank you,' cleared her throat again and swinging open a ledger, busied herself with some accounts. I plodded out over the thick carpet, started off despondently in no particular direction, and, surprisingly, found myself almost immediately back at the bulldog in his glass kennel. I realised now why he had been so sceptical of my appointment. Sarah P. was obviously not much of a one for callers.

CHAPTER TWO

Of course, as soon as my hopes had been realised, I had qualms. These were increased in the Buckingham Palace Road, where I bought my uniform. The stockings were so very thick and black, the collar so very high and hard, the striped dress so very like a 1920 Kodak Girl advertisement. I tried the whole thing on at home, and took it off again quickly, before anyone could see. It made me look like one of the Noah family – as if I ought to be on a stand. Perhaps I would pass among a lot of others all dressed the same, and the cap might help. The shop had told me that I would be shown how to make it up at the hospital, but at the moment, it was just a flat linen semicircle that bore no resemblance at all to a Madeleine Carroll halo.

Sarah P. Churchman, orderly as a calendar, would not take me until the beginning of the month, so I had a few weeks to fill in before my incarceration. Following the current craze, I collected scrap-iron. I borrowed a barrow and a small hairy pony called Tiger from the local mews, and went from house to house annoying people. I usually managed to call at an inconvenient time: people were either out, or in the bath, or cooking the dinner, but even so, apart from a man who abused me for being a propagator of infernal machines, the response was soon too great for the pony. People began to unload boilers and bedsteads and garden rollers on to us, and poor Tiger just took one look and sagged at the knees. His union wouldn't allow it, he said, and I had to hurl the things feverishly on to the pavement again before he lay down in the shafts.

Then the Borough Council lent me a motor dustcart, complete with two dustmen called George and Arthur. George was waiting to be called up. He was young and earthy, with fair hair that sprang out in front of his cap like coiled wire. Arthur was older and more staid, the home philosopher type, who liked a kipper to his tea, and would trundle out quiet sagacities over the bones. We went round to all the residential hotels of Bayswater. Labyrinths of cellars under the pavement yielded tons of stuff that had been accumulating since accommodation was sold out for Queen Victoria's Jubilee. George and Arthur were just as keen to ferret it out as I. I suppose it was a change from cabbage stalks and tea-leaves wrapped in sodden newspaper.

At the Grand-Carlton, watched from behind the lace curtains of the lounge by mouldering old ladies, George kept staggering up with cistern after cistern, plug and all. Although they had been rusting there for years, they were in good shape, unused as far as one could see, and afterwards when we were knocking off for tea and hot pies at Andy's Café, we tried to fathom the mystery of the Seven Cisterns in a Cellar. Perhaps the owner of the Grand-Carlton had once come into money and had planned lavish expansion, beginning with the plumbing. In the first flush of enthusiasm, he had ordered these seven cisterns before the Will was proved, and when he found that he would not, after all, be able to build anywhere to put them, he had hanged himself with one of the chains, and his relations had not the heart to sell the cisterns. A ribald cousin called Cyril had suggested erecting one as a tombstone, but had been frowned down. Or, said Arthur, someone might've bought 'em cheap at an auction and put 'em by for a rainy day. He had a great uncle who would buy anything if it was a bargain and whose wife had left him when he came home with a mechanical bar-room piano that broke into the *Lily of Laguna* every time an underground train passed underneath the house.

After a few days, Arthur let me drive the lorry and even work the lever that tipped our load on to the dump. I could have gone on doing this for ever, but Redwood called and I had to leave off and start trying to get my hands clean again. We got a little paragraph in the local paper saying that we had collected ten tons of scrap-iron, and I got a furious letter from a man in Porchester Terrace, who said that the old bath I had removed from his cellar was his air-raid bunk.

I arrived at Redwood station on the evening of September 30th and didn't know what to do. I couldn't walk up the hill with my luggage, I couldn't see any buses, and I didn't think it would look right to sweep up to the Queen Adelaide in the dowager Rolls-Royce that seemed to be the only available taxi. I asked about buses and everyone told me something different, so eventually I decided to take the Rolls and get out before I got to the hospital. Perched on the worn beige whipcord, my nose almost touching the paper carnations, I clung on to the strap, tense with apprehension. It was drawing so near – the agony of being plunged into a new world, of being stared at and criticised, of only learning the right things to do by doing the wrong ones first. All too soon, we were at the top of the hill, and I must get out and be a nurse or else go home again and never know what it was like. The iron gates towered above me as I went through, and I felt very exposed as I lugged my suitcases across the gravel and presented myself at the glass box.

The blood pressure seemed worse. Surely more veins flamed round his nose now than before.

14

'New nurse?' he panted. 'Wrong door. Nurses don't use main door. Round to your right.' He motioned with his arm and then leaned back, exhausted, against a notice board. I slunk away, thankful that at least I had not arrived in the Rolls. Following the grey wall of the hospital, past all the doors with their different prohibitive notices, I came at last to one larger and heavier than the rest, with a great lock on it.

'NURSES' HOSTEL', it said, but it might just as well have said 'GAOL'. A smaller door within the big one was ajar, but I didn't like to go in. I rang. Nothing happened, and I knocked with the same result. I was beginning to feel unwanted, when I heard footsteps behind me and turned to see two nurses arm in arm, wearing red cloaks over more convincing replicas of the uniform that weighted my suitcase. They stopped giggling to give me a silent stare as I stepped respectfully back, then they pushed open the little door and went giggling inside. I followed them and stood in a dim, square hall, trying to make out what sort of a place I was in. Dusk had drifted in from outside and there was no electric light to chivvy it out. Instead, dim blue bulbs made the ghostly twilight of a photographer's dark room. Evidently this was their way of saving blackout material and I wondered if the bedroom lights were the same.

Before me, the lights made fading pools down the polished wood of a long corridor, and on my left, stairs turned upwards into obscurity. The two nurses had gone this way and looking after them, I saw a blur of face hanging over the banister at the top.

'I say,' said a very young voice, 'did you want something?'

'Well, yes, I – er – I mean, I'm a new nurse. I've come.'

'Oh, bad luck,' she said depressingly. 'Still, I suppose you want to find your room. I wonder where they've put you. Half a mo – I'll come down and look on the board. You go and make the coff, Con,' she called back as she came downstairs, 'I shan't be a jiff.' Everything with her was an abbreviation. Striking a match by the notice board, she searched for the number of my room. 'Presuming the Ass Mat's remembered.'

The who?'

'Assistant Matron; old Fanny Harriman. Mad as a hat.'

Nevertheless I was prepared to like her for having the same name as my mother. It was only later that I discovered that Fanny is a derisive applied to any Sister. Seeing my name on the list gave me a thrill of belonging, and removed some of that feeling of having come on the wrong day. The nurse led me down the long blue tunnel of the corridor. 'There's hardly anyone about now,' she said. They're not off dute. Here you are, here's your boud.' She opened the door and sniffed. 'Furniture pol. They only clean your room when you first come here. Makes a good impresh,' she said and disappeared.

The light was not dazzling, but at least it was not blue. When I had climbed on a chair and removed the green shroud from it, I could see quite a lot. Thank goodness, anyway, one had a room to oneself. I was dreading getting up at six o'clock, but it would be impossible in company. It's bad enough to have to see one's own face at that hour, let alone anybody else's.

The *décor* of my little home was simple. Wardrobe, black iron bed on wheels, chair and dressing-table with swing mirror that overswung itself and reflected only your stomach. Behind the cupboard door there was a long list of rules, starting with 'Nurses must throw open their windows and turn their mattresses before going to breakfast,' and ending with: 'No nails to be driven into walls,' and 'trunks and boxes to be sent to boxroom and not kept under the bed.' That was to stop anyone flitting in the night. I felt rather harassed and homesick, did a little desultory unpacking, sat down on the bed and brooded, read the rules again and wondered whether I ought to tell anyone I had come.

Then the noise began. At first it was just an odd shout, a heavy tread, a door banging. Soon it had swelled to a crescendo of voices, door-slamming that made my mirror swing farther each time, and tramping feet that could be nothing else but the nurses coming off duty. My door burst open and a fat girl with a shiny face filled the doorway. Her apron bulged before her as if it held all the family washing.

'Oh, hallo,' she said. 'Are you a new Pro?' I supposed I was.

'D'you know how to put on your uniform?' I thought so.

'D'you know how to make up your cap?' I didn't.

'Well, you'd better come along and I'll show all of you together.' I was relieved to hear that there were other new girls besides me. It made me feel less inferior, but when we met, in the fat girl's bedroom that smelt of cheap powder and tea-leaves, I began to feel inferior again. There were three of them, two Welsh and one Yorkshire, called Gunter. They had all been nursing before – the Welsh girls at a maternity home in Caerphilly, and the other one at some hospital unspecified. She was completely silent, but managed to convey the impression of knowing a lot. Whenever our fat instructress, while she was sewing a specimen cap, told us some rule or point of etiquette, the Welsh girls would say: 'Yes, we know. Like at Caerphilly,' and the dumb one would nod and drop her heavy lids, as if it were an old story. I wanted to ask a lot of questions, including: 'When do we eat?' but when the senior nurse asked if we had had supper, the others all said they had, so I did too.

I looked hideous in the cap she made up for me, because she would try it on right down over my eyes. The others didn't look too bad; they had more curls or something, and the Yorkshire girl was hideous anyway, with or without a cap. Afterwards, she and I went out for a silent walk. At least, I went out for some air and she loomed beside me and stuck, like some large dog on a string. The air on the hill was cool and fresh. 'I like the night,' said Gunter. 'It's more quiet than the day.' With which simple truth her conversation ended and we returned in silence through the little door and were parting halfway down the long corridor, at the door of my room, before she spoke again.

'I'll call for you on the way to breakfast,' she said. 'You and I'll be friends, shall we?'

Thump – crash! 'Six o'clock, Nurse!' – crash! as the door shut again. Whoever it was had given me the shock of my life. I thought I had only just gone to sleep – a heavy, weighted sleep from which awakening was unbearable. I lay for a while, stunned, unable to believe that my night was at an end. So this was what it was like to rise at six!

Only the thought that Gunter might be upon me before I was dressed, forced me out of bed and into my clothes. My fingers were still numb with sleep and fumbled with the studs and buttons that caged me in. Remembering one or two astringent remarks from Sarah Churchman on the subject of make-up, I washed my face and let it shine on. Now for the cap. The more I fiddled with it, the more shapeless it became. I pushed it forward, I tipped it back. One way I looked like a half-witted waitress, the other like a half-wit. It was all very well for Madeleine Carroll; she had probably had hers made up by Adrian, not by a girl with fingers like half a pound of sausages. A door banged and feet hurried past my room. In a sudden panic that I was late, I left the cap to its own devices, rocking insecurely somewhere on the top of my head, and trod into my respectable black shoes. No time to wait for Gunter, even if I had wanted to, but when I opened the door, there she was, waiting outside like the Rock of Ages, with her heavy jaw slightly dropped and her eyes like lead coins.

Nurses were coming out of doors all along the corridor and we followed the stream away from the entrance hall, through a door and up endless flights of stone stairs. Gunter climbed like a stayer, but I felt exhausted for the day. In the dining-room, there must have been about fifty nurses, gathering round the three long tables like a flock of white birds. It's a funny thing that whatever nurses may look like individually, *en masse* they make an oddly pure effect, like a billowing flight of doves, that belies their conversation.

Someone shoved me into a place and we all stood behind chairs while a pretty little Sister with a tired face said Grace. The tables were covered with green oilcloth and set with crockery that looked as if it ought to have GWR on it. The empty table across the end of the room had a tablecloth and napkins; evidently the Sisters breakfasted later. Breakfast was strong tea, a brittle bit of bacon with the rind on, and as much bread and margarine as you could eat. And could some of them eat it! The doorsteps that they got through at an hour when my stomach was only just stirring in its sleep, were staggering. Gunter told me she could never fancy marge from a child, so she ate her way solidly through three hunks of dry bread. I looked at the other nurses and wondered whether I should ever be able to tell them apart. Thank goodness, they took no notice of us new girls. They just ate and drank and passed the bread up and down the table and said: 'Sugar, please,' more like pigeons now than doves. Opposite me, the two Welsh girls were talking away, unawed, about Caerphilly, with which Redwood evidently compared unfavourably.

Degrees of seniority were marked by the number of red stars you wore on the bib of your apron. At my table, they had none, at the table beyond, they all had one and beyond that, two. At a smaller table in the bay of the window, sat a dozen awesome girls with no less than three stars and special caps to boot. Among the two-pips, I spotted the abbreviating girl of the night before. She looked young and fresh, like a baby waked up for its bottle. She was talking to a girl who stood out from the others, not from particularly striking looks, but from an enviable air of not belonging to the herd, of looking at it from outside and probably laughing at it. I didn't think I liked her.

When Sister called the roll, she paused at my name, which sounded as odd as one's own name always does in public. 'You go to William Forrest Ward, Nurse,' she said. Gunter was destined for Herbert Waterlow, which was a relief. After Grace, I went into the corridor with the mob, which dispersed in all directions, while I stood lost. Someone grabbed my arm. It was the girl I had noticed at breakfast. She had straight fair hair, like clear honey, and a bony face, plain but attractive.

'Come on,' she said; 'you're on my ward.' She caught up someone on the stairs and they went down talking, while I followed behind like a servant. I felt terribly shy going into the ward and thought that the eyes of all the beds were upon me. I hardly dared look to see whether they were male or female eyes, and I was relieved to find that in spite of William Forrest, it was a women's ward – that was slightly less unnerving. I felt all hands and would have felt all feet too if my dress had not been long enough to shelter them. The others stood about for a moment yawning and calling good-morning to some of the patients, then we took off our stiff cuffs, rolled up our sleeves and began to make beds. That is to say, Nurse Richardson (square, with a healthy crop of black hair on her upper lip) took one side of the bed and did miraculous things like mitreing corners and whipping draw sheets in and out under obediently raised bottoms, while I, on the other side, fumbled and muddled, tore my nails and was convinced that I should never make a nurse.

Each hour of that first day strengthened my conviction. I could do nothing right, it seemed, and everything wrong. I was always either in the way or not there when I was wanted. I had always either not given enough time and trouble to something or else should have been finished an hour ago.

I can give no very coherent account of that first day, because it was a completely incoherent day. It seemed that I had special duties – the most menial, I could see that all right. The Staff Nurse, one of those with three stars and frills on her cap, strung off to me what these duties were, but I couldn't take them all in at once. Simple items that even I could do, like sweeping the floor, and cutting bread and butter, alternated with mysteries like 'doing one's side', 'seeing to the gastric feeds' and 'getting diabetic specimens'. I spent most of the day pottering about after somebody, saying: 'What do I do next?' and in this way discovered what the nurses were like.

The Staff Nurse, who was called Nurse Ketch, was slick and soulless. She was usually too busy doing something frightfully responsible to reply. When I came trotting up with my innocent question, expecting some commendation for having finished the job before, she said: 'I told you what to do once,' and went on being highly skilled with glass trolleys and bits of rubber tubing. It seemed that no comment other than adverse was ever made on your work, and that it was not what you did but what you did not do that attracted notice. If you were told to do twice as much, and, by a superhuman effort, achieved it, it would be taken as much for granted as your heartbeat.

Nurse Richardson was kinder. She would tell me, when she had time, but then she never had time. She was always scudding about, with two furrows between her heavy brows, throwing desperate glances at the clock and muttering: 'Oh, Glory, I'll never get done. I've got that ear to dress ... inhalations ... all those temps to take ... that leg – Heavens! I've forgotten the diabetic specimens. Have I got time to test them before I do that leg? I shan't go to tea ...'

I was rather afraid of asking Nurse Parry, the girl who had brought me down. She seemed so sure of herself, and I gathered she thought me a panicking fool. She herself strolled through her work, unperturbed by crises, and letting fall appalling language, more from habit than provocation. 'For Christ's sake, woman,' she kept saying, 'calm down. We don't work very hard here on a Sunday.' That was all very well. We did, and I wanted to know what to do next before I was cursed for not having done it. I envied her her easy familiarity with the patients. She didn't mind what she said to them and they seemed to love it. I myself was terrified of the thirty odd female bodies that were our charge. *Sister Fairchild* had said, in Chapter Two: 'Never let the patient know that you are nervous or do not know what to do. You will sap his confidence in you and so delay, or even prevent his recovery.' But they could have had no confidence in me to be sapped. I didn't even know what was wrong with them and was frightened of touching the wrong end.

How did one ever learn their names? Except people like Mrs Greenbaum, whose name was indelibly printed on my mind after I had given her the wrong dinner tray. Knowing full well that it was not hers, she had eaten it and had nurtured the consequent pain until her doctor came round and she could tell him exactly how she got it.

The two other nurses on the ward were fairly junior. They had no stars and seemed to do almost as much cleaning and polishing as I did. Nurse Donavan was jolly and cockney and rather dirty and would sooner wipe a plate on her apron than walk two yards to the sink to wash it. She answered my questions with loud laughter and: 'Good Grycious, don't ask *me*. I only work here.'

Nurse Drew was saccharine. 'Ask me anything you want to know,' she kept insisting. 'I can remember what it was like to be strange,' she said, as one looking down the years and stretching out a hand from the summit of experience. She didn't have far to stretch, as I presently discovered, for she had only been there three weeks longer than I had.

These were the nurses on William Forrest Ward. William Forrest himself was a man who had lost his wife there, of a pulmonary embolism, and had endowed the ward in questionable gratitude. Of Sister Lewis, the dictator of the ward, I knew no more at the end of the day than the beginning, for she had not spoken one word to me. They told me she never did under a week. Nurse Parry insisted that there was once a nurse about whom, at the end of two months, she was still asking: 'Who is that?' with the same look of delicate distaste that I had seen her direct at me. She was a frail-looking woman, a mere anaemic drift, and completely unnatural. She struck poses and wove sentences of elaborate refinement. She didn't look strong enough to be a hospital nurse, unless her frailty was also a pose.

By the end of the day, my mind and body were in such a chaos of fatigue that I couldn't think of anything but my bed, black iron or not. I just had the strength to stagger to a phone box, accompanied of course, like a solid shadow, by Gunter, and tell my family: 'I love it.' Because I did. That was the one thing that emerged clearly.

CHAPTER THREE

For the first few days I groped my way through a dust-storm of new impressions, baffling orders and mystic phraseology, but gradually the dust began to settle into the pattern of hospital life. What had seemed chaos at first emerged as a routine so rigid that it superseded any eventuality. The Ward Work must go On. That locker must be polished without and scoured within, though Death and Tragedy lie in beds on either side.

Soon I could hardly imagine a time when I had not been doing exactly the same things at the same time each day. I sometimes caught myself thinking how deadly the work would be if it were not for the patients, forgetting that without patients there would be no work, for it seemed to have an independent existence, which nothing could ever stop. If all the beds were empty, one would still come on at seven o'clock and push them backwards and forwards and kick the wheels straight.

As it was, life became more bearable with each day's knowledge of the patients and the realisation that they were people, not just bodies under counterpanes whose corners had to be geometrical. Of course, there was hardly any time to talk to them, but sometimes, closeted behind screens to give a blanket bath, you could get down to a good gossip, until a long white hand drew back the screen to admit the ivory face with its fluted nostrils and fastidious lips.

'Neu-rse' – Sister Lewis's voice had a kind of disdainful creak – you're giving a blanket bath, not paying a social call.' She was on speaking terms with me by now, at least on telling-off terms. I was responsible for an unmentionable little apartment called the sluice, which she would enter every morning at nine o'clock, almost changing into old shoes to do so. She would sniff delicately and touch things with her fingertips, but her eye was ruthless. There was usually something to be cleaned again and I would have to miss part of the half-hour's break we were allowed for making our beds, changing into a clean apron and having a cup of coffee.

If I had been surprised by the capacity of the nurses' stomachs at breakfast, I was staggered when I did get time to go to the dining-room for what was known as 'Lunch'. The ends of yesterday's long loaves were on the table, with a mound of margarine and a bowl of dripping. I tasted the dripping once, and tasted it all day in consequence. Gunter used to take her plate to the end of the table where there was plenty of elbow room and eat bread and dripping like a starving refugee.

This being Lunch, the next meal was called Dinner. This was at midday, except for the senior nurses, and there were all the white pigeons again, ready to make up for only two slices of meat by quantities of potatoes and as many goes of rice pudding as they could manage before Sister said Grace. Tea was at four and the bread was new and doughy and had to be cut in hunks anyway, and supper was at half past eight, when one came off duty. It was usually sausages and disguised pies, and perhaps blancmange or cold rice pudding left over from dinner. One thing that hospital taught me was to eat the sort of puddings I had been refusing since the nursery. Hunger compelled it. My appetite grew enormous and I saw myself becoming one of the doorstep-and-dripping brigade, with my apron growing tighter each day and my dress straining its seams.

Seven a.m. to 8.30 p.m. sounds a long time, but we got three hours off during the day, either morning, afternoon or evening. Evenings were the best, because there was no coming back on duty, and sometimes I used to dash down to London in order to get a decent dinner and dash back again to get in before they locked the little door. It was not until later that I discovered the bathroom window. We also had one whole day off a week – a day of eating, drinking and sleeping. Words cannot describe the joy of wearing human clothes.

All the same, I was quite proud of my uniform and was getting used to the sight of myself in it, although I still felt like somebody masquerading as a nurse. The mysteries of William Forrest Ward were being slowly revealed to me; it was a medical ward, I discovered. This sounded well to tell at home: 'I'm on the women's medical ward.' Nurse Richardson was kind to me. When we were making beds together, which was the only time she ever got a moment to talk, she would drill me in the patients' complaints. Half the time I had not the faintest idea what the words meant but it pleased her to hear me say: 'This patient is suffering from acute leukaemia with enlargement of the spleen and oedema of the lower limbs.'

'When I was a new Pro,' she told me, 'nobody would tell me anything. I know what it's like.' She had me on her conscience and was determined to bring me up right. When she was not reckoning out loud the jobs ahead of her, she would keep up a running commentary on my work.

'Now the draw sheet – straighten the mac, pull from me, tuck in – now you shake the pillows, then *up* the bed with the patient – that's right – arm under her axilla. Now turn in the wheels, pull that locker forward, has she got water? Here's a torn pillowcase ... Oh, Glory, we'll never get these beds finished and I shan't get the flowers done before Sister comes on. Off you go to the linen cupboard, Nurse. *That's* right – pop it on – open end away from the door, don't forget. Now, Mrs Brownlees. Now, Nurse, what did I tell you about this patient's hand?'

'Cellulose,' I would say sleepily, snatching at the corner of a blanket as she whipped it through the air.

'Oh, Glory, you must try and remember – cellulitis.'

'Fancy,' said Mrs Brownlees, 'cellophane,' and stored it up to tell Ethel on Visitors' Day.

Next to Mrs Brownlees was a Polish woman, a Jewish refugee from Warsaw, who when she had a pain, would keen like the lost tribes of Israel: 'Oi-yoi, oi-yoi, yoi-yoi-oi!' Her English was not good enough for her to enter into the sociability of the ward and the conversation that broke out whenever Sister was off duty. She would lie with only her chin above the sheet, following the exchange of symptoms from bed to bed with eyes like black currants. Mrs Brownlees, who was fat and wobbly, tried to jolly her along and called her Miss Clean dearie, but as Miss Klein only stared at her suspiciously, she soon turned to Mrs Russell on the other side, who would swop a fibroid for a confinement any day.

One day, I found Miss Klein crying and oi-yoi-ing as if her heart would break. 'What's the matter?' I asked, nonplussed. Sister had told me to find out what she wanted for dinner. 'Have you got a pain?'

'No.'

'What's the matter then?'

'Pleess?'

'Come on, cheer up,' I said. 'I want to know what you'd like for dinner. There's some lovely fish – well, anyway, there's fish—'

'Na!' She shrugged off my hand and turned her face into the pillow.

'Well, would you rather have meat? Would you like fish or

meat, Miss Klein,' I persevered. I thought perhaps she didn't understand me because she was usually keen on her food, so, without thinking, I tried her with: 'Wollen Sie fisch oder fleisch—' She was round on me in a moment, with her hair on end and her eyes flashing in her stricken face, 'Ah!' she cried, thrusting me away, 'You too! You think it too!'

'Think what?'

'All these woman—' she darted a look round at all the figures sitting up harmlessly eating stew off painted tin trays, 'they think I am a spy.' She nodded vigorously and a great teardrop fell into her thick lower lip. 'Oh, yah,' she interrupted my protestations, 'you can say and say and say. Don' tell me. I have heard them talk about me and say: "she is a spy". They don' like I am here. How I can get well?'

'But that's ridiculous, Miss Klein. Nobody talks about you. We're all very fond of you. Who do you think doesn't like you?'

'Her, and her next.' She nodded towards Mrs Brownlees and Mrs Russell who were whiling away the time between courses with the subject of varicose veins. 'All day they talk and say: "She is a spy, she talk fonny," so now I don' speak any more, but still they talk. You shall see – they will tell the politz. Yoi-oi-yoi—' She began to sob again.

It was no use trying to reason with her. She was obsessed. Small wonder that she had this persecution mania after what she had probably been through. The Warsaw from which she had fled must have been a city of spying and treachery and suspicion, of whispers in cafés and meaning glances and abusive notices mysteriously appearing on walls. How could you trust anybody when people that you knew, even your friends, appeared from one day to the next in Nazi uniform, and even your old servant turned informer?

For several days she lay in a huddled ball, sobbing off and on, and then early one morning, she suddenly hopped out of bed, scooted for the door and was off down the passage in her crumpled nightgown and bare feet before anyone could stop her. When she was brought back, struggling and shrieking in Polish, they put boards round the sides of the bed so that she couldn't get out, and she lay like a trapped animal, with only her eyes moving. She had no people over here and the mistress for whom she had worked came to see her once and stood looking vaguely down at the bed and saying: 'Oh, dear, it's all very unfortunate, but I don't see what I can do – I'm not responsible for her.' Soon after that, they took Miss Klein away, I don't know where to.

At one end of the ward, glass doors led to a stone-floored balcony, where half a dozen convalescents and chest cases were protected from the hilltop winds by yellow army horse-blankets. The balcony had three glass sides, like a conservatory. When the windows were open you could see the hospital's vegetable garden, full of cabbages and rhubarb, and beyond that the descending roofs of residential Redwood, and when they were shut the anti-shatter coating gave you the impression of being in a Swiss mist.

In a corner of this balcony, surrounded by fourpenny novelties, bags of gummy sweets and half-empty pots of anchovy paste, was my greatest friend, Mabel Mutch, a convalescent Appendix. She had a face like a slab of concrete, a powerful cockney accent and a sense of humour that lit up the balcony. Her husband was called 'Cicil', and was very flash with a three-wheel car and mauve trousers, and she used to tell me long stories of how he had courted her at the White City and how she had finally said yes at the Palace, while Robert Taylor was at Garbo's deathbed.

It was one of my jobs to sweep and dust the balcony in the mornings, and I used to spend as long as possible over it, talking to Mabel about food and drink. Once Cicil brought in half a bottle of port, and when Sister had gone to supper we had quite a party. The woman in the next bed had some too and it made her cough worse than ever and the bright spots on her cheeks flamed.

There was not much time for sociability in William Forrest, however, even when the Staff Nurse wasn't whisking up and treating you like dirt or Sister appearing silently with her: 'Neurse, since you appear to have plenty of spare time, you had better go and employ it in turning out the splint cupboard.' I was always in a desperate hurry to get done.

'Getting done' is the purpose of every nurse. You have so much work to do by a certain time and not long enough in which to do it. If anything untoward happens, or extra work crops up, it throws you out and you rush about saying: 'I'll never get done!' and nobody pays any attention because they are too busy trying to get done themselves. I was terribly slow at first and permanently harassed. I could cheerfully have killed any patient who delayed me by upsetting a glass of water or fancying a slice more bread and butter when there wasn't any cut, or any of the hundred things I was sure they did on purpose to annoy. Ordinary working tempo doesn't do for hospitals. After a while, I got the knack of keeping up such a speed that it was impossible to stop going. My feet became scorched by the friction and were balls of fire at night. I tried sleeping with them on a pillow, and even raising the foot of my bed on books, higher and higher, until Nurse Drew told me my heart would slip.

I was growing to dislike Nurse Drew. She and I were supposed to work together in the evenings – taking round the suppers, tidying the ward and cleaning things that all had to be cleaned again anyway in the morning. She had a happy knack of looking very busy about doing nothing, being closeted behind screens holding a leg while it was dressed, or running back and forth with hot fomentations for Nurse Ketch. By the time I had pushed round the trolley, with my chant of: 'Cocoa, Bovril, hot milk, cold milk,' gone back to the kitchen half a dozen times for things I had forgotten, weighed out the special suppers for Diabetics and opened a sardine tin with a pair of scissors for Mabel, the maid would often have gone off duty and I would have to wash up. Nurse Drew would come mincing in with her head on one side just as I had finished, and offer to help me. I could have pushed her simpering face in if I hadn't been too tired.

However, she was senior to me and I had to stand back for her at doors. It was rigid, this hospital etiquette. I was always dropping bricks and addressing people as equals or helping myself to salt before someone who had a red star. Once I answered the telephone and took a message for a doctor who was doing his round in the ward. Most respectful, I went up to him with lowered eyes and hands behind my back, waited for his attention, said: 'Excuse me,' delivered the message in a hushed voice and thought I had done rather well. Afterwards, Sister beckoned me over to where she was sitting with one elbow on the desk and her fingers arranged in the air like a ballet dancer's.

'Nurse,' she said, looking at the dirt on my apron from under her mauve lids. 'You must never, never, do such a thing again.' I was staggered. I asked her what I had done, what she meant?

'You know perfectly well what I mean,' she said. 'I am exceedingly shocked.' So was I, but with surprise, not horror.

'But really, Sister,' I began, 'I don't know—'

'*How* long have you been here, Nurse?'

'Two months.'

'And you mean to stand there and tell me that you don't know that you may not address a member of the medical staff directly, but only through the medium of someone senior to yourself?' I gaped.

'How you could do it, Nurse, I don't know. How you could bring yourself to do such a thing —' She looked at me as if I were a bad smell.

I went away and cried in the sluice and Nurse Drew came and

patted my shoulder and said: 'Cheer up, we all have our little troubles. I'm sure you didn't mean to break that thermometer.'

The amount of time one wasted putting on and taking off one's stiff cuffs for the sake of etiquette was endless. Once, a patient was having a terrific nose-bleed and I was sent hurrying up to the kitchen for some ice. Remembering that the only two occasions on which a nurse may run are fire and haemorrhage, I pelted off and ran into a Sister on the stairs who held me back by the arm and said: 'Nurse! whatever are you doing outside a ward without your cuffs?' Breathlessly I tried to explain, but she wouldn't even listen until I had gone back for them and confronted her again decently dressed. By the time I got back to the ward with the ice. Sister said: 'I suppose a patient might die before you'd hurry yourself,' and the patient, who was farther from dying than I was, looked as smug as was possible with a large wad of cotton wool under her nose and moaned pitifully. She was my *bête noire*, this woman. She would keep on calling, calling for me in a hoarse voice when I couldn't possibly come. 'What is it, Mrs Kirby?' I would throw over my shoulder as I dashed by. She would never answer – just beckon with a horny finger. 'Nurse, I wants yer.' As often as not when I did go to her, all she wanted was to know the time, or to ask me what was for dinner. One morning, she had been particularly trying. I had remade her bed twice, because she said crumbs were fretting her bottom, and countless were the times I had trailed to the kitchen, either to refill her glass or to heat up her cocoa which she had allowed to grow cold. Two casualties were coming in and I was trying to make up beds for them and at the same time keep an eye on a mad woman who would keep tearing off her bandages.

'Nurse!'

'Oh, you can wait a moment, Mrs Kirby.'

'Nurse, I wants yer.' Out of the corner of my eye I could see her beckoning, but I pretended not to hear. I had to pass her bed on the way to get sheets out of the linen cupboard.

'Nurse – 'ere – Nurse—' It was like a hand jerking at my skirt. 'Oh, *wait* a minute, Mrs Kirby,' I said. 'Can't you see I'm busy?' She was still beckoning, undeterred, when I came back. Sister was looking my way, so I had to go to her. 'Well, what is it now?' I snapped. I was furious with the woman. Everything had gone wrong this morning. I was hot and tired and hungry and my cap would keep slipping off the back of my head. 'What is it?' I said, dumping the sheets heavily on to her legs while I jabbed at my cap.

She beckoned me closer. ' 'Ere,' she croaked, ' 'ere, dearie, I've got a stick of chocolate for you.' My soul craved for nut milk chocolate, but I was ashamed to take it. I had to pretend I never ate chocolate and she turned up her eyes at me, hurt. When she left hospital, her nephew, who was in the trade, brought her in a whole parcel of chocolate, which she distributed to all the nurses – except me, of course.

Some mornings, before she said Grace after breakfast, Night Sister would read out the names of those whom Matron wished to see. This usually meant trouble and there would be craning necks and stares of gloating sympathy at the unfortunates, who would pretend it was about holidays. One morning, it was Nurse Dickens to see Matron at ten o'clock. I froze with horror, a fork-ful of solidified scrambled egg substitute halfway to my mouth. What had I done? Or rather, what had been discovered? Could anyone have found out that I had been cleaning the bath with pure Dettol to save elbow grease, or about that medicine glass – had I not buried the pieces deep enough in the bin? Gunter was staring at me, the primary stage of digestion visible in her open mouth.

'It's all right,' said Evans. 'I had to go yesterday. It's only to sign on.' She and her Caerphilly colleague were not so thick these days, since they each discovered that the boy from the 2d. library

33

had been taking the other one out. He must now have been concentrating on Evans, for she was quite bouncing, while the other drooped, rather spotty, farther down the table.

'What's signing on?' I asked.

It appeared that your first few months were a kind of trial on both sides. You could leave or be thrown out without notice, but once you had signed on, it was a month's notice on either side and you could not leave without a good reason.

'Do you have to sign on?' I asked the girl next to me, a little bustling body who may have had legs somewhere under the voluminous apron that would have gladdened the heart of *Sister Fairchild*.

'Well, you don't have to,' she said. 'She gives some people longer if they can't make up their minds.'

'I shan't sign on,' I boasted. It was a claustrophobic idea. When I went into Sarah P.'s office, she was scratching away at one of her interminable ledgers; the desk was littered with them and with notebooks and sheaves of lists. I thought sadly of the paper shortage and of the scrappy bundles that Bert and Arthur and I had pounced on with such pride in my salvage days. Matron gave me a quick glint from her thick lenses and said: 'You had better come back and see me in a clean apron, Nurse.' She talked like a ventriloquist – her lips rigid and her epiglottis sliding up and down her scrawny throat.

I didn't feel like a fagging all the way down to my room. 'Please Ma'am,' I said, 'I haven't got a clean one till the laundry comes back.'

The laundry came back yesterday, Nurse.'

'Mine wasn't there, please Ma'am.'

'I checked the laundry myself. There was none missing. You can come back to me with a clean apron or a better excuse.' If there was a spark of humour in her eyes, the thick lenses concealed it.

I went. I might have known how useless it was to try and pit oneself against authority and a system that had been going on long before one thought nurses were only things with laps and warm towels. Several people had told me that they tried to resist the hospital system at first and had ideas about revolutionising the whole thing. But you can't; it's too big and too rooted. You may think it absurd that grown-up girls who are considered responsible enough to deal with life and death should have their bedroom lights turned off at the main at half-past ten every night, but there's nothing you can do about it. After a while you get quite good at doing your hair in the dark.

When I returned, crackling with starch, Matron just handed me a piece of paper and said: 'Sign here,' and of course I signed meekly. The net was closing round me.

Once I had signed on, I realised that I had let myself in for exams and lectures. You had to attend these three days a week, in your off-duty time. The final examination was three years ahead, with its remote possibilities of becoming State Registered and wearing frills and medals, but there was something called 'the Pree-lim', which you took after a year, and could take as many times as you could afford the entrance fee until you passed. Some of the nurses had been taking it cheerfully and unsuccessfully for years. Their swotting, or 'studying' as it was known at Queen Adelaide, was done communally. They would sit on each other's beds, drinking tea out of tooth mugs and eating large dry cakes from the busmen's café across the road. They would start off quite earnestly with: 'What is a cell now, Jones?' . . . 'A cell is a minute living organism consisting of a nucleus and protoplasm enclosed in a stroma, or envelope' . . . 'Brilliant, now, let's have about tissues,' but the conversation would soon drift on to what I said to Sister and how Dr Pascoe said: 'Thank you, Nurse,' from behind his mask in Theatre.

The lectures were on Hygiene, Nursing, and Anatomy and

Physiology. Hygiene was all right if you happened to be keen on sewage and Activated Sludge. A knowledge of plumbing is apparently essential to a good nurse and soon I could not pass a house without gauging the efficiency of its outside pipe system. Nursing was mostly practical work – bandaging each other and making the bed of a lay figure that was known as Old Mother Riley and appeared to be a maternity case.

The Sister Tutor who taught us was so fat, that once between her desk and the blackboard she was wedged there for the whole lecture. She liked to illustrate various bones on herself, and would poke and prod at her cushiony hips for ages, trying to find her Iliac Crest. She always spoke in technicalities, even in ordinary conversation: she was dehydrated instead of being thirsty, and rotated the Axis on the odontoid process of the Atlas when she wanted to turn her head.

Anatomy was fascinating. I started to write a story entitled: *The Skeleton in the Cupboard*, in which the hero was called Pyloric Sphincter and the heroine Hernia Bistoury. There was a beautiful spy called Vena Cava and a will-o'-the-wisp creature called Poly O'Myelitis, who led a gipsy life on a Cavernous Sinus. The heroine's unattractive friend, who was always tagging along as an unwanted third, was Ulna Tuberosity, and there was a dapper old gentleman called Sir Glenoid Fossa, who collected antiques and owned the inlaid ivory Malleolus, the blunt instrument that silenced the barking of Hernia's faithful Mastoid.

There were about a dozen nurses in my lecture class: the Welsh girls and Gunter, who couldn't spell, four new girls, even newer than me, and a few oddments from higher up who had arrived too late to go into the class above. One of these was a conversational girl called Kelly, with wild hair and soft brown eyes and an irrepressible sociability. She would interrupt Sister halfway through a dissertation on ears to say: 'I must just tell you about my aunt, Sister. I'm sure you'd be awfully interested. So would the class, perhaps.' Her smile flashed over our inert figures like the beam of a lighthouse on a shuttered village.

'Not now, Nurse,' said Sister impatiently. 'Afterwards, if you like.'

'Oh, but Sister, I must just tell you. It was so queer. This aunt, you see – she lived in Dublin – she'd been deaf for years and never thought anything of it, till one day, her nephew who'd just qualified at the Rotunda, said: "Why don't you let me take the syringe to it, Auntie?" She'd try anything once, she said, so he did, and what d'you think? Out came a blue bead. It must have been there for ages, because it was years since she wore that necklace. Wasn't that amazing?' The beam swung round on us again.

'Fancy,' said Sister and tapped on the blackboard with her pointer. 'Now the external auditory meatus—' I liked Nurse Kelly. She brought a freshness to the sterility of the lectures that Sister had been delivering without variation ever since she gave up the post as Junior Night Sister at the Birmingham General because of heart trouble.

'Describe this bone,' she would say, rootling in her gruesome box and thrusting one at Nurse Kelly, who would handle it like an amusing toy. 'There's a funny little knob at the end here – well more of a hump I'd call it, wouldn't you, Sister?'

'That's a tubercle, Nurse.'

'Oh, but it isn't exactly. It's more like those sorts of warts that grow on trees – and look! There's a little ditch – where the other bone fits in, I suppose.'

'I don't know what the examiners will say to you, Nurse, I'm sure. You must try and be more technical.'

'Oh, but they won't mind surely, if I explain in my own words—'

'Sit down, Nurse. Nurse Jones, go on describing the bone.'

'Oh, but I do know it – really,' said Kelly, jumping up again and waving her hand.

'This is the lateral epicondyle,' pronounced Nurse Jones, stabbing it with a dogmatic forefinger.

'Oh no, Nurse, surely—'

'Sit *down*, Nurse Kelly!' She would eventually subside and go on talking to me, unabashed, while Jones rattled crisply through the salient points. She was a menace, a know-all with a glistening face and important figure. She liked to be thought keen, and when the lecture was over, would delay our escape by asking unnecessary questions, while we muttered and shuffled our feet.

It was bad enough having to attend lectures in your off duty, but when they fell on your day off, it was infuriating. At first, I used to miss them and go home as usual, but I soon found myself before Sarah P. at ten o'clock in a clean apron. Having a lecture on my day off meant either that I could not go home for the night or that I had to come back from London in the morning. For the hundredth time I wished that nurses had a Union. No other trade would allow one's free time to be encroached upon like this. I collected a repertoire of excuses – dentist's appointments, long-lost relations, a mythical fiancé, which I trotted out from time to time in order to get my day unspoiled. The exam was nearly a year off, anyway, and I didn't think I would still be there, even if the war lasted. Every morning, as I fought my way out of sleep at six o'clock, I resolved to give in my notice, but as the agony wore off my resolve weakened and the interest of the day began to take hold of me. I made a bet with Nurse Parry that I would not stay a year.

'You won't have the initiative not to,' she said. 'They get you into a rut and then you haven't the energy to cut free. I used to think I'd go mad if I stayed another day, but now I've settled down, like a cow.'

It was visitors' day and we were in the bathroom making plaster bandages and having a few surreptitious puffs at a cigarette. I can't think of anything less cowlike than this leggy creature with her attractive, dark blonde hair and her casual talk. She had been trying to shock me with improbable stories of her pre-hospital life. 'I came here to expiate my sins,' she said, 'like a ruddy nunnery – look out!' We hurled our cigarettes out of the window.

'I can smell smoke,' said Sister, coming in and finding us rubbing plaster into the stiff gauze strips like mad things.

'It was that porter,' said Parry, 'when he came through to fetch the laundry.'

'You may stop the bandages now,' said Sister, still sniffing unconvinced. 'I'm going to ring the bell for the visitors to go.' She drifted away.

'Dirty swine,' said Parry. 'It's only five to four.' Sister resented the visitors and would always try to cheat them of five minutes at either end of their time. She thought they spoiled the appearance of the ward, and after they had gone we would have to mop the floor because she fancied they left muddy footmarks, even on a dry day.

I loved visitors' day. Long before two o'clock the crowd would begin to collect in the corridor outside the ward, peering and waving through the glass doors, while we were tidying and retidying lockers, changing the bedjacket of Mrs Grant who had dribbled her mince again – anything that Sister could think of to keep them out a little longer. At last the doors were opened and they poured in, making a beeline, or hesitating if they had not been before, usually too shy to ask. Straw hats with roses on, knitted berets with brooches, best black coats, paper carriers crammed with food, flowers of all kinds from great sprays to wilting little bundles in brown paper. Men with their caps held in front of them, lurching from foot to foot, girls smart and made up, chatting brightly to Ma, but looking round all the time and fiddling with their curls, old men with dim eyes, who were managing alone at home and probably not getting enough to eat.

A young husband would go up to his wife's bed on tiptoe,

clutch her hand and hang on to it for the full two hours, both of them practically speechless. Children were not allowed into the ward, but sometimes they would be brought to the door to wave at Gran and hustled away when they set up a yell to see her lying there as if she belonged to the hospital, and not to them any more. That must be the worst part of having someone in hospital. You have surrendered them, body and soul, to this alien, intimidating institution, that only lends them to you grudgingly for two hours twice a week.

CHAPTER FOUR

Women were not meant to live *en masse* – except in harems. They inflate the importance of their own little centre of activity until it eclipses the rest of the world. Men manage to pigeonhole their life: work, domesticity, romance, relaxation, but a woman's life is usually as untidy as her desk. She either fails ever to concentrate on one thing at a time, or else fills one pigeonhole so full that it overflows into the others.

I don't know whether the nurses at Redwood were typical of the whole profession, but most of them had no interest in anything that happened a yard outside the iron railings. They never read a paper, except the *Nursing Times*, and only turned on the Common Room wireless when the nine o'clock news was safely over. They were only interested in the war as far as it affected them personally – shortage of Dettol and cotton-wool perhaps, or jam for tea only once a week.

The ward beds had earphones fitted to them, connected with a central receiving set, and while I was dusting lockers, I used to enquire about the seven o'clock news. 'Why d'you always ask if there's any news?' a patient asked me one morning.

'Well, I don't know – because I'm interested, I suppose.'

'Funny,' she said, 'I shouldn't have thought a nurse would be interested.' That summed up the attitude of the outside world towards nurses and of nurses to the outside world. Nurse Donavan once asked me – I remember the day well; it was a red letter one, because she had washed her hair – 'Whatever were you talking to Sister Mason about at dinner?'

'Oh, the war,' I said vaguely. 'Settling world politics.'

'Good gracious,' she said, 'hadn't you got anything better to talk about than that?' I asked her what she would talk about when a German officer swaggered through the glass doors to take over the ward.

'I'd ask him if he'd had his bowels open,' she said and laughed coarsely.

Although they were so wrapped up in the hospital, some of the nurses grumbled incessantly. 'I hate it,' they would say. 'I hate the uniform, I hate the patients, I hate the Sisters and Fanny Churchman is a mean old witch.'

'But you like the work, don't you?'

'Loathe it. Sick people disgust me and operations are boring once you get over feeling faint.'

'Why ever be a nurse then?' one asked innocently. The nurse would stare. 'Well, what else could I possibly be?'

I should have thought almost anything rather than something so distasteful. They could have left; it was only a question of a month's notice and the Matron's odium. They can't have disliked it so much. In the same way, they grumbled about the food, while packing away mouthful after mouthful.

I asked a lot of them what originally made them take up nursing. Sometimes it was that they had been ill and had a very good nurse at an impressionable age. They rushed into hospital as soon as they were old enough, without seeing anything of the world or having any of the fun that is due to extreme youth. Naturally the restricted life irked them. They would have done far better to have seen a bit of life first and settled down in hospital afterwards if they had not yet worked the urge out of their system.

The war, of course, sends a lot of girls into hospital, but in normal times, apart from hero-worship and a semi-religious call, they go because nursing is about the only profession which you can enter entirely unqualified and not only get your training free but be paid while you are training. I never can see that nurses are so underpaid in the probationer stage. Besides their training, they get their keep, uniform and all medical treatment for nothing. I agree that the wages of a fully trained nurse are iniquitous; their skill and experience, acquired after three years of comparative slavery, should entitle them to more pay than a high-class parlourmaid.

I say all this now, rather smugly, but at the time, of course, I grumbled as much as anyone and disparaged the contents of my monthly envelope. Redwood was not a hub of entertainment but one can spend money anywhere. Apart from things like stamps and cigarettes and stockings, whose life was not lengthened by crawling about dusting bed wheels, there was always food. When the stomach wearied of a diet excessive, as *Sister Fairchild* would say, in carbohydrates and deficient in Vitamins C and D, we used to live for a while on coffee and buns and snacks and whatever we could afford. At the beginning of the month we used to go to the Blue Lady Café and Biddle's Restaurant and the tearoom above Hooper's, the only department shop in the town – all places where you got a tablecloth and a couple of flowers in a vase and a reasonable amount of currants in the cakes and tea per pot, not per cup. By the end of the month, we would be sneaking out after dark to 'Fried fish, Wet or Dry, Chips 2d., newspapers urgently required', or to 'Jock's Box' and 'Jack's Snacks', where the sandcake was really made of sand and the coffee came syrupy out of a bottle, but the beans and sausages were heaven at ninepence a go. We never went to the Rowan Arms – why, there was a set price for dinner there and two ancient waiters and an idiot boy in tail-coats, not our style at all. There was a cosy bar, though, upstairs and along the passage past the engravings of the various stages of Queen Victoria's coronation, and, as the barmaid had once been a patient on William Forrest, it made a good excuse for Parry and me to call in there occasionally with coats over our uniforms. She and I had got as far as Christian names – definitely not done at the hospital, however great a friendship. Her name was Chris. I liked her a lot and wondered why I had felt an aversion to her at first. Envy, I suppose, because she seemed so at home. She told me that she had hated me, too, and thought I looked sour and con-ceited. There had recently been a fruity scandal at the hospital, just before I came unfortunately, and now everyone was on the lookout for people to be 'queer'. One night, the guns round the nearby aerodrome were very noisy, and I went into Chris's room for company. What with this and the Christian names, we were quite a bit of gossip until Nurse Grainger provided a fresh subject by running off and marrying Nurse Larkin's fiancé, an unap-petising man called Gander, who had had half of his stomach removed on Herbert Waterlow Ward.

Just about this time, I was feeling quite pleased with life. I had got an amusing friend to work with, and had found one or two others who were good for a laugh; I was no longer the most junior on the ward: there was a pathetic, half-drowned little thing called Weekes, who never spoke above a whisper and who knew no better than to ask me what to do; I was beginning to learn my way about the work of the ward, and had picked up one or two of the basic rules of nursing. My complacency was doomed to shock, however.

One evening, the Senior Staff Nurse, the fat girl who had ini-tiated us on our first evening, summoned me to her room. The basin was still choked up with tea-leaves, and her smalls were drying on hangers, festooned round the top of the cupboard.

'Just a hint, old thing.' She was fearfully matey, as matey as her sister, whose photograph rollicked at me from the dressing-table. 'You won't make yourself popular here by being too friendly with the seniors. It isn't done, you know, really.' She undid her belt, and the studs popped gratefully.

'D'you mean Nurse Parry?' I was staggered.

'Oh, come on, I didn't mean anything personal,' she said, red in the face, as she struggled with her apron straps. 'Just a hint.'

'Who may I be friendly with, then?'

She released the strain from one overworked safety-pin. 'Well, your own set.' The other safety-pin relaxed and her apron bib fell forward, exhausted.

'Oh, my own set. People like Gunter.'

'Yes, old thing.' She could breathe more easily now. 'When you're as junior as you are, it's better to stick among the juniors.' I noticed that her mother and father were laughing at me from sagging deckchairs on the windowsill. She had undone her collar, and as there seemed nothing more to say, I thought I had better go before she started on the buttons of her dress.

When I had got over my amazement, I looked forward to telling Chris about it. She had gone out with an airman that night, but I would see her on the ward in the morning. We would make beds together, and I would tell her then. While we were doing poor old Mrs Morey, perhaps, who had morphia every four hours to sweeten the dregs of her life and thought that Chris and I were Snow White and Tinkerbell.

I had forgotten that it was the first of the month. I could have cried when Night Sister read out the Change List: ' . . . Nurse Dickens to go to Herbert Waterlow.' It looked like fate. Gunter leaned across the table to say: 'I'm not changed. You're on my ward.'

I returned her widespread smile with a sickly one, and slumped down to the Men's Surgical Ward in a furious temper, prepared to hate all the Surgical Men. I thought that I had been changed because I was Too Familiar with the Seniors. How petty these women were! All right, I thought – ten times as petty myself, but one's sense of values is groggy at that hour of the morning – all right, I won't try. Sister had the day off, and Nurse Sowerby, the Staff Nurse, was a feeble creature with swollen ankles, whom everyone called Sow. I slopped through what work I could not avoid, snapping at the men and not attempting to learn their names or ailments. Gunter was always underfoot and the other nurses seemed a deadly lot. The First Nurse, a raw-boned, ginger Scotch girl called Ross, said: 'None of your dirty William Forrest ways on this ward,' before I had even started, and I knew we were enemies. She had long yellow teeth and red wrists.

The day seemed endless, because I was clock-watching all the time, and at half-past five, I dropped what I was doing, excused myself abruptly to Nurse Sowerby and rushed off the ward, only to be recalled halfway down the corridor by Nurse Ross, to come back and wring out the sheet I had left in the sink.

'I said, none of your dirty William Forrest ways,' she said. 'You dare to treat Sister Martin as I've no doubt you treated Sister Lewis.' I bent over the sheet, with tears of rage burning my eyes. I prayed that she would give a man the wrong medicine and be publicly disgraced.

The next day was my day off, and when I got out into the great world things clicked back into proportion and I saw how wee I had been and how dangerously far on the road to becoming one of those whose limitations so irked me. Thank heaven for these days off, and for the sanity of a long sleep. I returned to Herbert Waterlow prepared to like it, and soon discovered that I was on the best ward in the hospital, with the most lovable patients. I had to work like stink to counteract the bad impression I had made on my first day.

There was always something going on on this ward. As well as operation cases, we received all the casualties – the car smashes, the drunks, the would-be suicides and the accidents from all the factories within twenty miles. It was quite exciting going on duty in the morning, because hardly a night went by without an admittance, and you might find anything from another perforated gastric ulcer, propped wanly upright with a saline transfusion dripping into the vein of his arm, to an unconscious man with two black eyes in something that was just recognisable as a face.

Scottie was one of these – a brawny giant with red hair ramping all over his chin and chest. He had been embroiled with a lorry on the way home from The Running Horse. He lay for two weeks like a happy baby, taking the nourishment that was fed to him and giving an occasional prehistoric grunt, but otherwise completely insensible. His tough little wife used to visit him every day and talked to him in the hope of waking him. Sometimes she would bring the baby and shake it under his nose, but he would just stare with empty blue eyes. Once, when I was pouring some Guinness down his throat, he smiled at me and winked, and I ran for Sister, thinking he was coming round at last. When we got back to him, he was more deeply unconscious than ever, possibly due to the stout, and she delivered me a short lecture on the strict observations of symptoms. I should like to be able to record that it was his wife and baby that at last pierced the Lethe of Scottie's brain, and that he opened his arms and cried 'Wee Teanie!' but what actually happened was that he suddenly grabbed Gunter's skirt as she was passing by, and said: 'Hullo, darling, it's a dark night for a nice wee lassie like you to be out by herself.'

There was plenty of work on that ward. We always had a few more patients than we could comfortably manage. More came in, and we still managed somehow. You never got off duty to time, but you didn't mind because what kept you was real nursing – something more than going over and over the same bit of brass with a duster. Working hard with people creates a bond, and I grew to find something in common with all the nurses – Sowerby, with her air of an overworked charwoman; Ross, who was deadly efficient; little Robins, the new Pro, who used to giggle and slap the men; Howes, whose apron and deportment were always spotless; even old Gunter, who continued to be as indigestible as the puddings that were our daily diet now that winter was drawing on.

I had not been long on the ward before I realised that it was Sister Martin who was responsible for the unusual atmosphere of willingness. She had the knack of getting work out of people without goading them, and of making them feel that they were co-operating in a united effort, instead of being pawns without initiative. She was a rare specimen.

She had the energy of the small, wiry person, and shot about from bed to bed like those cash holders on wires in old-fashioned drapers' shops. Each patient was in the nature of a personal challenge to herself. If anyone could save a man's life, Fanny Martin could – even the nurses admitted that. I have seen her miss all her off duty for five days, staying on the ward from eight in the morning until after ten at night, nursing a man who you would have thought was the core of her heart. When he died, she ran off and changed her apron, and was back again to see about rallying old Hoskins, who had been shrugged over hopelessly by the House Surgeon. She didn't think much of House Surgeons. She chivvied them all over the ward, and when at last they escaped, making, perhaps, for their dinner, she would run after them and drag them back to see a patient they had missed. She accorded a certain amount of deference to the Honorary Surgeons, but she was almost the only Sister who didn't either toady to them, or bridle, or hero-worship and probably make up long stories in bed about them. She treated them as equals, and if she thought they were wrong she said so, and they liked her. I once saw that eminent surgeon, Mr Harvey

Watkins, pinch her in the doorway of the Specimen Room, after she had worsted him in some argument. I looked at her with new eyes, and saw that she was quite young enough to be pinched. She might be quite pretty if she would only stand still long enough for you to see.

Chris's airman had asked her to bring a couple of friends to a concert at the aerodrome. She asked me to go, and Barnett, the baby-faced girl who had found me my room on that first evening. At first I said I would not go. I was always too tired these days to do more than a few minutes' homework for Sister Tutor, soak in a bath with the morning paper I had got from one of the men on the ward, and fall gasping into bed. Chris drew me terrifying pictures of myself in a rut, cutting myself off from the outside world through mental inertia, and ending up with social paralysis, a stammer and a twitching face when publicly addressed. I allowed myself to be persuaded, and began to look forward to it. It was ages since I had been out anywhere, and I had to spend all my off duty on the day of the concert trying to make up for the neglect of my nails and hair. Of course, the ward was busier than ever that day: two emergency cases for operation and a casualty admitted who never recovered consciousness before he died. As the evening wore on, I kept looking at the clock as I scurried about, knowing that I would never be finished by half-past eight, and ready to be picked up in the airman's tinny Austin at nine.

By an immense effort I was ready to go at a quarter to nine. I was dropping with fatigue, and would have given anything not to be going out. I kept thinking of my bed. On my way to Sister, old Hoskins called me. I pretended not to hear, but a smug man in the next bed sang out: 'Hoskins wants you, Nurse!' By the time I had attended to the old man, who fussed and fidgeted and couldn't be made comfortable, it was nearly nine.

'Please, Sister, may I—' I began.

'Nearly finished, Nurse?' she said. 'You've done that poliomyeletis boy's legs, haven't you?'

I had forgotten all about it. 'Just going to do it now,' I said, cursing inwardly, and dragged myself off to the back-breaking task, of rebandaging a couple of legs to splints, firmly and thoroughly so that the little devil couldn't kick them off.

By the time I was changed, Chris had been in and out of my room six times and had eventually gone out to appease the impatient Arthur, who wanted to go without me rather than be late for the concert. I rushed out, feeling a mess, piled into the back of the car on top of Barney, who said: 'Look out for my coiff!' and we rattled off down the dark hill towards the aerodrome.

Arthur had provided two exuberant friends called Tom and Gigs, for Barney and me. We seemed to have a lot of drinks quickly, and I was surprised that I could ever have felt tired. That must have been some other evening. The hospital seemed very far away, and I told Chris that she was right; I should do this sort of thing more often.

'Shut up,' she said, 'there's a man singing.' So there was. We were all sitting on rows of benches in a hangar, and a huge man in uniform was standing on a platform with a Union Jack behind him, his eyes tight shut and his fists clenched, singing 'There'll Always be a Nengland' as if it were being pumped out of him. After him there was a Sergeant-Pilot who tap-danced, and then a quartette harmonised interminably and nasally. They were evidently popular, because the audience stamped their feet and whistled and would not let them go until they had given a rendering of *Dinah*, cribbed from a record of the Mills Brothers. There was a conjurer, and a small thin boy who recited, and then it was the interval and we had more drink and sausage rolls. I missed the rest of the concert, as the one who was called Gigs, because he wore glasses, insisted that I would like to see his aeroplane, which was standing all by itself in the farthest corner of a very damp field.

I enjoyed my evening tremendously. The thought of six o'clock in the morning left me unruffled. Barney and I slept on each other all the way home, and I woke with a start from a beautiful dream to hear Arthur saying: 'Are you getting out, you two? This is as far as we go.' He had stopped in a side street just before the hospital, and we fell out only half-awake. It was bitterly cold and the stars were scattered prodigally on a black velvet sky, but I was too concerned with getting to my bed to notice the beauty of the night. The main gates were open, but we had to creep round the edge of the gravel to get to the little back courtyard and the convenient bathroom window.

'My God,' whispered Chris, 'the night nurses are busy.' Two ambulances were drawn up outside the main door and another turned in at the gates after us, its headlamp painting an arc on the gravel as it swung round.

'I bet they're all going to Herb Waterlow,' I said. 'I wonder what it is. There hasn't been a raid or anything.'

We could see shadowy figures and the humped shapes of stretchers, touched here and there by the red glow from a tail-lamp. Muttering voices and exhortations came across the gravel, but it all seemed remote from us, like a scene in a play. We crept on, falling over things, giggling and shivering, found our window and pushed it up cautiously, to avoid its treacherous squeak. I heard a hollow clang as Chris reached the bath, and then we heard her: 'What on earth – Here, come on in, quick, there's something up. Don't make a row.' I climbed sleepily in after Barney and sat on the edge of the bath to put on my shoes again. I didn't care what was up so long as I could get to bed. I didn't realise at first that all the blue lights in the passage were on, that people were running up and down and calling out, that the place was alive, in fact, at two o'clock in the morning, when it should have been dead in sleep.

I thought I had better get to my room before I was seen, but as

I turned into my corridor, someone grabbed my arm. It was Nurse Ross, half in and half out of her uniform dress. She didn't seem to notice that I was in outdoor clothes.

'There you are!' she said breathlessly. 'You've got to get into uniform and go on the ward.'

'*What?*' I must be dreaming.

'Hurry, now!'

'What's happened?' But she was gone already. The door of Robins's room was open and I looked in. 'Rob, what on earth's happened?'

'Don't you know?' She looked at me with enormous eyes, as she pinned the straps of her apron behind. 'There's been the most frightful explosion at one of the factories. Everyone on the men's wards has got to go on. There's twenty burn cases coming in, they say.'

How I got myself to my room and into my uniform, I don't know. I was almost crying with tiredness and my head throbbed like a machine. Through half-shut eyes, I saw my reflection in the mirror, grey and old, more like a patient than a nurse. I hardly had the strength to raise my arms long enough to fix my cap. No satin couch could have looked more tempting than my ugly, long-legged bed, with its jumble of cases and shoes underneath. I kept my eyes averted from it while I pinned on a dirty apron – I couldn't be bothered to look for a clean one – and stumbled out of the room, wondering how I was ever going to keep awake long enough to be any use.

The ward was in chaos. All the lights were on, and every patient awake and goggling. The two night nurses were dashing about aloofly, half resenting the day nurses' intrusion, half thankful for help in a situation with which, they told themselves, they could somehow have coped alone. Extra beds were being put up at the far end of the ward, and patients who were well enough were being moved into these so as to leave ten empty beds at the top of the ward. Four of the casualties were in already, and a stretcher was waiting on the floor in the passage. Sister was on her knees beside it. 'Quickly, Nurse,' she said, without looking up as I passed her, 'bring me the hypodermic tray – and the adrenalin.' But when I got back, she was standing up, just going back into the ward. 'I'm afraid it's too late,' she said, with a grim little smile. There were already three screens round one of the beds in the ward. I knew what that meant. Nurse Sowerby came out from behind them. Her mouth was quivering and she was on the verge of panic. 'Oh, Sister, they should never have brought them on to the ward,' she gabbled. 'They're bringing in dead men, that's all. Whatever shall we do – oh look – there's another stretcher and no bed ready. Oh, Sister, what shall we do—?' Her hair was in wild wisps and her cap askew.

'Pull yourself together, Nurse, for Heaven's sake,' said Sister, sharply. 'You'll have to go back to bed if you can't control yourself.' Poor old Sow gasped and wavered, and eventually saved herself on the rock of Sister's astringent calm. She spent the rest of the time being elaborately composed, doing everything with maddening deliberation and telling people to keep calm who had no intention of doing anything else. Some of the burns were not serious, others were a nightmare. They nearly all had to go up to the Theatre to be dressed and treated, and the blinds were going up on a slanting winter sun before we were anything like straight. Two more of the men had died before morning. It must have been a terrific explosion. People were talking about sabotage, but it was never proved.

As far as possible, Sister gave us a man each to attend to, while she herself dashed about from bed to bed, just in time wherever she was wanted.

'Get this man into bed,' she told me, as another stretcher loomed in the doorway. 'That bed there. Get him ready for Theatre; they'll all go up as quickly as they can be taken. I'll come and see him in a— Mr Briant! Here a minute!' She grabbed at the House Surgeon's white coat.

'They want me on Secker ward,' he said.

'They can go on wanting,' she snapped, and dragged him behind a screen.

Between us, the porters and I got my man on to the bed and heaped blankets on him. I was terrified. I had never seen a bad burn case before and I hardly dared to touch him. I looked round, but everybody was busy. It was up to me to look after him, and I suddenly felt proud and excited. This one shouldn't die. He was unconscious, but breathing, his face waxy and an ominous blue shadow round his nose and lips. I could just feel his pulse. His face was untouched and his eyes seemed all right, but it was his body ... I couldn't undress him; his overalls were burnt into his skin in places. I cut them away as well as I could. He was quite young, with a fine straight nose and curly mouth and brown, soft, boy's hair.

Sister came up to give him an injection. 'More blankets, Nurse,' she said, 'and hot bottles if you can find any. He's terribly shocked.' There was only one bottle in the cupboard, but I snatched another out of Robins's hand, cursed her as she grabbed at it, and I believe I hit her before I rushed off with it, leaving her twittering with rage. Mr Briant was examining my man sketchily when I got back. 'None of them are fit to go to Theatre,' he muttered, 'but I daren't leave them.' His long chin was dark with a stubble of beard and his eyes bloodshot. I remembered that the night nurse on Maternity had told me he had been up all the night before with a Caesarean. 'Get him up as soon as you can,' he said. 'He's got a chance.'

I saw Nurse Howes coming into the ward at one end of the Theatre trolley. She looked as neat and spotless as ever, her madonna face unruffled. As soon as she had got her man into bed, I grabbed the porter.

'Here, this one's next, come on.'

54

'Sister said that chap over there,' he said stolidly.

'No, no – she meant this one. Really, she told me.' I dragged him unwillingly over to the bed. There was no one free to help us, but between us we managed to get him on to the trolley. In the lift he suddenly opened his eyes and moaned.

'Hullo,' I said.

'Lo,' he said, and closed his eyes and moaned again, complainingly, pouting like a hurt child.

In the anaesthetic room, there was another trolley waiting, with a nurse from another ward. 'How many have you got?' she asked.

'Ten,' I said. 'At least, ten came in. How many have you?'

'Six. Secker have got some, too. Where's yours burnt?'

'Body.'

'Face and eyes, mine.' She sighed. 'Gosh, I'm tired, aren't you?'

I remembered with a shock that two hours ago I had been on the point of death. I didn't feel a bit tired now; there hadn't been time. Surely it couldn't have been only two hours ago. I could hardly remember it, it seemed so far away.

The sliding doors opened and one of the Theatre nurses came through. I caught a glimpse of the usually speckless and orderly Theatre. Chaos was an understatement.

'Hullo,' said the nurse, as she took hold of the other trolley. It was Barney. 'How d'you feel?' I said.

'Terrif. What a night!' She grinned, and they went into the Theatre, and the doors slid to behind them.

The youngest and newest of the House Surgeons came in, swinging his stethoscope and looking as nonchalant as a Harley Street surgeon.

'Is this chap identified yet, Nurse?'

I shook my head.

'Some of the relations are here. There's a woman outside who hasn't found her husband yet. I think she'd better have a look at him before he goes under.' He called through the door behind him: 'Come in, Mrs – er ...' She came in, a little brown-eyed fieldmouse, who was going to have a baby, clutching her handbag in front of her and tiptoeing. She took one look and sucked in her breath, nodding and looking from one to the other of us. 'Jack,' she said shyly, and touched his face. 'I'nt 'e cold?'

'He'll be all right,' said the doctor, with over-loud assurance. 'You tell Nurse his name and all that, and then you'd better go and wait downstairs.'

'Roper's the name,' she whispered.

'Right you are,' he said. 'You tell Nurse, I've got to go and—' He escaped, still swinging his stethoscope, determinedly jaunty.

I found a bit of paper and put down the particulars she gave me, to fill in later on his chart. She answered me earnestly, anxious to do the right thing, awed by the hospital. She kept touching him wonderingly, as if unable to believe that this was really the man who should just about now be calling her name as he stamped into the house, home from the night shift.

'The doctor said he'd be all right—' she whispered, as if to reassure herself.

'Yes, I'm sure he will. You'd better go and wait downstairs now, Mrs Roper. We'll look after him.'

'Yes,' she said, touching him once more before she went out of the door. 'But i'nt 'e cold ... i'nt 'e terrible cold?'

Barney came in soon, and we wheeled him into the littered Theatre. Mr Sickert, the Resident Surgical Officer, was sitting in a corner, in his sterile cap and gown and mask, with his gloved hands clasped in front of him, like a good little boy. When we had got Roper on to the table, the anaesthetist clapped down the rubber mask. 'I'll only give him a whiff of gas,' he said. 'Just enough to keep him under. His condition's pretty poor.'

Mr Sickert got up wearily. 'Better cut down for an intravenous up here, I suppose. Why wasn't it done on the ward, Nurse?'

56

'Well,' I mumbled through my mask, 'I don't know really, sir. It's such a muddle down there—' I had said the wrong thing.

'Muddle, muddle, muddle – it's always the same. Expose his leg, Nurse – come on, hurry up. What it would be like here in a bad air-raid, God only knows.' He grumbled away to himself as he began to cut down to the vein.

I went into the sluice to find the stand for the saline bottles. I could hardly get in for the piles of towels and gowns and dirty swabs overflowing from the sinks and bins. Through the far door I could see them operating in the other Theatre. A nurse came out with a bucket of dirty towels, and I asked her where the stand was.

'Don't ask me,' she said, as she emptied the bucket despairingly on to one of the heaps. 'I'm either going or gone mad.'

They finished with Jack Roper at last. The saline had improved his pulse slightly, but his colour was still deathly. His arms and body were dark purple where they had coated him with Gentian Violet. It was already hardening into a sheeny skin like the tight-fitting costume of an acrobat.

I had to leave him when we got back to the ward, because there was so much sluicing and clearing up to do outside. I felt fiercely possessive about him and hated to take my eye from him or let anyone else touch him in spite of their knowledge compared to my ignorance.

In the sluice I flopped. Robins was flopping there, too, and we cried with exhaustion over a pile of sheets. I discovered that I was aching all over and I could do nothing but yawn and yawn.

Sister came out while we were coping half-heartedly. 'You can leave this lot for the moment,' she said. 'Dump it all in the bath, if you like. You can go off now and have a bath. There'll be breakfast at six, and you'll have to come back on the ward for a little, I'm afraid, but I'll let you all off in shifts during the day to sleep.'

There was porridge for breakfast, and sausages and bacon, and cups and cups of glorious coffee. Coming out of the dining-room, we met the other day nurses coming in for the ordinary breakfast. They were aliens – people who had slept all night. It was too much bother to appease their curiosity.

I had got beyond being tired now. I made beds and tidied the ward just as if it were an ordinary day, feeling that I didn't care if I never slept again. My legs didn't feel like my own, that was all; they carried me about like automatons. Some of the men, who hadn't slept all night, were peevish and tiresome, but most of them were grand. The ones who were allowed up helped us as much as they could: they swept the balcony and emptied ashtrays and ran errands for the other patients. They approached as near as they dared and stared in mute sympathy at the violet figures – there were only six of them now, and soon would be only five. Those with face burns had skin charred to black, and the pads over their eyes were startlingly white.

Sister sent me off at twelve o'clock. Jack Roper had woken up, and he was holding his own. He had said 'Hullo' again, and had taken a feeding cup of tea from me. I didn't dare ask Sister what she thought about him, in case she should shake her head.

I couldn't sleep for a long time, and when I did, I dreamed about him. I went back on to the ward in the evening, unrested, feeling as if I were moving about in a play. Sister was still there. I don't know when she slept.

Roper was the worst of the burn cases, and therefore Sister's pet. She nursed that man like her own son, and when she saw that I was interested in him, she let me do a lot for him. I used hardly to dare to go on the ward in the morning in case anything had happened in the night. I don't know why, but for some reason it meant more than anything to me that he should live. The oddly possessive feeling that I had for him made me almost oblivious of the other patients on the ward. I didn't care what happened to them, but Jack must not die. It was a kind of conflict between myself and the evil force that destroys youth.

Mrs Roper came every day to sit by his bed and to hold his hand mentally, since she couldn't hold his purple bandaged one. He was a cheerful boy, and used to make commonplace little jokes and smile politely when one tried to be funny for his benefit.

On the Friday evening before Sister's week-end off, Sowerby was already twittering in anticipation of being left in charge of the ward. She so far forgot her position as to show me her varicose veins in the bathroom.

'What would you do with legs like mine?' she moaned. 'Aren't they wicked?'

'Wicked,' I agreed.

'They always seem to get worse when Sister's off. Oh, dear, what'll go wrong this week-end, I wonder?' Last time, the pipes behind the sterilisers had burst and we had been practically flooded out, and the time before that, she had got a Catholic priest to give Extreme Unction to a rabid Methodist. It was just poor old Sow's luck.

However, this week-end seemed to be set fair. Sister went off quite happily on Friday afternoon, leaving the ward not over-full and all the burns progressing satisfactorily. Sir Curtis Rowntree came to do a round when he had finished operating and expressed himself as pleased with Jack Roper. Sow came beaming back into the ward after ushering him out. 'What a *nice* man he is,' she said, as she pottered back to the desk. 'He said "Good night, Nurse" ever so charmingly, just as if I'd been anyone.'

Saturday began badly. I tweaked a tube out of a man's stomach while I was making his bed, and Nurse Ross had to spend hours trying to get it back before the doctors came round.

'One little setback like this and the whole routine's thrown out,' fretted Sowerby. 'Look, you see, Nurse Ross should have started dressings hours ago. We'll never get them done before dinner. I suppose I'd better start them myself, but then the doctors'll come round, and then where'll I be? Oh, dear, I do wish you wouldn't be so careless, Dickens.'

'Well, I didn't do it on purpose,' I retorted. I was worried myself about what Mr Morris Evans would say to me if he discovered it.

'If you speak to me in that tone of voice, Nurse,' said Sow surprisingly, 'I shall have to send you to Matron.'

'But *Sow*—!'

'Oh, it's all right, dear,' she said hastily, horrified at herself. 'You know I'd die rather than get anyone into trouble. It's just that I get so worried sometimes I don't know what I'm saying.' She called round the screens to Ross. 'Have you done it yet, Nurse?'

'No,' said Ross angrily. 'I've a mind to leave it.'

'Oh, you'd better not do that. I don't know what Mr Morris Evans will say. Look, I'll start some of the dressings.' She sent me off to get the trolley, but, of course, no sooner had she got the bandage off the first man and her hands scrubbed, than a stout Surgeon in a hurry burst through into the ward with a small House Surgeon panting at his heels.

'Where's Sister?' he snapped, snatching down the chart of his first patient and scattering the notes all over the floor.

'Sister's off duty, sir,' said Howes politely, smoothing down her apron.

'Where's the Staff Nurse?' he demanded angrily, and Sow came hobbling breathlessly up with her hands red and dripping. Every time she started to do a dressing, something called her away, and she was still talking about starting them when it was time for her to serve out the patients' dinners.

'I've done all the dressings,' said Nurse Ross crisply, as she passed the kitchen on the way to her own lunch.

'Oh, have you? How splendid. That is a relief. I don't know how you've managed so well.'

'Method,' said Ross nastily, and went on.

'Well,' said Sowerby, on Sunday evening, when I brought her a cup of tea in Sister's sitting-room, 'that week-end's over, thank goodness, and we haven't got through too badly.' She sank into the wicker armchair and kicked off her shoes. 'I don't think Sister'll find anything wrong when she comes back to-morrow. I really do believe I'll be able to sleep tonight. What a nice cup of tea you make, dear. Just pop into the ward before you go and have a look at that appendix man! I'm not quite happy about him.'

I went and looked at the man, who was showing no cause for anxiety, said good night to Jack Roper and went off the ward.

Sowerby may have been able to sleep that night, but I certainly could not. I read for hours, and then kept dozing off into queer fragments of dream and waking in a fright with my heart thumping. I wondered whether my room were haunted; the wardrobe had a nasty looming look about it. I got out of bed and shut its door, in case a body should fall out, but it was still a sinister shape, and as the moon sailed in and out of the clouds, a tiny eye kept winking in the mirror.

I dreamed again, a vivid nightmare, and woke with a start. There was someone in my room.

I sat up, terrified. 'It's all right,' said a white shape. 'It's me, Andrews.' She was the Junior Night Nurse on the ward.

'What's the matter? Is it morning? What's happened?'

'We can't find the continuous nasal oxygen apparatus. I thought I saw you cleaning it last night.'

I told her where I had put it: in the wrong place, of course. 'Who's it for, Andrews?'

'Roper. He's collapsed.'

CHAPTER FIVE

Just before Christmas, Sister went on holiday, and a temporary woman called Sister Oates took charge. She was a snob of the highest order, so superior that she could never bother to learn anybody's right name. She had been relieving on the private wards, where apparently she had spent most of the time bridling and smoking cigarettes in the middle of her mouth in the room of Lady Mondsley, who was in hospital for hypochondria.

I was not looking forward to Christmas. It was the first I had ever spent away from home and I didn't think I would be very good at communal jollity. 'Christmas is such fun here,' people kept telling me.

'What do you do?'

'Well, for one thing, the nurses all have a Christmas dinner and the doctors wait on us. It's a scream, my dear, we all throw the food about. Last year we had wine.'

'What, Graves?' She nodded, awed.

'Oh, everyone goes perfectly *mad*, you know. We do the daftest things . . . we all throw the food about!' That seemed to be her criterion of wassail.

Because I could not be at home, I pig-headedly determined not to enjoy myself, but as the preparations advanced I began to be drawn in. You can't live in a place that takes up your whole time and interest without absorbing some of the current atmosphere. The men were out to have a good time; they accepted the situation in which they found themselves and determined to make the most of it. They had been getting out of hand for some time – ever since Sister Martin removed her velvet-gloved control. They mocked Sister Oates behind her back and called her 'Wild Oats', because she was so proper. There were quite a lot of them at this time who were allowed up, and it was the hardest thing in the world to get them into bed at all.

They were not allowed up between nine and twelve in the morning. 'Nurse Dickinson,' Sister would say, 'get all those men into bed. I'm going to have my coffee now and I don't want to see anyone running about when I get back.' Having her coffee was a morning ritual which took place in the sitting-room. No one must disturb this sacred rite, but Nurse Sowerby was graciously admitted to discuss the day's work, rather as if she were a cook coming up to settle the meals.

I managed to hound some of the meeker men into bed, but others would only say: 'Come orf it, Blondie, can't a chap get shaved in peace?'

'Well, mind you get into bed as soon as you've finished, and for heaven's sake don't smoke till she's inspected the ash-trays.'

I tried to chivvy them back by the time Sister came to do her stately morning round. She would be halfway round the beds, with her 'And how are you this morning, Jenkins?' or Fox, or Stuart, or whatever the name might *not* be, when a wild pyjama-ed figure would scuttle across the floor and bound into bed, emerging above the sheets with an innocent air, while Sister Oates would stop in her tracks, staring as if she had found bugs in her kitchen.

There was a man called Toller, a railwayman, who had lost an arm in a shunting accident. He had only three fingers on the remaining hand, but he could do more for himself than a lot of the patients did with ten. After a few days of drinking through a straw, he demanded a cup and taught his fingers to hold it. He would not even use a spoon for his meals, but managed to manipulate a fork like an American. It was agony sometimes to watch him struggling to strike a match, missing time after time, but it was as much as your life was worth to try to help him. He would deliver some goodsyard language that sent you away red to the ears. He had a vital, Latin appearance – black hair, brown skin and very white teeth, and his eyes were always up to something. He kept the whole ward alive, and his cheek was colossal. On Christmas Day he kissed Sister Oates, smack on the lips, which must have needed some courage.

'Nurse Dickinson and Nurse Bunter,' she said, on the day before Christmas Eve, 'this afternoon we will decorate the ward.' Mounds of holly and miles of coloured paper-chains were stacked in readiness in the splint cupboard, and there was a Christmas tree and a whole boxful of balloons. Sister began to blow one up, her pigeon chest poutering alarmingly. The whole ward was watching open-mouthed, wondering which would burst first – she or the balloon.

'There,' she said at last, panting and holding her hand to her heaving apron, 'that's the way to do it. I mustn't do any more, because of my heart.' Soon after that, she retired to her room to eat tea and buttered toast, leaving Gunter and me to cope with the decorations, and emerging when we had finished to say: 'Oh, no, I don't fancy that at *all*.' Fortunately, she couldn't make us rearrange them, because two of the results of a motor-cycle accident came in and kept us busy. So she was able to spend the rest of the Christmas days saying: 'Now, if only we'd had the Christmas tree at this end of the ward—,' and 'If you'd put those balloons where I wanted them, the men wouldn't have been able to reach them with their cigarettes.'

On Christmas Eve there was a dress rehearsal of the concert that we were to give to the patients – as if their suffering were not enough. Chris and Barney and I had been asked to go to a dance at the aerodrome that night, and as the other two were not in the concert they refused to let me make us all late by staying on for the rehearsal.

'No one'll notice if you're not there,' said Barney.

'But I daren't not go. What'll Beaver say?'

'Oh – her,' said Chris, and Barney said: 'Anyone would think you were the flaming princ. boy, the way you go on.' Actually, I was in the back row of the chorus: 'The Redwood Juveniles', in knee-length operating gowns and big white bows of bandage in our hair. After a day of running about after Wild Oats, I was as keen to get out of the hospital as the others. I had just decided to cut the rehearsal and was going into my room to change, when Beaver, the Senior Staff Nurse, gave me a slap on the back that pitched me through the doorway. 'That's right, old thing,' she said, bursting with Christmas Cheer, 'don't be late for rehearsal. I'm going to give you a line to say, as Jones is off sick,' she added, as if bestowing a colossal treat. I would have to go to the rehearsal now. Chris and Barney went on to the dance without me, as Arthur was champing outside, but he promised to come back for me later.

The rehearsal was held in the Common Room. Some people turned up in the strange garments that were their idea of a policeman or a soldier or a pirate; others, under the delusion that it would be All Right on the Day, had not yet thought about their costumes. Everyone talked the entire time.

Beaver kept telling us that a bad dress rehearsal made a good first night.

The House Surgeons were in the concert, too. They strolled in after dinner, guffawed their way through the sketches, but soon got bored with it and strolled out again. Miss Llewellyn, one of the female Housemen, stayed on till the bitter end, her spectacles and teeth flashing with keenness. She had been an awful nuisance all along, always having some ambitious idea about a thing long after it had been settled and wanting to argue it out. She kept urging us to have part songs, although none of us could sing in tune, much less keep a part.

'We always used to do them at the Royal Free,' she would say, with that nervous, pecking movement of her woolly head. 'They were a tremendous go, I can tell you.'

I escaped as soon as I could, and changed my silly operation gown and did something to the face which had obviously not been attended to since six o'clock that morning. On my way out, I ran into one of the Sisters and had to pretend that I was just going out to post a letter.

'There's no post out on Christmas Eve,' she said, eyeing my clothes suspiciously.

'Yes, there is, Sister,' I lied. 'Special wartime arrangement.'

'Well, in that case, you can post some for me.' I toiled up to her room with her to get the letters, which I forgot all about and found in my pocket weeks later.

When I reached the usual meeting place, out of sight of the hospital, there was no sign of Arthur and his biscuit tin on wheels. A large black car was waiting a little farther up, however, and as I approached, a head looked out of the driver's window.

"Devening,' it said. 'Are you Nurse somebody-or-other?'

'I expect so.'

'Hooray. Climb into the pumpkin, sweetheart, and I'll take you to the ball,' said the head, disappearing inside. It was obviously rather drunk.

Even I could see, however, that it sat on top of a uniform with far more stripes than I was accustomed to.

'Are you a pilot?' I probed, as we shot dangerously downhill. He laughed so long and boisterously that I didn't dare enquire any further, because it made the car lurch.

'Why did you come and fetch me?' I asked. We had left the dark, deserted Victorian streets and were levelling out into the suburbs.

'Heard someone say they were coming to fetch a nurse,' he said. 'Marvellous party, by the way. Never could resist a nurse, so I said I'd come. Chap didn't mind – too busy with a cracking blonde.' This must be one of the evenings on which Chris was being nice to Arthur.

The hangar was gay with holly and flags and hordes of sweating, pushing people dancing to a band that was only audible at one end. The shuffle, shuffle of their feet on the concrete almost deafened you as you came in, but after a bit, you didn't notice it.

'Straight to the bar,' said my boy-friend. He turned out to be a large, well-fed man, with a great head of curly, greying hair, which he held very high, like a horse.

'What is it?' I whispered to Gigs, whom I found in the crowd round the bar. He chuckled. 'It's a Wing-Commander. Doing well for yourself, aren't you?'

'Here you are, darling,' said the Wing-Commander, handing me a glass.

'Thank you, angel,' I said, and he roared with laughter and kept telling me what a wit I was. He was easily amused.

'Look out,' said Gigs in my ear. 'There's its wife over there.'

Sitting at a table by the wall, hemmed in by the standing crowd, was a superior little party, with Mrs Wing-Commander in the middle, skinny and upright, with red hair piled on top of a face that seemed to go on for ever vertically. She sipped her drink as if it had been poured out for her by a Borgia. I danced with her

67

husband and then escaped for a while, but he found me again and slapped me playfully.

'Naughty little girl to run away,' he said. 'I'll have to keep you on a collar and lead.' He was just as easily amused by his own wit as mine. He insisted that I should meet his wife, so that she could ask me to their house. He evidently didn't dare to ask me of his own accord. She was circling regally round the floor with a deferential young officer, who was under the delusion that he might thereby advance his career.

'This is Nurse What's-it, Mavis,' said the Wing-Commander – I hadn't yet discovered his name.

'Oh, yes?' she said, making inverted Vs of her eyebrows and looking at my swollen red nurse's hands as if she knew that I had corns on the soles of my feet.

'Yes,' he said, with his head higher than ever, not meeting her eye, 'she tells me they get God-awful food at the hospital, so I thought it would be fun if she came to dinner one night.' She was looking at him cannily, and he laughed uncomfortably, as much as to say: 'Yes, you're right, I am a bit tight.'

'So you're a nurse?' said his wife, and led me to a corner, where she questioned me with a kind of detached pity, as if I had been an unmarried mother. After a struggle between disinclination and her duty as a social worker, she fixed a date for me to dine on my evening off, and left me, her charitable conscience salved. I had no intention of going, but I thought it was simpler to accept now and cry off later.

Christmas Day. Noel. Sing Hey, the Holly, but I didn't feel like singing Hey anything when the Senior Night Nurse bawled: 'Six o'clock, Nurse,' maliciously across my sleep. One couldn't even go to church, to make it seem more like Christmas, because on Christmas and Boxing Day we had no off duty at all.

All the essential work of the ward, the dressings and treatments, had to be got through in the morning, so as to leave the afternoon free for jollity. Fortunately, we had only one very ill patient, but I didn't see how he was going to last out the day, with the noise that the men were already making. They had started the morning by dressing up and playing charades. Jackson, who could get about at a great rate on his crutches, had chased Gunter into the bathroom and relieved her of her cap and apron. I found her sitting resignedly on the edge of the bath, reading a two-days-old paper. She looked funny without her cap; her head was quite flat, like a boiled egg with the top sliced off.

In the middle of Toller's famous impersonation of herself, Wild Oats arrived on duty, with a majestic hangover from the Sisters' Christmas Eve party, at which they had had Empire Burgundy and Bagatalle. We had to tell her he was being Douglas Byng.

We had all to subscribe to a present for her, and Sowerby now presented it in the sitting-room, with much clearing of the throat. It was a tooled copy of Shakespeare's Comedies, which Ross had picked up cheap because it had a page missing. It was only one of the last pages and there was no reason, anyway, to suppose that she would ever read the book, and it looked handsome and expensive. She was pleased with it. She visualised it sitting behind a glass-fronted bookcase when her ex-patients came to tea with her.

Then she fished in the cupboard where she kept the tea and sugar locked away from us, and surprisingly presented us each with a bottle of eau-de-Cologne. 'A happy Christmas to you all,' she said, her gold back tooth glittering.

When she went for her elevenses later in the morning, we gathered in the kitchen to distribute our own gifts. To save having to buy five presents we had each bought one, and we jumbled them up in the bread bin and drew in turn. I had bought a bottle of complexion milk that I wanted myself. I thought I'd be able to recognise its shape. To my fury, who should draw it but Ross, whose face obviously had no dealings with such things. She unwrapped it in silence and went away to her work. I drew a beastly little memo book, with 'Lest I Forget' stamped across the cover. I was pretty sure it was Ross's contribution. Gunter drew a bit of bread the first time, but tried again and got a powder compact. Powder and scent – her young man would have had a fit if he had known. She had told me all about him. He was a male nurse in the RAMC who thought that clothes were for utility, not adornment. 'He likes women to be as God made them,' she said.

After the present-giving, she drew me into the linen cupboard. 'Something for you,' she said, fumbling under her apron and producing a very nice screw pencil. 'A Merry Xmas,' she said, taking my arm. She had a passion for touching you. Luckily she had not seen me draw the memo book, so I was able to say: 'And I've got something for *you!*' and produce it proudly.

The men's Christmas dinner was the high spot of the day. There was a huge turkey and a plum pudding, and a crate of bottled beer. The surgeons had to dress up in chef's caps and carve the turkeys. We had Mr Harvey Watkins, who wore a small frilly apron round his non-existent waist and was full of bonhomie. He carved the turkey on a table in the middle of the ward, and we all stood round him with trays, saying 'Ha-ha' to whatever he said. Sister ladled out the vegetables and sauces as if she were presiding at an East End soup kitchen, and we carried the plates round and opened the beer. There was big eating, and a certain amount of cheating among those who were on special diet. I got mixed up and gave Gastric a leg of turkey and three roast potatoes, but it didn't seem to do him any harm, and he was very difficult afterwards about his normal diet of flaked fish and purée.

The shattered turkey and the remains of the excellent rich dark plum pudding were taken out to the ward kitchen, and when Sister had taken Mr Harvey Watkins into her sitting-room for a glass of sherry and the men were busy pulling crackers, a disgraceful scene took place. All the nurses rushed for the kitchen, as fast as their various degrees of foot trouble allowed, and with silent accord we fell on the broken meats. You can get far more turkey and plum pudding by snatching it from the dish with your fingers than you ever could at table. Goodness knows how long we would have gone on stuffing if it had not been for the frenzied shouts of: 'Nurse!' from the ward. Old McGilligan had fallen out of bed and was sitting happily on the floor in his nightshirt, singing 'Come Back, Paddy Riley to Ballyjamesduff.'

Seeing that there were enough people to deal with him, Gunter hurried back to the kitchen, before the porter should come and take away the dishes.

The visitors came after lunch, bringing presents and strewing the ward with paper and string. I had to go off and get ready for the concert. I was feeling tired now, but I remembered that Chris's Maternity Ward had some bottles of port going in the Labour Ward. It was queer to find the hospital regulations so suddenly relaxed. Ordinarily, it was an appalling crime to go to another ward without a very good reason, but to-day, one could wander about anywhere and nobody even said: 'Where are your cuffs?'

By the time we had done the concert on all the five big wards, it seemed to be getting very stale, but the audience lapped it up. They enjoyed seeing the doctors and nurses, in whose power they normally were, making fools of themselves. The House Surgeons dashed off in between every performance to fortify themselves, taking some of the more attractive nurses with them. Poor Nurse Beaver was perpetually hunting for people, and when they didn't turn up in time to go on, Miss Llewellyn, who was anti-fortification, leaped into the breach and understudied, mouthing her words and doing a great deal of miming at the side of the stage when someone else was talking. After I had said my one line: 'But look, Princess, see who's coming!' I lost interest and used to go

71

and sit in the audience. There was never room for all the Redwood Juveniles in the space at the end of ward, anyway. Some of them would be going through the motions right out of sight, but quite happy.

Some of the Night Nurses had stayed up as it was Christmas and were sitting yawning, their eyes bright with lack of sleep. Andrews told me she had followed us round and seen the concert on every ward. She was in love with Mr Briant, and was torturing herself with the sight of him in a borrowed battledress, with a bandage round his head.

The Nurses' dinner party was as promised, except that it was cider, not Graves. There was plenty of food, both eaten and thrown about, and Mr Vavasour, the gynaecologist, was very giddy with a bit of mistletoe. Matron looked in to see how we were getting on, and we all had to give three cheers for her, goodness knows why, as she was not even responsible for the food. She had probably had a row with the Housekeeper about providing too much. Afterwards, there was dancing in the Common Room, with five times as many women as men. Etiquette decreed that the doctors should dance principally with the Sisters, and when one of them danced with a nurse, there was much jealous whispering: 'Look at Harrison. Isn't she soft? *I* wouldn't dance with Johnny Briant – conceited ass.' If a couple were so rash as to sit out somewhere, the Assistant Matron, a cushiony woman with abundant hair, would search for them and manoeuvre them back into the ballroom. With the nurses' bedrooms so close, you see … One never knew. These modern girls …

I enjoyed Boxing Day more than Christmas Day. Sister went off in the afternoon, and the men produced some beer from their lockers. Robins brought up her gramophone, and we moved the desk and cupboards from the centre of the ward and danced. Toller could rhumba. 'This is the other thing you don't need two arms for,' he grinned.

The ill patient had fortunately been given an injection of morphia after lunch, and slept like a log, even through the singing of the patients who couldn't get up to dance. Even Sow's varicose veins took the floor, and she polka'd with old Daddy Masters, who might never have heard of such a thing as Hernia. Jackson and I had discovered the delightful game of filling with water balloons for unsuspecting people to burst. I can't quite remember how it happened, but it ended in a rugger scrum with me underneath. I was lying on my face, screaming, when all the bodies on top of me suddenly melted away, and I rolled over to see Wild Oats looming above me in perspective. At the time, she only said: 'Put your cap on at once and go and change your apron,' but the next day she had me into the sitting-room.

'You see, Nurse Dixon, it isn't so much a question of bad behaviour. We won't go into that – that's your parents' responsibility. It's a question of your dignity as a Nurse. You're letting down the whole Profession, don't you see?'

I mumbled and shuffled my feet.

'It's playing for popularity, Nurse,' she went on, her eyes bulging like a Hyper-Thyroid, 'and it won't do. The men don't like you any the better for it – don't imagine that for a moment.'

'But, Sister—'

'I'm speaking, Nurse. I say they don't think any the more of you; they merely lose their respect for you. They remember, and they'll take advantage of you another time.'

'But, Sister, they wouldn't. After all, they are sensible.'

'They are not sensible, Nurse.' She looked up at me in surprise. 'And remember: whatever class a patient may be, and some of them may be very good class – *quite* good class – you must always keep yourself just that little bit above them. Dignity, Nurse – without it, you may be a nurse, but you'll never be a good nurse, Nurse.' I edged towards the door, and she held up her hand. 'One more thing,' she said impressively. 'There might not always be other nurses there to back you up. Night Duty, for example. You might easily find yourself one day in a *very embarrassing position.*' She pronounced the last words with a ponderous horror, and I left her, slightly out of breath, to contemplate this interesting possibility.

The aftermath of Christmas was as might be expected. Two days of thirteen hours apiece without a break had left everyone tired and irritable, and the patients were inclined to be whiny, like children overtired by a party. There was all the clearing up to do, a lot of extra cleaning, and all the decorations to take down.

'How about leaving them up for next year, Sister?' asked Robins, from the top of a step-ladder. 'It would save an awful lot of trouble.'

'I can't hear a word you say, Nurse Dobbin,' said Sister Oates, who was in no mood for joking. 'Mind what you're doing with that holly.' Robins dropped it on to the upturned face of a sleeping man, and he sat up with a yell.

'I don't know how Sister Martin puts up with such girls. Ah, there's Mr Harvey Watkins!' She steamed towards him, the badges and medals on her apron arriving long before she did. 'Good morning, Mr Harvey Watkins,' I heard her say. 'Just clearing away the traces of merriment, you see.'

The surgeon rubbed his hands and ha-ha'd, throwing out his legs as he walked. The House Surgeon lagged behind, looking as if he could have done with more sleep and less liquor.

This reaction was general, it seemed. One would not have thought Redwood to be a town of unbridled licence, nor of the temptation or facility to make a beast of oneself. Yet into the Out-patients' Department there poured a stream of black eyes, broken heads and acute abdominal disorders. One man, who was admitted to our ward as a query concussion, was found to be merely sleeping in the comfortable lap of Bacchus, and was fetched home, as soon as he had stopped being sick, by a harridan in a hard hat.

We also had an old man who had been knocked down by a car, and a couple of motor-cycle accidents. One of these was a Canadian soldier, whose right leg was amputated soon after he came in. He was a fine man in his prime, about thirty-five, weathered and independent, a man to lean on in a crisis. And now he was leaning on me, asking me whether his leg was there, for of course he could still feel it.

I didn't know what to say. He was only just round from the anaesthetic and very shocked. They were going to give him a blood transfusion as soon as Mr Briant could get down. I hedged. 'You'll be all right. All you've got to do is just not to worry. Try and get some sleep.'

The words sounded trite and silly as I said them. He was not a man to be fobbed off with glib hospital jargon.

He gave me a look that he had probably given a lot of brainless women, and said: 'Come on now, Honey. Don't stall. I can take it.'

'We're not allowed to tell patients anything. You have to ask Sister, or a doctor.'

'They've chopped it off, then,' he said, fixing a cold blue eye on me. I nodded.

'Yeah.' It was more a long-drawn expiration than a word. 'Yeah. Thanks for telling me.'

In spite of his ability to bear pain, he was a difficult patient. He was autocratic and grumbled about everything except his leg. He had the aggressive Canadian conviction of supremacy and was quick to criticise anything that displeased him. Wild Oats mistrusted him because she felt he had got her number, and I think all the nurses except Ross were a little afraid of him. He made one feel somehow pettily feminine, and rather ridiculous for being occupied most of the day with trifling details. Unlike the other men, he would not accept a rule because it was a rule, unless he approved of it.

'If he wants to have things his own way,' Sister kept saying, 'he ought to go into a private ward. But I don't suppose even the Canadian Army is mad enough for that. The man's only a Private, after all.'

Laurence Cowley – that was the Canadian's name – had had a knock on the head that had wiped out all recollection of the accident or what led up to it. The Police had been to see him once with notebooks, and boots that resounded through the ward, but he had been unable to tell them anything. He was very tactless with them, and started to quote the Canadian highway laws and they went away, their boots a little subdued by pique.

It was more than a week after his operation before something clicked in Cowley's brain and he remembered part of what he had forgotten. I was feeding him his dinner, for one of his wrists was broken and the other hand bandaged. We had got beyond the preliminary 'Hell, where do they get this stuff, anyway?' stage, and he was taking the spoonfuls sulkily and abstractedly, as if he were trying to keep his mind on more pleasant things. Feeding somebody is very boring. Because you are impatient to be finished, you try to make them take the food faster than they want, and they either choke or take it slower than ever – on purpose, I believe. Cowley had two teeth knocked out, which did not help matters much. I shovelled in as large a mouthful as he would take without protest, and while he dealt with it, shifted my weight from foot to foot, leaned against the bed and gazed round the ward with ennui. I was watching old Daddy James trying to retrieve a piece of meat that had fallen down the front of his nightshirt, when Cowley suddenly gave the impression of having leapt six feet in the air, although he was actually unable to move.

'Jumping Jesus!' he said, 'I knew there was something!'

'What—'

'Maisie!' he almost shouted. 'What happened to her? Why in Hell didn't they tell me what happened to her?'

'What happened to who? Who's Maisie?'

'Why, the kid who was riding pillion on the bike. I forgot she was with me till just now. I guess that bang on the head – but they could have told me about her, they could have told me what happened.'

'Perhaps she wasn't hurt,' I suggested.

'She must have been. She'd have come around to see me. Listen, maybe she's hurt bad. Maybe she's even dead – Jeeze, poor little Mais. Poor kid—'

'If she was hurt, she's probably in this hospital. I'll ask Sister if I can ask at the Secretary's office.'

'Keep that old battleship out of this, will you? She'd have the enquiry scheduled in triplicate and sent up to the Ministry of Information. Find out yourself – it'll be much quicker. Jeeze, I'm going to feel badly if—'

'I'll try, but we're not supposed to give information about patients, you know.'

'Don't pull that on me,' he said, magnetising me with an eye.

'All right,' I said. 'I'll find out at teatime. Look, you haven't had your pudding. I'll go and get it.'

'If you do,' he said, 'I'll sling it in your pan. Listen, Honey, it's not pudding I want, it's Mais.'

Maisie was in Jane English Ward, with compound fractures of both legs. At first they had thought she would not live, and it was nature, not she herself, who had made the effort and proved them wrong. She had been told about Cowley, though not yet about the amputation. Evans, one of the Welsh girls who had come with me, was on Jane English, and she told me all I wanted to know while we squatted in front of the gas-fire making toast.

Above the fire, a notice in a looping hand was pinned to the wall with drawing-pins:

Owing to damage to the Asbestos
NO NURSE MAY MAKE TOAST AT THE GAS FIRE
Bread is more nourishing than toast
E. Harriman, Ass. Mat.

There were dozens of these little texts, all over the hospital and nurses' hostel. Sister Harriman's duties seemed to be wholly deterrent, but she was evidently of the school that thinks children should be told Why, and nearly every one improved the occasion with a little free information. One of the notices in the bathroom read:

DO NOT USE TOO MUCH HOT WATER
There are others to come after you

also

Too hot a bath lowers the vitality
and reduces resistance to infection

and another on the board in the entrance hall read:

NURSES ARE RESPONSIBLE FOR THEIR OWN BLACKOUT
ALSO FOR ANY FINE INCURRED IN CONNEXION WITH SAME

Carelessness in such matters is more than unpatriotic

IT IS TREACHEROUS

After I had found out all I could about Maisie, I sounded Sister Oates. I was helping her to put away the clean linen – at least, she was telling me where to put it and I was running up and down the step-ladder to reach the top shelves.

'Sister,' I said casually, with my face in the linen basket, 'does Cowley know about that girl who was injured with him?'

'No,' she said. 'He remembers nothing about her, and Sir Curtis Rowntree doesn't want him told yet. How many pillow-cases have you?'

'Forty-two.' Sister ticked it off on her list. 'How did you know about the girl, Nurse Dixon?' she asked. 'He hasn't said anything about her, has he?'

'No,' I said. 'One of the nurses on Jane English was talking about her at tea.'

'There's a great deal too much shop talked at meals, in my opinion,' said Wild Oats. 'When I was doing my training, one of the Sisters used to listen to our talk and anyone who mentioned the wards was sent away from table. We used to have some very interesting conversations, I remember.' She sighed. 'But girls these days have no social manners at all.'

'I make that twenty-four drawsheets altogether,' I said coldly.

'Correct,' she said. 'Up on that top shelf, please.'

'Sister,' I pursued, when I was at the top of the steps, making piles of the fragrant-smelling linen, 'supposing Cowley remembers about the girl and asks, will you tell him?'

'I should certainly do nothing without Sir Curtis's permission, Nurse. He has given his orders and it is my duty to see that they are carried out. Surely there was a great deal of laundry this week. I shall have to see about making the nurses wash some of the things in future.'

When she was safely away at her supper, I told Cowley what Evans had told me. He considered the information, acclimatising himself to the idea of Maisie with a bruise on her forehead and both legs in plaster casts up to the hip.

'You won't tell anyone I told you, will you?' I said.

'Hell, no. You were great to do it. Listen, do one thing more for me, will you? Write a little note and have them give it her.'

'Quick, then,' I said, 'before Sister comes back.'

I got a bit of paper and he dictated to me:

HULLO, MAIS,

Sorry I busted you up. Keep your chin up, kid, and get well quick. Am feeling fine, but afraid I'll have to use cork on my right leg from now on.

. Be seeing you soon, Honey.

LARRY

I took the note round when I went off duty, and had to dodge in the shadows out of Sister Porter's way until Evans came out of the ward. She made some excuse to go back again, and came out after a while with another bit of paper, folded very small. 'She's crying,' said Evans.

I sneaked back to Herbert Waterlow, and gave the note to the Junior Night Nurse, who was making Horlicks in the kitchen. As I came out, Sister was just coming off duty with a great bunch of chrysanthemums that I could almost have sworn were the ones Mrs Lockyer had brought for Lockyer.

'I sent you off duty hours ago, Nurse Dickinson,' she said. 'What on earth are you doing?'

'I forgot my lecture book, Sister,' I answered. 'I was just asking Nurse Andrews if she'd seen it, because I want to do some work to-night.' I did not want to have to walk majestically to the hostel with her, so I hurried on ahead to get dressed for the Police Dance at the Rowan Arms.

It strikes me now how very often I failed to obey *Sister Fairchild*'s injunction to 'cultivate scrupulously the habit of accurate statement.' Unless it meant harm to anyone else, it was always much simpler to make an excuse, if you had a convincing one, than to go through the fatigue of another row. I probably never deviated from the accurate statement so often in my life before, not even at school. But in hospital you have got to look after your own interests. Nobody else will.

I carried several notes backwards and forwards for Larry before Sir Curtis Rowntree decreed that the taboo subject might be broached. Larry put up a very good pantomime of surprise and gradually dawning memory, and immediately began to make himself a nuisance. He wanted to be put on a trolley and wheeled round to call on Maisie. He could see no reason why it should not be allowed. If it came to that, nor could I, but I realised that it could not be done. It was just one of those things that weren't.

'I came over here to fight for liberty,' he told Sir Curtis, who stood over him with his elegant length and proud face, his black hair flicked carefully up over each ear. 'For liberty,' continued Larry aggressively, 'and what do I get? First thing I know, I'm in a prison camp. Don't talk to me of the Motherland. When can I get up, Doc?'

'Take it easy, son,' said Sir Curtis, whose daughter sometimes took him to the cinema, 'we've got to get you a new leg first.'

'Say, do I have to wait for a cork leg before I can see Maisie? Now see here, Doc—'

Across the bed, Sister Oates threw a glance which said: 'What can one do with such a man?' but the Surgeon ignored her and turned round to ask me politely to bring screens.

Sister Martin came back at the end of that week, much to the relief of everyone, including Sister Oates, who was going to the Maternity Ward, where she hoped to find some high-class babies. She had despaired of ever finding any high-class Surgical Men.

Sister Martin made a brisk tour of the premises on the first day and announced that we had been slacking, which was true, but somehow one felt that she blamed Wild Oats as much as us. There were indigestion tablets loose in her desk drawer and a ring from a hot coffee jug on her sitting-room table. Once one got used to the idea of working harder, it was nice to see the ward return to its old efficiency and the stimulating air of enthusiasm come creeping back. Even Larry noticed that difference and became more amenable. Then, just when I had got to the stage of waking each day with anticipation instead of distaste, my happiness was neatly whisked away.

There was only one announcement after roll-call at breakfast. 'Nurse Dickens to go on Night Duty to-night. For what we have received, the Lord make us truly thankful.'

CHAPTER SIX

One of the stock phrases at the Queen Adelaide Hospital was: 'I can't stick this hole any longer.' Everybody said it, even those who were obviously destined to pass their State exams brilliantly, become Sisters and go on upwards, nursing their lives away but deriving great satisfaction and happiness thereby. Nobody, however, ever admitted to anticipation of this, or to the smallest ambition. If one wanted to pass an exam, it was only so as not to waste the fees, or be outdone by that conceited Wyman or give Toots – Sister Tutor – the satisfaction of seeing her prophecy fulfilled. However much you liked nursing, the thing was to pretend that you hated it and were only there under some unfair compulsion.

'I'm going to hand in my notice,' was another favourite remark, but it rarely came to more than an extravagant account of the interview with Matron, in which the triumphant nurse had consented to stay out of gracious condescension to the War.

There was one girl who lived permanently on the eve of departure, crouched, so to speak, like a runner, ready to spring off in a moment. It was said that she always kept her suitcase half-packed, and if you asked her to do anything, even if it was only a week ahead, she would say: 'My dear, I can't fix anything. I probably shan't be here by then.'

Her name was Dawlish, and she was quite handsome in an over-ripe way. She dressed her thick black hair in as many sweeps and coils as the shortage of hairpins allowed and perched her cap on top like a crown. She had a superior way of talking and a trick of slowly lowering her eyelids as if you came far below her estimation of herself. She seemed to be a good nurse, and if she were only half as skilful and knowledgeable as she thought, that still made her very efficient.

I am sure she enjoyed the work. One sometimes caught her in a complacent song, that would give place at anyone's approach to: 'I can't stick this hole any longer. I'm going to give Fanny Churchman my notice to-morrow.'

'But you did that last week,' one would say.

'I know, but this time I'm not going to relent. I'm not going to stay here and be bossed by uneducated women with no breeding. Sister was abominably rude to me this morning about the broken thermometer. She as good as told me I was a liar. "How dare you speak to me like that, Sister?" I said. She didn't know what to say to that, so she said: "I merely asked you, Nurse, if you knew anything about the thermometer." "Pardon me, Sister," I said, "you accused me of lying – I suppose because it's what you yourself would have done under the circumstances."' Dawlish paused, to make certain that one was impressed.

'So Sister said, in that voice – you know, trying to disguise the cockney accent – "Very well, Nurse," she said, "You can go to Matron's office to-morrow morning." "I shall be only too glad to," I said, "to hand in my notice and tell her exactly why I'm leaving."'

At dinner the next day, I heard her describing the interview with Matron: 'So I said to her: "I'm not accustomed to such treatment, Matron," I said. "I don't like your tone, Nurse," she said.

"No, Matron," I said, "and I'm afraid I don't like yours." I did, really,' she replied to the exclamations of incredulity, muted by macaroni pudding.

"'If you're not careful, Nurse," she said, "I shall have to give you a month's notice." "Thank you, Matron," I said, "but I came here for that purpose this morning.'"

I had been waiting outside Matron's Office myself that morning, but Dawlish didn't like to be addressed by Juniors and anyway, I didn't think it worth asking her how she had got all this into the half-minute or so within which I had seen her go in with a shilling and a broken thermometer in her hand and come out with a new one.

Whenever, in my moments of depression or rebellion, or simply fatigue, I considered giving in my notice, I had always ended by deciding to stay until I had to go on Night Duty. I hated the idea of staying up all night from compulsion not choice, and of having to spend precious daylight hours in bed. One would be completely cut off from the world, a demi-civilised, underworld creature, out of touch with normality for three weary months. Recent notices had hinted that, owing to shortage of staff, this might even be extended to four months. 'Many factory workers have been on Night Shifts for more than a year without complaint. E. Harriman, Ass. Mat.'

I was quite willing to give the thing a try, but I didn't see how I should ever keep awake. I went off Herbert Waterlow Ward at two o'clock in the afternoon, supposedly to get some of the sleep that I should miss that night. Night nurses had rooms in a different part of the hostel, behind a baize door, but I had not yet had time to change my room. I had not been in bed ten minutes before three of the maids settled down outside my door for a long gossip, whose punctuation marks were shrieks of laughter. I stood it for a while, and then opened the door and gave them what angry people in hotels give to belated revellers who are being awfully amusing with the boots and shoes. They stared at me in silence and I slammed the door and went back to bed, feeling rather a fool.

'Ee,' said Janet, who came from Tyneside and had stunted legs and not a sound tooth in her head, 'ee, that Na-a-as Dickens, who does shay think shay is? What a cha-ayk!' They talked on for a bit, to make it quite clear that when they did move away it was only because they wished to do so. I burrowed my head down and concentrated on sleep. It was bitterly cold; perhaps that was why I could not get off. I went out to the bathroom and filled my hot bottle.

'Hullo,' said Richardson in the corridor, surprised to see me in a dressing-gown, 'are you ill?'

'Night duty.'

'Oh, Glory, how *awful*. D'you know what ward you're on? I expect you'll be on Maternity – MacDonald's off sick. I say, bad *luck*.'

Thoroughly depressed, I got back into bed with a jersey over my nightgown and lay tense until I could relax in the slow return of warmth. I knew what Night Duty on Maternity meant: a baby born every night and all the mess for me, as junior, to clear up. Anything up to ten babies yelling all night long, and Night Sister coming round at intervals to say: 'Call yourself a nurse and you can't even keep a few babies quiet!'

I had just fallen into a shallow doze when somebody came down the corridor with her voice raised in song. I dozed again, and she returned, still singing the same song. After that, it was the nurses coming over for their teatime cigarette. Three and a half hours until getting-up time. If I could get off now, it would still do some good. The more I worried about it, the more restless I became. My head was like a factory working overtime. How often, on the ward at this time, I had felt that I would give anything to get into bed and sleep for ever. When the workmen began mending the pipes in the bathroom opposite, I gave it up and switched on the light to read. I was just nodding pleasantly over the book, reading whole pages without taking in a word, when a battering ram struck my door and Janet's 'Uff pust sevvun, Na-a-as!' stabbed me into the horror of reality.

This, I thought, as I got dressed, was the body that I had got to drag round with me all night. Please God, don't let any babies be born to-night. Hold up the course of nature until daytime; it can't make any difference.

The junior night nurses' breakfast was at eight o'clock and we had to be on the wards at twenty-five past, so that the day nurses could get off. There were nine of us, and we sat at one end of a table, while a maid laid the places for the day nurses' supper.

Tea and porridge and bread and margarine did not go down very well at this hour, but I was pleased to discover that Kelly, the Irish girl who brightened Toots's lectures, was also on night duty. She arrived late, in a sweet disorder, and helped herself to an immense plate of porridge, saying: 'Just got here before Fanny Adams, God be praised.'

Fanny Adams was the Senior Night Sister, a nut-coloured raw-boned woman, who prowled round the hospital on silent feet, with a venomous fang for a tongue. When she took morning breakfast on the Junior Night Sister's night off, people hardly dared to speak. She came in to-night, just as Kelly rammed in the last of her porridge, and we all stood up as if we had sat on drawing pins. She was very tall and looked, in her uniform, like an iron column, because she had no ins and outs and her apron did not stick out like other people's, but hung rigidly tubular.

She looked us over in silence and ticked off our names in a book.

'Nurse Dickens,' she said sharply, pronouncing it 'Diggins', 'you're on Jane English.' I could not help a broad smile spreading with relief at my escape from the babies, but she wiped it off with: 'I don't know what you're grinning at. You'll find plenty of work to do there. Busiest ward in the hospital at night usually.' Then she gave us a short lecture on blackout carelessness, threatened us all with prison, and thanked the Lord tartly for our tea and porridge.

Sister on Jane English was sitting at the desk writing the report when I reported for duty. She was quite young; she had done her training in this hospital and had only recently been promoted from Staff Nurse, and was very conscious of her status. She spoke primly, folding her mouth after each remark, in the same way that one felt she would never leave a drawer or a cupboard door open. She told me to go and ask the day nurses if I could help them finish up. I found them in the sluice, reading the paper.

'Is it half-past? Thank God,' they said, and hurried away to go off duty. I could have told them there was nothing to hurry for, because I had seen the maid dumping on the supper tables the great bowls of beetroot which always accompanied the pink rubbery circles known as Luncheon Sausage.

Sister Porter told me to go round the beds to see if the patients were comfortable. All the ward lights were out, except one or two, green-shrouded, over the beds of very ill patients and the shaded lamp on the desk, which picked out Sister's small hand, writing carefully, and one side of the neat roll of dark hair which surrounded her head in front of her cap. Just behind the desk, in the middle of the ward, a fire was burning low in the tiled stove, but beyond this, the beds were in complete darkness. I knocked into one or two, and fell over a chair, but most of the women were awake anyway, and the one or two who groaned were probably chronic grumblers. They all seemed very nice, with that undefensive friendliness that unfolds when the lights are out, and they all wanted to hear what had happened to poor little Nurse Siddons. They were very upset to lose her; it seemed she had

88

made life pleasant for them, and I suppose they doubted my ability to do the same.

'Always remembered I liked my egg more set than the others, little Nurse Siddons did,' sighed a woman who was no more to me than a vast mound, a tangle of black hair and a breathy whisper. I promised her that I would remember, too. I knew I was more likely to forget, but it seemed a pity to spoil her night.

In the kitchen, there was a list of those who had hot milk drinks before settling. I was just putting the saucepan on the stove, when Maxton, who was my Senior Night Nurse, arrived with a small suitcase and a cross expression. She went into the linen cupboard to deposit her cloak and case. I wondered what was in it.

'Good evening, Nurse,' I said politely, determined to start out right at least, however casual I might become later, under stress or exhaustion.

'What are you doing?' she said. 'You'd better stop it now and come into the ward while Sister gives the report.' In order to hear the report, one had to put on one's cuffs, and we stood, hands behind backs, one on either side of Sister while she read it. My mind wandered. It was no use feeling tired now, I told myself, with eleven hours to go, but my whole system insisted that it was time to finish work now, not to start.

'I hope you're listening carefully, Nurse Dickens,' said Sister, looking up. 'This is the only way of getting to know the patients, you know.' I brought my brain back. 'Do you know what Osteomyelitis is?' she asked.

'No, Sister.'

'Well, why didn't you ask, then, when I was reading the report on Mrs Rudolph? I don't want any carelessness from you, Nurse. This is a methodical ward, as Nurse Maxton will tell you.' Nurse Maxton lowered her pale eyes, which were always rather red, as though she had been crying. It was now that I first sensed the faint antagonism that all Day Sisters have for the night nurses on their ward. There is the suspicion that, behind their back, one will trifle with their beloved machine. Wherever possible, the blame for a mishap is pinned on to the night nurses. It is they who have broken that syringe to which no one will confess; they who ate that jelly and stole Sister's ginger biscuits. Sister Porter was quick to champion the day nurses, as she never would be to their faces, telling us how frequent treatment had improved the condition of Miss Murphy's back and how everything possible had been done to make Miss Griggs more comfortable, and hoping, though not expecting, that we should be as conscientious.

She rose and gathered up a neat pile of books and papers from the desk. 'When I come on in the morning,' she said, looking up at me, for she was very short, 'I do a complete round of kitchen, sluice, bathroom, specimen room – everything, to make sure you leave everything clean and tidy as the day staff leave it for you. Good night, Nurses.' She walked off as if she were in a deportment class with a book on her head. The long night had begun.

She was another of these notice addicts, I discovered. You could not open the door of any cupboard without being told to replace things in it tidily, and the walls of the sluice were papered with instructions to go easy on the Vim, to keep the steriliser filled up, and which disinfectant to use for what. Nurse Maxton told me vaguely what my duties were, but her mind seemed to be elsewhere. When I had given out the hot drinks and helped her rub the backs and heels of immobile patients, I had to do a spot of cleaning and then wash and iron some linen bandages. I was tiptoeing through the ward, dismayed to find that my shoes squeaked, which I had not noticed in the daytime, when a hoarse whisper came from the gloom at the end of the ward.

'Nurse!' Mrs Riscoe was sitting up in bed, two long plaits of dark hair hanging over the shoulders of her white nightgown.

'I say, dear,' she whispered, 'we always has a nice cup of tea round about now, them what's awake.' I was sure this was not official, but I couldn't fall short of Nurse Siddons, so I went to the kitchen to put on the kettle.

'And what is Nurse Diggins doing?' No footfall had announced the approach of Sister Adams.

'Oh, nothing, Sister.' I could feel myself blushing. 'I – I was just going to fill up the Sterile Water bottles.'

'You come into the ward while I do my round with Nurse Maxton,' she said. 'Cuffs on, please.' I had to stand sedately in the middle of the ward while the other two went round the beds, although in the kitchen I could hear the kettle boiling over and hissing on to the gas. Sister Adams carried a great torch like a lighthouse, which she flashed on to the patients' faces, waking them up to enquire if they could not sleep. Afterwards, she and Maxton went into the little room where the drug cupboard was, and I heard her telling Maxton off about something while she gave out the prescribed drugs. By the time she had gone, more than half the ward was awake and wanting tea. I resolved to take it round before eleven o'clock the next night

If it was difficult to learn patients' names and ailments in the daytime, it was impossible at night. I didn't think I would ever get them straight; I kept coming across a patient who should not be there, by my reckoning, and the five Fractured Femurs, with legs strung up to beams, were as one to me. For all I knew, I might have been giving out tea to Gastric Ulcers, but I couldn't keep asking Maxton, who was closeted behind screens with a fomentation, and who anyway moved in a brooding world of her own.

'What do I do now?' I asked her, as she was replacing the bowls in the steriliser.

'Oh, I don't care,' she said. 'You'd better come and sit at the desk and get on with the mending, while I write the midnight report.'

She dashed off a few words about the ill patients and said:

'Now for a bit of peace, thank goodness,' and went to fetch her suitcase. It held what seemed to be all her correspondence for the last year, an apple, a half-eaten bar of chocolate, a bag of macaroons and some khaki knitting. This knitting was her passion. She hated to be called away from it and kept dashing back to it at every opportunity throughout the night.

'Who's it for?' I asked, finishing off a darn which I knew would never satisfy Sister Porter.

'My sweetie,' said Maxton, and sighed. I would have liked to hear about him, but feared to be thought oncoming. A plaintive voice called from one of the beds and I had to get up to attend to it, and to two others who were struck with the same idea. Maxton was still clicking away furiously as I sat down and started on another operation sock. She sighed. Presently she sighed again, and said: 'Aren't men unreasonable?'

'Frightfully,' I said, and waited for more. Sure enough, it came, pouring out in a whispered torrent, to the unceasing accompaniment of the pecking needles and whirling wool. Sweetie, it transpired, was in an Anti-Aircraft unit near Redwood and had fallen for Maxton while having his tonsils out on Secker Ward. He was a man of fierce passions, and would flare up in an instant if Maxton so much as spoke to a bus conductor. The quarrel which was weighing on her tonight was such a complication of misunderstandings, wrong telephone messages and female cousins mistaken for males that I could not follow it closely. This evening, Maxton had received a stilted letter saying that she need not bother to meet George same time same place Saturday. I had to read this and many others that had gone before, some tender, some disagreeable and some embarrassing, while all the time Maxton knitted away at the pullover as if it were already imbued with some of the glamour of George's person.

I was to get sick of the sound of his name before long. Never did a couple have so many quarrels, so many reconciliations or so many tedious conversations which had to be retailed to me verbatim. Never was a couple more boring.

At twelve o'clock, Maxton finished a row, dabbed a grubby felt puff on to a solid powder compact and dabbed it on her nose and went up to the Midnight Meal. I felt rather big at being left in charge of the ward and strolled importantly round once or twice.

'Where's the other nurse – the sandy-haired one?' asked one of the Fractured Femurs. 'I wish she'd come and fix my leg; it's tormenting me.'

'I'll do it,' I said, though baffled by the network of strings and pulleys and bandages.

'Don't you touch it, my girl,' said the woman. 'The other nurse understands it. I want her.'

'She's gone to her supper.' The woman groaned. 'Oh dear,' I said, 'is it very painful?'

'It's perjury, that's what it is, Nurse. Perjury.'

Someone came into the ward and I saw it was the very young House Surgeon, Mr Ridley. I went up to him.

'Anything you want, Nurse? I'm just going to bed.' I remembered that Maxton had told me that if any of the House Surgeons came down, I was to ask them to chart Mrs Rudolph for something. I had not the slightest idea what that meant, but I repeated the message, and he yawned and said: 'OK. Where's her chart?'

Her chart? I didn't even know where her bed was. I wandered ineffectually round for a bit, peering at the names on the charts, and at last he went over to the right bed and got the chart himself. I felt an awful fool.

'What d'you want for her?' he asked, bending over the desk and shaking his fountain pen dangerously near Sweetie's pullover.

'Well, I – er—'

'Pot Brom and Chloral, I should think,' he said, making cryptic signs on the back of the chart. 'Yes, please,' said I, although he might have been prescribing weed-killer for all I knew. He was just going, when another groan of Perjury came from halfway down the ward.

'Oh, would you just look at this woman's leg, sir?' I asked. 'She says it's painful and she won't let me touch it.'

'Hullo, Mrs Davenport,' he said, going up to the bed and flashing a pencil torch on her. 'What's the trouble?'

'Me leg again,' she said. 'Here I lay, week after week, and it gets no easier. It don't seem right, you know. You'd think they could do something.' She looked like one of those potatoes that people photograph and send to the papers because it bears a curious resemblance to a human face.

'I'll soon fix that,' said Mr Ridley. 'Hold the torch a sec, Nurse.' He began sorting out the strings that slung Mrs Davenport's leg to the beam. 'Now then, young man,' she began querulously, 'don't you touch they cords – ouch!' With a quick wrench, he had hauled her foot about six inches higher and straightened it.

'There! That's better, isn't it?' She hated having to admit it, but it was.

Maxton came back as the House Surgeon was sauntering away. 'What did *he* want?' she asked, chasing the remains of her meal with her tongue.

'He was fixing Mrs Davenport's leg; she was making an awful fuss.'

'Silly idiot,' said Maxton. 'I wish he'd leave things alone; she's not his patient.'

'Well, he made it all right, anyway,' I said. 'I think he's rather nice.'

'I could have done it,' she said, picking up her knitting. 'I hate these Housemen – stuck-up little boys, they think they know everything. Give me an older man, a man with experience—'

'Like George?' I suggested, knowing that it was time for me to go up to the dining-room, and escaping before she could get going on the subject.

94

'Well, how's Sweetie?' Kelly asked me, as I came into the dining-room. He was evidently a notorious figure. The night duty maid dumped a tin pie dish down in front of Flowers, who sat at the head, and she doled out an ambiguous concoction with a ladle. It was vegetables cooked in water, and then the water thickened and coloured with browning to look like gravy. Afterwards, we had cold rice pudding. We were allowed half an hour away from the ward, and we spun it out with cups of tea and desultory conversation, but they all seemed pretty bored with each other and inclined to bicker. Night duty makes you like that. For one thing, you are always tired, and the comparatively few people with whom you mix get on your nerves far more than the large, assorted day staff. After a time, you feel you must scream and throw chairs if you have to sit once more at table with the same eight girls. Every mannerism is a prong, and their table manners nauseatingly familiar. You listen for the dreadful clicking of Ringer's jaw, you long to tell Flowers not to hold her knife as if she were going to eat peas off it, and you know that at any moment Jones will say: 'I always say a cup of tea bucks you up.'

Someone once burst out to me: 'Oh, for God's sake, Dickens, don't keep kicking your chair like that!' I never knew I did it. I was devastated; I knew exactly how she felt.

When I got back to the ward, it was very cold. The fire had gone out and there was a bleak draught that hit you as you sat at the desk. I went and got my cloak and then leaned against one of the radiators for a while, yawning. Soon I was so sleepy that I had to sit down, and I put my head on my arms on the desk and floated peacefully away. The words 'Fanny Adams' dropped into my sleep like stones into a lake, and a dig in the ribs sent me jumping to my feet just in time to see Maxton going forward to meet Night Sister on her early morning round. I stood by the desk swaying and shivering, and when she drew level with me on the way back, Sister stopped and flashed her torch on my sleepy face.

'And who is this Nurse with the bad manners? Ah, yes, Nurse Dickens; we shall have to keep an eye on you.' She stayed a moment longer, as if expecting something from me, and then, as I wasn't worth wasting her battery on, clicked off her torch and walked on.

'You soft thing, why didn't you take off your cloak?' asked Maxton when she had gone.

'Good Lord, is that what she meant? I didn't even know I had it on.'

'Well, I'm sorry for you if she gets a grudge against you. She knows how to make life Hell.' She picked up her knitting again, and I slumped down beside her. 'Maxton, I'm so tired, I think I'm going to die. I'll never last out. Isn't it nearly time to start waking them up?'

'We're not supposed to start before five o'clock, but it's impossible to get done if you wait till then. You just have to look out one of the Night Sisters doesn't catch you. Siddons used to start by washing the ill people. They don't know whether it's Christmas or Easter, anyway.'

'Can I start now?'

'Heavens, no. Not for at least another hour.' I sat and brooded for a bit, fell asleep, woke up and sat on my hands to try and warm them. I prayed that nobody would call, because, apart from being too tired, I was too cold to move. I was numb with despair. I knew now, for certain, that the night would never end.

'D'you think that'll be long enough to his armpit?' asked Maxton.

'Uh-huh,' I said without looking. The thought of Sweetie's armpit made me quite ill.

'If I were you,' she said, 'I'd go and cut the bread-and-butter and lay the trolley for breakfast. You'll never have time later on.'

In the kitchen I was struck by the brilliant idea of a cup of tea and wished I had thought of it before. Maxton would not come and have one, because she wanted to get over a tricky bit of arm-hole. She kept telling me to hurry up with the bread-and-butter because while I was in the kitchen she had to answer all the calls in the ward.

On night duty, you reach the nadir of vitality at about half-past three. Your system is barely ticking over; you think you are alive but you couldn't swear to it. Soon after that, you have to start work and there is so much to do that you have to start at top speed and keep up the pace until eight o'clock or later, when you go off duty. The initial effort is agony, like the moving of a limb that has been numbed with cramp, but once you have forced yourself into motion, you can keep it up if only you go fast enough. Maxton and I scuttled about like mad things. We each had our own work to do, mine more domestic and hers more skilled, and we only spoke occasionally as we flashed past, or pushed each other out of the way in the sluice, to fling over our shoulders that despairing cry: 'I'll never get done!'

Being strange to the ward, I had no system. My hair escaped from under my cap and I could see my face shining out of the corner of my eye. To think that a short time ago I had been frozen solid! I constantly caught the name 'Nurse Siddons' in a regretful tone as I muddled along, and when it came to breakfast time, the murmurs swelled to protest. The patients had to pro-vide their own eggs, and in my frenzy to get the breakfasts in and out before the day staff arrived, I got mixed and gave them out at random, so that rightful egg-owners at the far end of the ward were cheated. Added to this, I had hard-boiled them all by mis-take, and I pretended not to hear the murmurs of 'Wicked waste, with eggs so scarce', and 'I been looking forward to that egg for days'.

'What, no porridge, Nurse? We always have porridge.'

'I'm so sorry, I'm so sorry,' I almost sobbed, as I poured out tea and got mixed up with those I had sugared and those I hadn't and

97

gave a sugared one to a Diabetic. The atmosphere all round me was pregnant with the uneasiness of a ship whose crew is about to mutiny, and just as I was making up my mind to the fact that they would all complain to Sister and probably even to Matron, Mrs Wilson, blessed Mrs Wilson, stemmed the growing tide and turned it in my favour. She was the woman who liked her egg well set, and she had got it; the tea was black and the sugar allowance exhausted by the time I reached her, but she liked it strong and unsweetened, and she detested porridge. So she raised her voice and stood up for me, and as she was respected for her size and the length of time she had been in hospital, they gradually came round and I loved them all instead of wanting to shoot them. One or two who were allowed up even volunteered to help me clear away, and Miss Holloway, who was very refined in a green kimono and slippers with rosettes, padded from bed to bed saying: 'Are you *quaite* sure you've finished? Ah, then I'll take your tray. Just like the cafeteria, isn't it, Nurse?' Her giggle was like the whinny of a catarrhal horse.

The Day Staff came on at seven, yawning and aloof, and we went on making our side of beds, secure in the superiority of having kept all these people alive while the others were callously asleep. We came to a bed with a wide cradle over two legs, ele-phantine with plaster of paris. I looked at the chart. 'Maisie Griggs'. Of course! I had forgotten that she was on this ward. But she was not at all as I had pictured her; she was quite young, but, perhaps because pain had settled in her face and eyes, she looked as old, even older than Larry. He had told me he was going to marry her, and I mentioned it, and the women on either side took it up delightedly and teased her. I was surprised to find that nobody except Evans, who had carried the notes, knew about Larry.

'Why didn't you tell them?' I asked Maisie. 'I'd boast about a man like that.'

'What's he like?' asked Maxton, heaving up one of the cumbrous legs while I turned the pillow underneath.

'Marvellous,' I said, and enlarged on him.

'Man to leave home for, eh?' said Mrs Rudolph.

'Rather. Isn't he, Mais?'

'Yes,' she said, in her quiet, toneless voice. 'Oh, don't touch that leg, Nurse – I can't bear you to touch that leg.'

None of the other Sisters ever came on duty before a quarter-past eight, but Sister Porter arrived punctually at eight, looking as neat as a doll that doesn't undress. I had forgotten about her inspection and had to dash round trying to create order, but she arrived too soon and said: 'I will not have my ward untidied. You must work *my* way here, Nurse, whatever you do on other wards.' She had already discovered that I had given an egg to a woman on sulphanilamide tablets, an unforgivable crime, apparently.

'I'm sorry,' I said, 'I didn't know—'

'You should have,' said Sister, thoroughly shocked, although it could not have been so long since she herself had discovered this fact with equal surprise. I suspected that she was younger than me, but she made me feel half her age. It is depressing to see someone cast off Youth almost unworn. It usually means they try to dress up in it again much later on when it doesn't suit them any more.

After this, I went to ask Maxton if there was anything else I had to do. 'What a night,' I said, 'I'm dead to the world.'

'What a night?' She looked at me in surprise. 'Why, that was one of the easiest nights I've ever had. You wait till we're busy.'

I was too tired to be hungry, but I had to go up to the dining-room and face rabbit stew and ginger pudding, which, at half-past eight in the morning, seemed queer eating. One of the Seniors, a girl called McLeod, with arms like a blacksmith and a blooming complexion that did not look as if it had been up all night, did miracles with the food and ate on unabashed long after we had all finished.

Afterwards, when I was changing my room to the night nurses' section, I passed by her open door and saw her sitting on the bed with a friend, eating salmon out of a tin with tin-openers.

When I had adjusted myself to living upside down, I began to like nursing at night. It meant you were free to go about during the day as long as you could stay awake, and I found that by the time I had come off the ward and had a bath, I had got my second wind and enough energy to go out. It was spurious energy, that wore off after a time, leaving one limp and dull-witted, but it was enough to start off with. Officially, of course, we were supposed to be in bed by eleven o'clock, but drawn curtains and a bolster in the bed satisfied Sister Harriman's short sight. The wife of the Wing-Commander whom I had met at the Air Force dance had twice asked me to her house, and eventually I accepted an invitation for Sunday lunch. Chris was off that morning, and she and I walked in the town and had coffee at the Blue Lady to keep me awake. Then I changed and bicycled off down the hill, with the wind making havoc of my carefully set hair.

Wing-Commander and Mrs Fellowes lived on the outskirts of the town in the sort of house that you find on big golf-course estates. My heart sank at the sight of two cars outside the door. I didn't feel equal to a party. There they all were, in the lounge or drawing-room or whatever they called it, drinking cocktails and making booming conversation. Mrs Fellowes, with her hair in a lot of little curls like rusty iron filings, stressed the fact that I was a nurse, which made my hands feel larger and redder than ever. Bertie Fellowes had not the faintest idea who I was, but greeted me jovially with his horse laugh and gave me a large strong cocktail. There were one or two other Air Force officers, a pink and white soldier and a high-pitched young man from some Ministry. There were also some women in towny tweeds, and a girl for whose enhancement the WAAF uniform might have been designed. There was a broken-down relation somewhere about, and two dogs that lay on the furniture.

At lunch they all talked about the war, and as I had not seen a paper for days, I kept out of it and concentrated on the food, until Mrs Fellowes called the maid back with a dish and said loudly: 'Now, you *must* have some more. Don't worry about us, we'll wait for you. I know nurses always have enormous appetites.'

Everyone stopped talking and stared, and Bertie said: 'Yes, by Jove, remember that female we had in the house while you were having the Twins? Ate like a horse, you never saw anything like it,' he assured the company.

'Yes, and d'you remember how awful it was at meals, Uncle Bertie?' said the girl in WAAF uniform, 'how she only had two topics of conversation – the Royal Family and disgusting details of her other cases?'

'God, yes,' said her uncle. 'I never knew which I disliked most – the Little Princesses or Lady Sidebotham's operation. She began on regurgitation once, at breakfast . . .'

'They're all the same, aren't they?' said the tweedy woman with the regimental badges, 'a race of screaming bores—' She suddenly noticed what I had been aware of for some time: Mrs Fellowes making pulled-down faces and tapping on the table to remind them of me. The tweedy woman laughed nervously, cleared her throat and began to talk very fast about bridge.

It was the fact that they thought I minded which made me so furious. I resolved to leave as soon as possible. However, in a comfortable armchair in the drawing-room, I became so comatose that I had not the gumption to get up and break into the talk with good-byes. Somebody came and sat down by me and began to talk, and I had to fight to keep my eyes open. I felt stupid and plain, and I wanted to powder my nose but didn't know where I had put my bag. 'You look sleepy,' somebody said. 'Too much lunch.'

'I'm all right,' I said, 'you get tired being on night duty.'

'You mean you've been up all night? How ghastly.' But it didn't really penetrate. They all felt too well and self-confident to imagine a dreariness of spirit such as mine. With an effort, I got up and went over to Mrs Fellowes. 'I really must go now,' I began, but Bertie cut in with: 'Go? Good Heavens, what are you talking about? You can't go yet. We're all going over to see a display by a new type of Fighter.'

'Oh, but really, I don't think I—'

'Nonsense. Of course you must come. I'll take you in the Buick with me. Off you go upstairs with the other gels and do whatever it is women take such hours over.' His laughter made my head reel.

Up in Mrs Fellowes's bedroom, I sat on the bed while the other women chattered and tried on each other's hats. I felt exactly as I used to at the age of eighteen, when I had gone dumbly to parties and every female, including the cloakroom attendant, had made me feel inferior. I was out of touch with the world all right, if this was the world. Somehow I survived the rest of the afternoon, tagging along and yawning when no one was looking, and then we all had to go back to tea at 'Four Winds', which was the name of the Fellowes' house. I might have gone home then, but my resistance was shattered.

Mrs Fellowes sat very upright behind silver teapots, and we sat round balancing things on our knees and there was much passing of food. They were talking about the War again, and it seemed odd that we should be eating three kinds of cake. They went on talking about the War and it seemed that the pink-and-white soldier ran the Army and the high-pitched youth ran the Civil Service and the others ran the Air Force, which was nice for them. Tea woke me up slightly and I began to talk about the hospital. I found I could talk quite a lot about that before I realised I was being a bore. I had given up all thought of ever getting to bed, when some of them began to say they had to get back to the aerodrome and miraculously the party broke up.

Bertie's niece offered to give me a lift, as she was taking the Civil Servant to the station.

I explained about my bicycle.

'Leave it here, my dear,' said Bertie. 'You can pick it up any time.'

'Oh no, thanks awfully. I don't mind a bit. I like bicycling.' I didn't want to come again.

'Now be sure and come and see us another time,' said Mrs Fellowes, smiling her charity smile at me as I said good-bye. 'Whenever you want a good meal, just ring up. We're in the book.' The niece pressed me once more to come in the car, and I again insisted that I liked bicycling and pedalled away into the biting wind that is always in your face when you're bicycling, whichever way you go. I had dismounted and was pushing the bike up the steep part of the hill, when the WAAF roared past me in an Air Force car. She waved and I waved back to show that I was happy.

Maxton and I were fairly busy these nights and Sweetie's sweater was making poor progress. We had several operations at night and one or two desperately ill patients who had kept us fussed and caused Sister Adams to be in and out of the ward all night, which was enough to break anyone's nerve.

I liked going to the Theatre at night: it was exciting, and the operations, being nearly all emergency ones, were imbued with a sense of urgency. Also, there was only one Theatre Nurse on at night, so that the nurse who brought the patient from the ward had to stay and assist in all the little things that the theatre staff did in the daytime. When I ran about with drums, brought in the saline bowl or held a leg, I felt as important as if I were doing the whole operation. It was nerve-racking, because I did not know what to do, and with a dangerously ill patient on the table, the atmosphere tense with the surgeon's nervous irritability, and someone hissing from behind a mask, 'Quick, Nurse! Give her an injection of Atropine!' I nearly had a stroke.

Usually, Mr Sickert, the Resident Surgical Officer, or one of the other Housemen did the night operations, but sometimes one of the Honoraries was called from his after-dinner chair or even from his bed. Nurse Bonar, the Night Theatre Nurse who assisted with the cases, handing instruments and swabs, had a wholesale disdain for all these men, and the more eminent they were, the more she despised them. Each one had some idiosyncrasy in the theatre – Sir Curtis Rowntree hummed all the time, Mr Harvey Watkins would not allow iodine on the patient's skin, and the gynaecologist flew into a rage if anyone spoke. Nurse Bonar would imitate them before, during and after the operation for the benefit of the House Surgeons, the porters, or whoever was about. If the operation was complicated and took a long time, Bonar would begin looking at the clock, raising her eyes to heaven and making pushing gestures in the direction of the unsuspecting surgeon. Afterwards, while she and I were bandaging the patient, she would begin to revile him almost before he was out of the door. One of the House Surgeons would stroll in. 'Treat for you, Nurse Bonar. Vav's going to do a Caesar in half an hour's time.' He would withdraw hurriedly, because Bonar sometimes threw instruments when she was in a temper.

I personally was terrified of all surgeons and hated having to go near enough to do up their sterile gowns or to wipe sweat from their brows. Once or twice I had touched them and made them unsterile and I wished myself dead as I received their reaction at having to go through the whole scrubbing-up business again. My greatest shame, however, was when one of them suddenly shot at me through his mask: 'Fetch me the proctoscope!' and never having heard of the instrument before, I heard it as something else and came trotting faithfully back with the white coat of the night porter which I had dragged off his indignant back.

On the night after the Fellowes party, we had an acute appendix and an amputation of a finger, and it was nearly midnight before I got back to the ward. I was not feeling nearly as tired as I expected after only two hours' sleep, but Maxton assured me that I should feel worse later. When she had gone up to 'Meal' and I was sitting at the desk reading the paper in an attempt to make myself more up to date than the afternoon had shown me to be, I heard sounds behind me that required investigation.

It was Maisie, with the sheet stuffed into her mouth to muffle the tearing sobs that were shaking her. Two days ago, they had decided that her left leg was not satisfactory, and needed extending. So they had driven a skewer through the heel – right through the bone and out at the other side, and from the ends of the skewer a cord let over a pulley to a fifteen-pound weight that hung clear over the head of the bed.

'Poor Mais,' I said. 'Is it very painful? Have you had your Veganin?'

'It isn't any good,' she sobbed. 'Nothing's any good any more. I wish I was dead.'

'You mustn't talk like that. You've got to get well for Larry.'

She looked at me with her swollen eyes, her sobs momentarily checked. 'But didn't you know?' she whispered. 'Larry's dead.'

'But Maisie, he's not!'

'Oh yes, he is,' she went on in that toneless voice. 'I saw him. There was an accident, you know. There's blood all over his head.' She began to cry again. I didn't know what to do. I thought if I talked to her steadily, it might penetrate, but she only said: 'Poor Larry. Poor Larry. There's blood on my face too, Nurse. I wish you'd wash it off.'

'No, there isn't, Mais.'

'Yes, yes, can't you see?' She rubbed at her forehead with frenzied fingers. 'All over here – blood – ugh! Horrible, sticky. Look, it's all over my hand.' She held it out and then turned it backwards and forwards under her own eyes. 'All over blood,' she said pitifully.

I took hold of her hand. 'It's not your head that hurts, Maisie,' I said, 'it's your poor legs, and they're going to be all right pretty soon.'

'No, no,' she wailed, 'they'll never be all right. I don't want anything done to them. I can't ...' She was sobbing uncontrollably now, dry-eyed and hysterical. I went to the telephone and rang for Night Sister to come, and Sister Gilbert, who was Fanny Adams's junior, came and gave me some morphia for her and Maisie slept for a while and woke again to pain.

She had to have morphia every night for a long time. Nights and days of continual pain drew her face into sharp planes and hollows, and even when the pain was temporarily easier, she thought of nothing but its return. The news of Larry was good. He was being discharged soon to a convalescent home, but she would not talk of him now and refused to write to him. Often, in the creeping hours after midnight when Maxton was knitting away at the Balaclava helmet that was the pullover's successor, I used to sit by Maisie's bed and we would have tea and talk until someone called me away.

'Larry's going out to-morrow,' I told her one night. 'I suppose you'll get married as soon as you're well.'

'No,' she said. 'I'll never marry him.'

'But I thought it was all arranged. He told me—'

'You don't understand, Nurse. There was never any question of it before the accident – well, we were friendly, and he used to take me out because he was grateful to us when he was billeted on us – but not marriage. I'm too old for him, anyway.'

'But he wants you to – he told me.'

'Can't you *see?*' she said, fiddling with the bedclothes as she always did when the pain was returning. 'It's obvious enough, surely.' She gave a short laugh. 'He only asked me out of pity – to try and make up for what he'd done to me.'

I was glad when Sister moved Maisie's bed away from the neighbours who tried to cheer her up by teasing her and calling her 'the bride'. Sister put her out on the balcony to see if she would improve, but it was a long, long time before she went home, with her left leg still in plaster. I went to tea with her once and she told me that Larry had tried everything he knew to get a Staff job but had been passed out of the Army as unfit and had gone back to Canada.

'He wanted Maisie to go out to him,' broke in her mother, untying her apron as she came out of the kitchen. 'Her father and I both think she ought to go.'

'Don't be silly, Mother. A man doesn't want a wife with a use-less leg.'

'Sister was telling me that Mr Sickert wants you to come back for more treatment,' I said.

'I won't go. I've had enough of being messed about. It wouldn't be any good anyway.'

'Oh, Maisie,' said her mother, pushing the cups and saucers about ineffectually, 'I wish you wouldn't talk like that. Can't you persuade her, Nurse? She's so difficult.'

'Oh, Mother, *don't*,' said Maisie.

Instead of getting one night off a week, we got three nights run-ning each month. When Maxton had hers, her place on Jane English was taken by McLeod, the girl with the stomach like a Gladstone bag. She ate all night long, starting with tea and toast as soon as Sister had done her first round and keeping up her strength with a succession of snacks until I had made the break-fast porridge. I learned after the first night to make a double quantity. We were officially allowed to have our tea on the ward between four and five in the morning, and as this was our busiest time, Maxton and I used to snatch at it, dashing into the ward between each sip of tea and dashing back to the kitchen for another bite of macaroon. No matter how busy we were, however, McLeod would solemnly take her full twenty minutes in the kitchen, consuming vast quantities of bread and toast, which I, to my annoyance, had to make for her, and even afterwards, wandering dissatisfiedly into the larder and picking bits off the loaf.

Maxton had stayed with Sweetie's people for her nights off, as she had wangled them to coincide with his weekend leave. A horrid scene had taken place in the drawing-room after everyone had gone to bed and of course I was spared none of the grisly details.

'D'you think you ought to be telling me all this?' I asked, fidgeting uncomfortably.

'I thought you'd like me to tell you. Of course, if you don't want to hear about it—' she said stuffily.

Anything was better than to put Maxton in a temper for the night. It made her impossible to work with; she would delay taking the temperatures because she knew I could not take the breakfasts round and give the patients hot tea before their temperatures were taken, and I would be feverishly collecting cups and plates while the day nurses were already making beds, and the Staff Nurse would tell Sister I was inefficient.

'Go on, go on,' I sighed. 'I love it.' I wondered whether Sweetie was similarly regaling the boys of the Ack-Ack unit.

At the end of the month, I had my nights off, and Maxton was due to be back on day duty by the time I returned. A certain limited friendship had grown between us; you can't work hard together for night after night without developing some sort of bond, and I would miss her macaroons.

It was terrible coming back after three nights at home. It was just long enough to give one a tantalising glimpse of the delight-ful, forgotten life that used to be, before the curtain fell and one was walking down the blue-lit corridor of the Nurses' Hostel as if one had never been away. Tantalising too to have slept at night and been civilised during the day. I had slept late on my last morning, and taken the last possible train to Redwood, and Janet's 'Uff-past sev-vun, Na-a-as!' found me dolefully unpacking my case.

'Ee, not in bed?' she said, coming in and folding her arms over a shape of which everyone was suspicious until they discovered that it remained like that, year in, year out. ' 'Ad a good time, Honey? How's your yoong man?' she said, referring to the picture on my dressing-table which she would never accept as my brother-in-law.

'I've given my notice,' she said, accepting a cigarette. 'I told Sister Urriman to her face: "this place is a doomp," I said.' This was a ritual that occurred monthly, just before pay-day. Sister Harriman would have felt quite lost without it. I made the nec-essary sounds of regret.

'Ee well, ' said Janet. 'I suppose I must go and wake the other booggers.' I could hear her knocking and yelling all down the cor-ridor, returning with an ear-splitting rendering of 'A Pair of Silver Wings'.

Same old faces at breakfast, same old shop talk. Somehow one expected them to be different each time one came back. It was disheartening to think that they had all been circling around as usual within the confines, while I had been discovering that there were, after all, things going on outside. Nobody knew who was the new Senior on Jane English, but it was bound to be somebody frightful. I went about my early duties, prepared to be sickened by what nine o'clock should bring me. Sister called me over to the desk to inform me that Nurse Jones, who had taken my place while I was away, had made the tea ration go nearly twice as far, and why couldn't I, etc., etc. Catch Jones giving the patients tea in the middle of the night, I thought, and then I wasn't listening to Sister any more, for coming through the door, shooting her cuffs in that familiar way, was – of all people – Chris! Last Sunday, the stars had foretold that I would have a stroke of luck in mid-week that would alter my outlook on life. Here it was; I only hope that the prophecy was also fulfilled for the million other children of the sign of Taurus. It was a beautiful thought to think of all our fortunes turning simultaneously, like furrows in a ploughed field, and leading on up to better things, until at the week-end, we all met discouragement in our home circles and fell out, temporarily, with a Loved One.

The ward was still very busy, but the work was less oppressive when you could laugh about it. Nothing had ever been amusing to Maxton. She had not even thought it funny when the drug-addict came in with a broken hypodermic needle at large in her hind-quarters, or when Sister Adams slipped on a boiled sweet and shattered the darkness with a crash like the unloading of scrap iron, or when Paraldehyde went to Mrs Saxby's head and she made passionate advances to Mr Briant.

Mr Briant fancied Chris and was constantly on the ward. She called it a 'mental affinity', but whatever it was, I was always having to get up from the desk and occupy myself with chores while they talked and talked, he with his chair tipped, his feet on the night report book and his pipe alight, and Chris with her cap off and the desk lamp making her hair look like a jar of honey in the sun. I usually had to occupy myself in the kitchen, so that I could announce the approach of Sister Adams by dropping a plate, and then Chris would jam her cap on over one eye and Mr Briant would begin furiously writing up case histories with a pen with no ink in it. Sometimes, I would answer the telephone to Andrews' plaintive voice from Herbert Waterlow inquiring when Mr Briant was coming down to see their Peritonitis boy.

'Is it urgent?' I would ask.

'Well, not actually *urgent*, really – I – er – suppose he's frightfully busy with you?' I could picture her squirming and pulling up her stockings.

'Well, he is rather.'

'Could you ask him to come as soon as he can? I don't think he ought to leave it much longer.' I knew that she wanted him to go down while the other nurse on the ward was still away at supper. Then the telephone would ring again and the hoarse voice of Tivy, the night duty maid, would pant that Nurse Parry had better come up to the dining-room quick, as Sister Adams was up there to see Oo didn't turn up.

Once Chris came back from her burnt baked beans and waxy potatoes just in time to save me from a predicament. One of the night porters, a burly man with a cauliflower ear and an aboriginal brow, was in the habit of coming up to Jane English for a cup of tea at intervals during the night. The ward was quiet, so I stayed in the kitchen with him and got on with my bread and butter, while he drew in his tea by suction. The doings of his relations were a serial story of which he gave me an instalment every time he came up, whether on business or pleasure. I was supposed to be *au fait* with the Clan Harper, but would sometimes absently ask: 'Who's Harry?' or 'Where does Lilian live?' '*You* know,' Harper would insist over his shoulder, from the other end of the trolley that we were wheeling along from the lift. 'I told you about Harry. He's the one that's an ARP Warden down Bromley way – I *told* you. And Lilian, you know where Lilian lives – not a stone's-throw from the King and Queen, as she always says. Which bed is it, Nurse?'

'Yes,' he would continue, while we bent over the trolley, struggling to get our arms underneath the unconscious body to lift her on to the bed, 'yes, she's a London girl, our Lilian. Got a nice little business, too – Ready, Nurse? *Hup* she goes – Invisible Mending.'

We staggered to the bed. 'But she's not like Else. I told you about Else – Want her over on 'er side? Lilian never had her head for figures—' Thump, we lowered our burden and I pulled the blankets over her. 'Works in a cash desk, Else does. I say this old dame's a bit blue, 'n't she?'

'Yes, she is rather. D'you think you could get the oxygen cylinder while I hold her jaw up?'

'Sits in a cash desk,' he continued, trundling up the oxygen stand, 'with her hair all in curls, as smart as you like. She's the one I told you that married that chap in the RASC.' He leaned over my shoulder breathing heavily while I tried to push the thin rubber tube up the patient's nose. 'Got a nice little place out Burnham Beeches – turn it on now? Right, here it comes, Ma – or the Beeches, as some call it. But, of course, come the war they had to move out. Got a nice Let for it, though, trust Else for that – 'Ere, aren't you giving her a bit much, Nurse? She's not a barridge balloon.'

On this particular night, when Chris was at supper and Harper and I together in the kitchen, he suddenly broke off an account of Cousin Arthur's wedding to stride swiftly to the door, shut it and stand against it, breathing heavily and saying, 'You don't leave this kitchen without you give us a kiss.'

I tried to laugh it off, but he held his ground, half surprised at himself but determined to go through with it.

'Oh, come on, Harp,' I said, 'don't play the fool. Let me out. Let me *out!*' I said, getting annoyed, for I could hear someone calling from the ward.

'Give us a kiss, then.'

'Oh, stop it. Listen, there's someone calling for me. They might die and it would be your fault.'

'All right. You can go out – when you've given us a kiss.' He was still rather sheepish about it. I picked up a fork to jab into the hamlike hand that held the door knob, but as I approached him, he grabbed me, chuckling with delight at himself, and Chris opened the door on a most undignified struggle.

'I'm so sorry,' she said, with a bland, social smile. 'Am I intruding?'

'Yes,' said Harper, still holding my arm.

'Oh. I only looked in to say that Sweet Fanny Adams is on her way round to find out why there's no one looking after the switchboard. She wants to ring Mr Sickert's bedroom and ask him if to-night's the night, but she can't get through.'

Early that morning, while I was washing Mrs Saxby, assuring her that I was doing her early so that she could have a nice little sleep until breakfast time, a large figure shambled into the still-darkened ward and stood with hanging hands, waiting to be noticed. It was Harper, come to apologise. He was horrified at himself, for in spite of his stature he was as mild as a doe.

He was quite useful. He used to fetch up coal for us, so that as soon as Sister Porter had gone off, we could fall on the fire and nurse and nourish the dying embers into something that lasted us all night. Then, if Mr Briant came down with some beer, we could pull the settee across the fire and be as cosy as anything. Sometimes Chris and I took turns to have a sleep there, regretting it on waking to a sick headache and the sense of doom that hangs about before the dawn.

Certain nights stand out now from the endless succession that rolled by until I began to forget what it was like to work in the daytime. There was the night when a girl who had been in a collision on the way home from a dance was admitted at eleven o'clock with what was collectively called a fractured skull. Her mother didn't recognise her at first. Soon after midnight, the stertorous breathing suddenly choked on a dreadful noise and then stopped.

The kind little Junior Night Sister took the mother away, and Tivy rang down from the dining-room to say that Sister Adams was up there and creating for Nurse Parry. It was a freezing night; the fire was out, and there was a chill in the ward that seemed to have reached the core of my being. I sat at the desk, with my back resolutely turned on the bed that had three screens round it and tried to concentrate on the paper. I would have welcomed even Mrs Dummett's cough, to break the stillness of the ward. The silence was full of little half-heard sounds – creaks and rustlings and the breath of a sigh that might be only in one's head. In my imagination, I could hear the pad of feet on the floor behind me. Look round, I kept telling myself. You'll feel much better when you know it's only your imagination. You won't hear it any more. But I didn't dare look round in case I should discover that it was not imagination.

It was not imagination. I could hear it quite plainly now – the pad, pad of bare feet approaching me – I could feel it in my spine, paralysing me in my chair. Slowly, slowly, I turned my head, with my eyes following last, and then, in a moment, I had leaped to my feet with a smothered yell and my hand to my mouth, petrified by the white figure that was feeling its way up the ward from bed to bed.

Serenely unconscious that she had nearly killed me of fright, Mrs Montgomery proceeded on her way. 'Just going to the toilet, Nurse,' she whispered, as she passed the chair into which I had sunk with a cold sweat breaking out and my heart hammering. After that, I sat facing the screens until Chris came back.

When you have laid out a dead person at night, especially a casualty, you know that nothing that anybody could ever ask you to do would be impossible.

I felt shaky long after Harper had taken the girl away, and Chris and I were having cigarettes by the sterilisers, when I heard the faint creak and swish of the swing doors that led into the ward.

'Christ,' said Chris, 'who's that?' She stubbed out her cigarette and looked into the ward. 'The Terror that Walks by Night,' she said, and went out to meet her. I could see that Sister Adams was annoyed about something. She stood holding her torch like a weapon while she talked, and Chris seemed to be arguing with her. At length, she raised her voice and I heard her say: 'See that it's done at once, Nurse,' before she turned abruptly and went out of the ward.

'I'm terribly sorry—' Chris hardly knew how to say it. 'I tried to make her let me go but she won't let me leave the ward.' It appeared that we had not done our job properly; Sister had been to look, and the bandages were coming through. I had got to go down to the Mortuary with wool and packing and put it right. 'I asked her to let you take another nurse with you,' said Chris, 'but she wouldn't. Here,' she said, grimly, handing me the great torch, 'she left you this for company.'

When I came back, I looked to see if my hair had gone white. I almost wished it had; it might have got Sister Adams into trouble.

I never went to the Fellowes' house again. The nearest I got to them was meeting the down-trodden relation in the town in a hopeless sort of hat, and she took me into Hooper's for a cup of coffee. She liked to talk; she didn't get much chance at 'Four Winds'; and over the second cup she became very confiding and told me that Mrs Fellowes had married beneath her. 'The family was very upset at the time. She could have married anyone, you know.'

'But he's very nice, I thought,' I said tentatively.

'Yes, but there's a common streak. Also—' She managed to convey that her coffee cup was a glass.

'Oh, no!' I said. 'Surely not. He doesn't drink more than lots of people. After all, everyone drinks more in wartime.'

'Oh, my dear,' she said earnestly, pushing her glasses back, 'you wouldn't say that if you'd seen what I've seen. It's the stuff of ruin, that's what it is. The stuff of ruin. Insidious, don't you see? My social work has brought me in touch with so much of that sort of thing. It's been the cause of more unhappiness—'

'Perhaps *you* could talk to him,' I suggested.

She shook her head and pushed her glasses back again. 'I did once. He was terribly rude. As good as told me I was living on their charity. After all, as I said to him, it isn't as if Catherine hadn't insisted that I go there at the beginning of the War. I believe she wanted me, don't you see, to stand by her.' She made the lifting motion with her coffee cup again. 'Of course, I needn't stay – I've got my own place – but Catherine insisted.'

So that was Mrs Fellowes's Wartime Social Work. That and having me to lunch.

I wasn't going to repeat that experience again, but towards the end of my Night Duty time, I found I could do with less and less sleep. I was so thoroughly tired – not just a tiredness that a good sleep can erase, but a deep-seated fatigue to which I had grown accustomed. I had forgotten what it was like to feel fresh, and even if I went to bed early these days, I could not sleep for long. Once, I went up to London for the day and came back just in time to change into my uniform. I knew it would be a busy night – it always was when I had had no sleep, therefore I was not surprised to see, as I turned the corner, the blaze of light on the ward which indicated that something was up. The day nurses were behind with their work, and Chris had arrived before they had settled the ward into darkness and gone wearily off duty.

They had had several operation cases in the late afternoon and evening, and the last one, an old lady of seventy, had come back from the Theatre only just alive. 'She won't last long,' said Sister, getting up again to feel her barely perceptible pulse. 'I've rung up her people, but I doubt whether they'll get here in time.'

Automatically, she straightened the sheet over the dying woman and left us. There was nothing more she could do.

Sister Adams was off that night, and Sister Gilbert came tip-toeing up at ten o'clock with Mrs Colley's relations. The husband was a humble old man with faded blue eyes and the walk of a man who has spent his life with horses. His daughter was thin and tired-looking, her face blotched with crying, but she had put on her best coat and hat and was clutching an enormous battered handbag.

'I've brought Mum's bag along,' she whispered. 'She can't bear to be parted from it, but they took her off in such a hurry.' They stood by the bed and looked speechlessly at the old lady, her nose high and pinched in her waxy face, the collar of the white gown much too big for her.

Chris wanted to look at her dressing, and the husband and daughter went obediently to wait in Sister's sitting-room. The old man sat forward in his chair, his elbows on his knees, turning his cap round and round in his hands, and the daughter sat politely, with her hands in her lap as if she were making a call.

Chris had her hand on Mrs Colley's wrist, frowning.

'Not long,' she said. 'Christ, I hate to stand by and let someone just slip off like this. Here – stay with her a minute. That Appendix'll be out of bed if I don't give her her morphia.'

The green-shaded light over the bed fell on the old woman's face. You could trace the outline of every bone in her skull and her nose was typically sharp and prominent, as if the face had fallen away from it. Her skin was cold and faintly damp, and her pulse no more than a tremor and then not even that. I listened for her breathing and called Chris over. 'She's dead.'

'I wouldn't swear to it,' she said, and stood pensively tapping her foot. 'Look, get the hypo, syringe and the coramine. It couldn't hurt to give her a shot.'

'I suppose I'd better call her people in,' she said despondently, when she had given the injection. 'Oh, damn, here's Chubby. What the hell does he want?' Chubby was Mr Soames, the little new House Surgeon, just out of the egg, with fluffy hair that never would lie down on his round head. He was on for all surgical cases to-night, and was just going round to see if it was all right for him to go to bed. As we watched Mrs Colley, one of her eyelids fluttered and for a moment her breathing was audible.

'My God,' said Chris suddenly, 'I wonder—' She clutched hold of Chubby's arm. 'Listen,' she whispered urgently, 'couldn't we give her an intravenous? Couldn't we try it? Sister said it wasn't any use, but I don't know – *Please*, Mr Soames, do let's try. It seems awful just not to do anything when she's still alive.'

Chubby ran his fingers through his hair. 'I don't know,' he said, hesitatingly, 'it's not much good—' Chris's eyes were sparking at him, her face alive with urgency. 'All right,' he said and laughed nervously, 'I'll have a shot if you like.'

'I'll go and lay up the trolley,' she gabbled. 'Don't go away – I'll have it ready by the time you've scrubbed up. You put the electric heat cradle over her,' she told me, 'and tell her people they can't come in for a sec.'

'Is she—?' asked the daughter, getting up as I went into the sitting-room. 'We're going to try something,' I said. 'It might not be any good, but—' The old man was watching me like a trusting dog.

I wanted to stay and watch Chubby cut down into Mrs Colley's vein, where the saline was going to run in through the needle, but half the ward chose to be awake and kept me running about for the next half-hour. Mrs Davenport fussed and fretted and had me yanking her leg up and down five or six times. 'What's all that light at the top of the ward for?' she grumbled. 'A person can't sleep with all this running about.'

'We're trying to save someone's life,' I snapped.

'Poor soul,' she said. 'But me leg isn't right yet, Nurse, I don't know how it is—' I said something quite rude to her, I can't remember what, but it shocked her into silence, although she kept up a rhythmic, insistent moaning for as long as she could keep herself awake.

I went to hold Mrs Colley's arm for Chris, while she bandaged it to the splint to keep it still. Mr Soames was regulating the drip of the saline, his face flushed with excitement, for it was the first intravenous he had done since he had been here. Sister Gilbert came along to see why we had not rung her yet to say that Mrs Colley had died.

'I'll do the round while I'm here,' she said. 'All right, don't bother to come with me, Nurse,' and she tiptoed off down the ward alone.

When she came back, she found the three of us wild with excitement. Mrs Colley's skin was still cold, but it was no longer clammy. You could hear her breathing now; you could distinctly feel her pulse.

'Of course, it might be only a momentary rally,' Sister said doubtfully, but she obviously didn't think that.

'Keep her warm,' said Chubby, putting on his white coat, his chick's hair on end. 'I'll come back when I've finished my round. Let me know at once if anything happens, and for God's sake keep that drip running.'

'Tidy her up,' said Sister, 'and let her people come in.' While I was rearranging the sheets to hide a little blood that Chubby had spilt in his haste, I kept touching Mrs Colley, to feel her skin gradually losing its marble chill. Suddenly she opened her eyes and looked at me accusingly. 'Me arm,' she whispered, 'what you done to me arm?'

'Now you've got to keep that arm still, d'you hear? Don't you dare move it.' She raised a grizzled eyebrow at me.

'Hoity-toity,' she said faintly.

The husband and daughter came in, breathless with hope,

glancing uneasily at the bandaged arm rigidly outflung and the gibbet-like saline apparatus. 'She may not know you,' whispered Chris, and Mrs Colley unhooded one eye. 'Think I don't know Dad?' she mumbled. ' 'Ere, where's me 'andbag?'

'Here you are, Mum.' Her daughter laid it on the bed under her groping hand. 'Ah, that's more like it,' she said, and drifted off into her Limbo again. They sat by the bed for a while, and presently they went into the sitting-room and had some tea. They wouldn't go home. Mrs Colley's pulse continued to be satisfactory.

Soon after Chubby had gone to bed, the saline tube blocked. We took the whole apparatus to pieces to try and eliminate the air bubble, but still we could see in the glass connection that it wasn't dripping through. We conjured with it for hours, trying different connections and new bottles.

Chris left me fiddling with it while she went to do a Mastoid dressing. When Sister came down, Mrs Colley's colour was worse and her pulse weaker. 'Try rebandaging the arm,' she said. 'There may be too much pressure.' She spoke calmly, but I could see that she was as worried as we were. She gave Mrs Colley some more coramine, and then the telephone summoned her to another ward. I piled on more blankets, refilled the hot bottles, and tried the old lady with some oxygen.

The arm was exposed now, with the needle tied into the vein, but still the saline was not running. 'I believe we'll have to get Chubby out of bed to cut down again,' said Chris, and swore under her breath as she fiddled with the tube. I became aware that Mrs Davenport had been calling monotonously for some time and went to shut her up. When I got back, Chris was not swearing under her breath but humming triumphantly.

'Don't move, don't breathe,' she said. 'I don't know what I did, but I've done it.' One of us stayed with Mrs Colley all the time, watching her like a hawk, checking her pulse, keeping her arm still and regulating the oxygen. Presently, she was well enough to take half a feeding cup of tea and even to grumble that it was not sweet enough.

She got very naughty. That was the joy of it. As her strength returned, she began to throw her weight about, and we could not let her people sit with her because she became too lively if she thought she had an audience.

'What you done to me arm?' she kept demanding. 'Practising on me, that's all you girls are doing – practising nursing, and I won't have it.'

'You keep that arm still,' said Chris.

'Don't you order me about, Miss,' said the old lady. 'I'm very poorly. I'll have another cup of tea, that's what I'll have, and if I wants to move me arm, I'll move it, see?' Her voice rose to a squeak.

'Look here, granny,' said Chris. 'We saved your life. Now shut up.'

'Oh, don't be mean to her,' I said. 'I feel as if she were my child.'

'So do I. I feel marvellous about the old bird, don't you? We saved her life.'

'Chubby didn't do anything, of course.'

'Oh, well, he helped, I suppose,' she conceded grudgingly, 'but I feel as if I'd done it all myself, don't you.'

I couldn't describe my feelings. I was *exaltée* with achievement; I was on top of the world. We were hours behind with our routine ward work, and we scrambled to get it done before, all too soon, it was time to wake the patients and get on with the morning's work. Granny Colley was sleeping. Every time I hurried past and looked at her, my heart glowed. When I looked into the sitting-room, the husband and daughter were sleeping too, she bolt upright and he with his head on the table.

'I been praying for the repose of that poor soul,' said Mrs Davenport unctuously, as I took her washing bowl. 'Save your prayers for yourself,' I said. 'She's alive.'

'Well, I never! And all that noise too. "She's gone," I said to myself, when I saw the lights on and all the to-do. "She's gone, poor soul," I said. I don't think I feel strong enough to wash myself this morning, Nurse. I know you're busy, but I don't feel able for it. I didn't sleep, you see.'

When I was bringing in the breakfasts, Chris called to me from the cupboard where she was measuring medicines: 'D'you realise we haven't had a thing to eat all night?' Nor we had. There hadn't been time to be hungry.

'Tell you what we'll do,' she said, coming up and putting in the milk for me while I poured out the tea, 'instead of going to the dining-room when we go off, we'll go to Jock's Box and have the most enormous plate of sausages and chips ever seen.' My heart swelled to receive the idea. It seemed the best I had ever heard and it kept me going through the work that was still before us. If either of us wilted over the bedmaking, or dropped into that half-tempo from which it is so difficult to shake yourself when you're really tired, the other had only to murmur: 'Jock's Box.'

Mrs Colley's husband and daughter had some breakfast and then they came in to see her. 'It's like a miracle,' the daughter kept saying, but they both had a bewildered air. They had steeled themselves to meet tragedy and now they had got to get used to this new idea. We put screens round Mrs Colley's bed, because the Day Nurses were starting the work of the ward. When Sister came on, with every hair in place, she sought me out where I was doing a bit of rinsing in the sluice.

'Nurse,' she said, 'why haven't you put Mrs Colley's mattress and pillows outside the ward to be fumigated?'

'Because she's still using them,' I said, pushing up some hair with the back of a wet hand. It was one of the proudest moments of my life.

There was no air at all in Jock's Box; only the smell of food. Chris and I slumped down at a little table and gazed dreamily around.

We didn't mind waiting; it merely gave us longer to savour the anticipation. In one corner, two bus drivers and a Clippie were having tea and bread-and-butter. The girl had a lot of greasy little curls anchored with hairpins. She was evidently one of the jolly ones, and she had to keep sprightly all the time, laughing a lot, with a great display of teeth. There were two soldiers at another table. They sucked their teeth automatically at us and then real-ised that we were too tired even to be annoyed by it.

And then, here was Jock himself, in a filthy apron and badly in need of a shave, coming out of the kitchen with a tray that could only be for us. You could see the smoke curling out of the coffee cups. I had been looking forward to this for hours. The aes-thetic quality alone of those bursting sausages, those golden chips, the baked beans sweltering in their tomato sauce – it seemed almost desecration to attack them. Or was it because one was going to eat them that they seemed so beautiful?

I paused, halfway through, to get my second wind.

'You know,' I said, for the hundredth time, 'she was dead. I'm sure she was dead, just before you gave her the coramine. We dragged her back.'

'M-m,' said Chris with her mouth full, and then, a little later: 'Often I wonder why anyone is a Nurse – all the sordid part, and the drudgery, and the impossible women, and all that. Then something like this last night happens, and you see exactly why. Let's have some more coffee, shall we?'

CHAPTER SEVEN

Soon after the Mrs Colley episode, when she was definitely round the corner and getting perter every day, Chris and I got into a spot of trouble. I am not quite clear to this day what it was all about, but it culminated in each of us visiting Sarah P. Churchman at ten o'clock to receive the information that we should never make a nurse, Nurse.

One of the charges was that we had had orgies with the Housemen – but orgies! This figment of Sweet Fanny Adams's brain was possibly woven round the time when she found Mr Briant asleep on the couch in front of the fire, and three empty beer bottles among the Cascara, Acriflavine and Soda Bic in the dispensary basket.

I also gathered that the authorities resented the fact that Chris and I got on well together and hailed the faintest sound of laughter as a sign that we were not working properly. It was the old story, of course; Nurse Dickens had no idea of hospital etiquette, Nurse Dickens was too familiar with the Seniors, Nurse Dickens was too opinionated. Nurse D.'s name, in short, was Mud.

I was genuinely taken aback. I was longing to stand up for myself, but I thought innocence would be safer.

'I'm sorry, Ma'am,' I said, trying to look wide-eyed. 'I'd no idea I'd done anything wrong, but if I have, I'm awfully sorry.'

'You don't look sorry, Nurse,' said Matron, turning her thick lenses on me. 'Is that the face you make when you're sorry?' I unwidened my eyes and tried another expression. 'I really am sorry,' I repeated. 'I'll try to do better.' I saw no other way out except this rather nauseating abjection, for I was afraid of the desiccated female Fakir behind the desk. Life had whittled off her all the human qualities and left a rigorous kernel of asceticism, which offered no contact or understanding.

'I am very disappointed in you, Nurse,' she said, surveying me.

'I'm sure we weren't quite so bad as you seem to have heard, Ma'am,' I ventured. 'And we did work hard, honestly.'

'But that's what you're here for,' she said dryly, and then I had to swallow some personal remarks, before she dismissed me with: 'You'd better go and clean your shoes now, hadn't you?'

That night, after a breakfast of jam on something that was either toast or very stale bread, Sister Adams announced with glee and an eye fixed on me to see how I would take it, that I was to go to Secker Ward. This was a small, auxiliary Men's Ward, where there was nothing much to do, and I found the inaction much more trying than the busy nights I had been used to on Jane English. My Senior was an unpleasant girl with grand ideas about herself and an undisguised scorn for anyone whom she did not consider to be on her level. I suppose that was why I was sent there, because, from the point of view of work, it was a rest-cure. I got through a lot of reading and felt always thick-headed and often bored. I heard Fanny Adams telling Nurse Varney on my first night that I was to be kept in my place, and she obeyed implicitly. That sort of thing was right up her street.

Whatever I was doing, she would come along and tell me, always in front of the patients, that I was doing it wrong, and soon

I got to the stage of being uncertain of elementary things that once I had practically been able to do in my sleep. She always ordered me to do a thing just before I was going to do it of my own accord, and anything I had to do for her, from making tea to clearing up her dressing trolley, she took entirely for granted.

She spoke in a studied, high-flown voice and spent a lot of time with her cap off in front of the bathroom mirror, arranging her hair. She was trying to better herself, and sat at the desk during the long empty hours, surrounded by textbooks on grammar and elementary French. This would have been admirable, I suppose, if one had not gathered that she was activated less by a pure thirst for knowledge than by the desire to set herself on a higher plane than her fellows. Of course, I was not allowed to sit at the desk with her, but had to perch on a shelf in the linen cupboard, screwing up my eyes to read in the bad light. She would invariably find me a job just before my mealtime, so that by the time I got to the dining-room, the food was cold and the tea stewed and as likely as not, Fanny Adams waiting to condemn me for being late. When Varney came back from her meals, she always went straight to the bathroom and cleaned her teeth with her special hygienic toothbrush and the mouthwash that was kept for the Gastrics.

The men usually slept like hogs all night, and I regretted the days when there had always been someone awake and only too ready for a chat. I came to welcome the hour that I had once cursed, the hour that every sleeper-out knows, when just before the dawn, every living creature stirs in its sleep or wakes for a moment, as if Nature wanted to assure herself that everything is still alive.

On my last night, Varney unbent slightly and told me about her travels on the Continent, where she had visited several cathedrals, the Louvre and the battlefields of Flanders, which she described as grievous devastation and a standing reproach to those warmongers who might have done better this time had they seen what she had seen.

When we were consuming oxtail and haricot beans at nine o'clock that morning, Sister Adams rapped on the table with a spoon and told me that I was to get up at five o'clock and go on day duty on the Private wards. Everyone looked at me pityingly and assured me that I should be no more than a glorified house-parlourmaid, but I was not ill pleased. 'Going on the Privates', as it was called, had the charm of novelty, and, I thought, the possibilities of amusement.

I had not reckoned with the bells. They rang all day long, as provoking as mosquitoes, and each time, you had to trek to the bottom of the long passage to see what number was waggling on the indicator. If you forgot to reset the indicator, you found that next time a bell rang, there were several numbers showing, and you had to burst in and out of half the rooms on the corridor before you found the right one. In any case, you always waited for a moment, in the hope that someone else might answer it first, but as I was the most junior nurse I usually waited in vain.

I got to know the people who rang for the sake of ringing, and if I was busy, would merely reset the indicator with an oath and let them ring again. One might answer the bell six times to pick up wool, tell them the time, or assure them that yes, Sister would come and talk to them as soon as she had a moment, and the seventh time, when one decided to let them stew in their own juice for a while, they would be dying or have fallen out of bed. One morning, when I had answered No. 3's bell eight times in an hour, I let her number waggle itself nearly off the hook while I finished making a blancmange. When I did answer it, banging in at the door with an intimidating expression, I found Mr Harvey Watkins with his thumb on the bell and his blood pressure mounting. I had to pretend that the indicator was broken and that I had been panting up and down the corridor to see who was ringing.

There were twelve private patients. I often think that, except for the privacy, they would have done better to have saved their money and gone into the General Wards. The wedge of Red that nine months of hospital had inserted into my social outlook, made me resent them slightly, but I could appreciate that since they were paying it was a little hard that there were not enough nurses to give them their money's worth of attention. The majority put up with this, but a few did not, and compared the hospital unfavourably with Nursing Homes of their acquaintance, forgetting that the fees at the Queen Adelaide were only half as much. They were paying, that was the point that stuck in their heads, and a phrase that often sprang, unvoiced, to my lips, was 'This ain't the ruddy Ritz.'

As is often the case, unfortunately, the objectionable people got more attention than the pleasant, unassuming ones. Sister Graham, who was a nervous woman with a mania for lists, used to pin up in her sitting-room little bits of paper with the likes and dislikes of the more difficult patients. She lived in constant terror of a complaint to Matron and would fuss up and down the corridor like a demented hen in her anxiety that all should go well. She was terrified of the doctors and, I sometimes thought, of the nurses too. She was universally considered to be 'daft as a brush'. It is almost impossible for a Sister to hit the nail of popularity. If she is too strict and stand-offish, she is hated, and if she is too familiar she is despised. God forbid, I used to think, that I should ever be in their position, but when I got to the exams, I ceased to worry, for I saw that there was no likelihood of it.

All the Private rooms were occupied when I first started to work there and after a few muddled days of taking in the wrong trays and giving Mr Faversham's peaches to Mrs Yule, I gradually got them straight.

No. 1 was Mr Levine, a cheery little American Jew, who was retarding his convalescence by refusing to be parted from his business. His secretary used to come every day with dispatch cases full of papers and, even when she had gone, he would have his typewriter on his bed table and rattle away until the patient opposite complained.

No. 2 was a lustrous girl who managed to make even an appendicectomy seem glamorous. She always had a few strident friends sitting about on the bed, who stared inquisitively at the nurse, as if they wondered how anyone *could*. The same patient who complained about No. 1's typewriter constantly complained about No. 2's wireless. I liked Bibi Preston. She was amusing, in a slow drawl, and was always pressing impulsively on one anything from a pot plant to a lipstick. Because we were not allowed to wear make-up in uniform, I think she thought that I always looked like that, which depressed her. I didn't argue the point, because she might have stopped giving me creams and powder in the hope that I might do something about myself.

No. 3 was a mad old woman with a broken arm, who was always ringing her bell and then not having the faintest idea what she had rung for. Sometimes she could not find the bell and would thump on the wall with an ebony walking-stick which hung over the top of her bed and from which she refused to be parted. She had several relations in varying degrees of lunacy, and a friend who came every day and said: 'Here I am again, Nurse, you see, turned up like a bad penny.'

In No. 4 lived Mr Walter Faversham, who was not aware that he had passed his prime. He thought that all the nurses were mad for him and used to call us Little Girl and Sweetheart and pat the bed invitingly. He saw himself as no end of a roué and would regale me with stories of naughtinesses while I did his room in the morning. Whenever I had been to London for my day off, he would say, 'Bet you had a hell of a party,' and enquire if I had been to the good old Kit-Cat and other places long since defunct. He was married, to what he spoke of as 'the Encumbrance'. They had probably been Bright Young Things together in 1920, and he had never really grown out of it, although his body had let him down by bringing him into hospital with acute gout.

Next to him, in No. 5, was a Miss Pennefeather, a colourless and humble woman, who wished to give no trouble, and would lie and freeze to death sooner than ring for someone to shut the window, not realising that she would be far more trouble if she caught pneumonia.

Across the corridor, No. 6 held Mrs Yule, a fat, contented woman who had borne an operation with fortitude and now spent her time writing letters to her various children and children-in-law in all parts of the globe.

Her husband was an elderly Home Guard and used to come and see her in his uniform before he went on duty, which caused Sister to call him Major Yule and ask him if he knew her brother, who was also in the Army.

No. 7 was the door that every nurse went through at every possible opportunity. I never had to answer this bell, because someone always beat me to it. Lieutenant Oliver Carew lived inside, minus a cartilage in one knee, and with dark hair and a boy's brown face on the pillow that set the heart beneath the apron bib thumping. He was naturally polite, incapable of bad temper and altogether so like something out of 'Tell England' that nurses with boy friends began to look at them critically and those without to set their hair more carefully at night. He was also very free with his cigarettes. What more could any girl want?

Nos. 8 and 9 housed two children who had struck up a friendship without ever having seen each other by tapping on the dividing wall. The boy was angelic, but the girl spoilt and captious. Her throat only hurt her when her mother was there, and with a little encouragement she would cry abandonedly until she went over the top. Then the mother would go tapping about in very high heels, indignant there was not a doctor immediately on hand to attend to darling Dilys. Mr Garthwaite, the ear, nose and throat specialist, called her 'The Sickener' and used to hide from her so that poor Sister Graham would be at her wits' end to know which of them to appease.

In No. 10, the Headmistress of the Girls' School that was evacuated to Redwood Court lay majestically nursing kidney trouble, and in No. 11 was an old man, who would not be there much longer, which would be a merciful release, said his family, who were getting bored with trekking out from London to see him.

No. 12 was the plague spot, the conservatory of too-exotic scents in which Lady Mundsley sheltered from the fresh air and shattering afflictions of the outside world. This was the woman whom Sister Oates had so prized. She had her own private nurse; we were not meet to handle that precious bundle of neurasthenia, and when one did have occasion to go into No. 12, she would shudder under the bedclothes and say faintly, 'Such a *noise!*' Her nurse was the sort of woman who would undress under a dressing-gown even when alone, and made more commotion over her one patient than we did with our eleven. She was always in the way: in doorways, or wedged into the linen cupboard, or walking slowly down the middle of the corridor with a tray when you wanted to pass in a hurry. She used to commandeer the best crockery and medicine glasses and the only eyebath that didn't dribble. She was always cooking up refined little messes in the kitchen when one wanted to get at the stove, and if she used the last of the Liquid Paraffin, she would not dream of mentioning it until after the Dispensary was closed. Her interests centred round No. 12 and she expected ours to as well.

'May patient had a better night,' she would say, as if confiding thrilling news, or 'May patient quite fancied that junket I made her. She's going to have a little nap now, so perhaps you could see that there is absolute quiet on the corridor.'

One day, when she had provoked me to more rudeness than

usual, I thought I had better try and atone by a little polite conversation, so while I was getting the tea trays ready, I asked her where she had done her training.

'What do you want to know that for, pray?' she asked, measuring out Rennet to the fraction of a minim. 'Quite the Miss Nosey Parker, aren't we?'

My good intentions vanished. 'If you think I care two straws—' I began and was fortunately interrupted by the entrance of Nurse Horrocks. I went on cutting bread savagely and the Private Nurse stirred milk with pursed lips.

'My,' said Horrocks, sniffing, 'I smell an atmosphere. Is someone having a row? Don't let me miss anything.' She was endlessly tall and as bony as a horse on its way to the knackers, and she had a cheerful gregarious spirit that entered whole-heartedly into anyone's affairs. If you had a bit of gossip or scandal to impart, you were always sure of an audience from Horrocks. She fed on that sort of thing, and when there was none about would concoct some intrigue from the tiniest nucleus, to keep herself going. Let anyone mention in her hearing that they felt sick, and it would be all over the hospital that they were 'preggers', and once when she thought she detected a white ring on the holiday sunburn of the third finger of Nurse Ketch's left hand, Horrocks had her secretly married to a bigamist with a wife in a lunatic asylum.

The other nurses on the Private wards were the know-all Nurse Jones, a sanctimonious girl called Farren, whom the men on Herbert Waterlow had christened 'The Disciple', a sexy piece called Delphine Lorrimer, who used the bathroom window nearly every night, and Summers, who had one eye larger than the other and legs like quart beer bottles, but was a born nurse. She was a genius with ill people – knew how to make them comfortable and sensed what they did or did not want without having to ask. Her patience and her temper were unshakable and she did not mind how late she stayed on at night. She never seemed to have any friends, and went to bed directly after supper and spent her off time during the day mending stockings or writing up her lecture notes. She told me once that if she had the choice, she would sooner work all week than have a day off. She didn't really mind that she could never go home because the fare was expensive. Her life began and ended on the ward.

When she was speaking to me I used to wonder sometimes whether I were going deaf or whether it was her adenoids. She had a curious habit, too, of leaving out all her articles: 'I'm going down to linen cupboard to get pillowcase for new patient.' 'Has Sister checked laundry?' She talked about her night duty as 'When I was on nights.' She had worked on 'Children's, on Men's, on Women's, on Eyes.' Now she was 'On Privates, on days.'

People who told me I should be a house-parlourmaid 'on Privates' had overestimated. I was Dogsbody. There was not nearly so much genuine nursing to be done as on a General Ward and what there was never came my way, as Junior. I used to spend my day cleaning rooms, doing flowers, carrying trays, looking up addresses in the telephone book, making hot milk drinks for the weakly, tidying the kitchen and washing up when the maid had her Bolshie days – and, of course, the bells. The Bells! The Bells! I got to feel like Irving.

Even when I was off duty, my errands were not done. There were stamps to buy for Mrs Yule, comic papers for the little boy, elusive American magazines for Mr Levine, beer for Lieutenant Carew and cigarettes for the would-be roué – 'and ten for yourself Dickie darling.'

Sister Graham had a periodical game called 'Going through the store cupboard', which I had to play with her. Somebody had once told her that she should be more methodical and this, like the lists, was one of her attempts, but it never really got her anywhere.

On other wards, it was as much as one's life was worth not to put things back in the right place, but here, everyone followed their natural instincts, and replaced things at random or not at all.

'Oh, dear,' Sister would sigh, as I opened the store cupboard doors on the chaos inside, 'all our good work last week seems to have been undone. These nurses simply make a pigsty of the place. It seems some people are naturally slovenly, doesn't it, Nurse?' Often, in an attempt to be chummy with her gels, she violated the unwritten law that a Sister never criticised one nurse to another, especially if she were not prepared also to make that criticism direct. It wasn't done to answer such remarks, so one had to pretend not to hear, even when she repeated it, a little wistfully.

She had the inevitable pad of paper and pencil in her hand and while I went through the tins, she would list them and make strange signs which meant replenishment or discontinuance, or queries, which meant that she would put off her decision until next time. There were several unnecessary tins that I had been replacing, week after week, because she could not bear to throw anything away. 'You never know, it might come in sometime,' was one of her favourite remarks.

There were tins of congealing patent food, old lumps of salt, faddish preparations that had been ordered once for a special patient and never been used, a lump of diabetic chocolate. I would solemnly open the tins, she would peer inside, we would both have a sniff at it, and I would make a movement towards the pig-pail, but she stayed me with: 'No, put it back, Nurse. It might come in.'

Then we would inspect the sugar, the oatmeal, the beef extract, the Bengers, which were littered about, some with their lids off, some retrieved from various places – underneath the dresser, on top of the plate rack, anywhere but on that portion of the shelf marked by Sister Graham with its name on a piece of sticking plaster. She could never understand why the rusk tin was always empty, even when we had no gastric patients, or why the jam and the lemonade and the sponge fingers and anything else that was nice to eat was always used up so quickly. Or perhaps she did know but didn't want to be thought suspicious.

Sometimes, after we had straightened the cupboard, we would attack the larder, where any amount of little leftovers stood about on plates until a nurse felt hungry or they went bad.

'Shall I throw away this potato, Sister?' I would ask, producing a hardened lump.

'Oh *no*, Nurse,' she would say in her Lord Woolton voice. 'You could make it into bubble-and-squeak with those greens left over from lunch and it would be a little extra for the patients' suppers.' I don't know when she thought I would have either the time or the inclination to do this, but I would probably be saved answering by one of the bells, which had been calling me away repeatedly ever since we started.

When I got back from having held little Dilys's head while she tried hard to make herself sick, Sister would be toying with the various jugs which were always standing about with the dregs of some beverage in them.

'I can't make out whether this is Bovril or coffee, Nurse.'

'Perhaps it's cocoa. Mr Faversham sometimes has some in the middle of the morning.'

'Does he?' And while I went to No. 2 to hand Bibi Preston 'that box of powder off the dressing-table and my nail things, and while you're here, could you be an absolute angel and get me out a clean nightie; this one looks like the wrath of God and I've got someone rather special coming to see me,' Sister would go into her room and add: 'Cocoa in mid-morning' to the other fancies on No. 4's list.

Poor Mr Faversham. He tried so hard and got so little encouragement from the nurses, except from Delphine, who responded automatically to any male, gouty or otherwise. One of his openings was to start an abstract discussion of the eternal theme and then work it round to personalities. We would be having quite an interesting conversation about repressions until he began to suggest that that was what I suffered from, and he was always starting on the effect of nursing on a woman's outlook, so that he could lead up to his favourite aphorism: 'You're a woman and I'm a man. You can't get away from that.'

'You know,' he said one morning, watching me idly while I fiddled around with a duster among the novels and magazines, slabs of chocolate, cigarettes and expensive fruit with which he sought to cheer his confinement, 'You know, my wife and I don't really get on together.'

'Oh, not that *again*,' I said wearily, polishing up his tooth glass. 'Say something a bit more original.' He never minded how rude you were. He liked it, in fact; it made him feel dangerous.

'So we made an arrangement,' he went on. 'She has her boy friends and I have my girl friends, and neither of us gets in the other's way.'

'Why not get divorced and have done with it?'

'Well, we've talked about it,' he said, reaching over for a grape, 'but it wouldn't be fair on the kiddie. One has one's principles, such as they are.'

I strongly suspected that he and the Encumbrance had never actually been unfaithful to each other. People who talk such a lot about it seldom get farther than talking. He was probably of a most domesticated nature and pushed the pram out on Sundays when he thought no one was looking. As if he guessed what I was thinking, he assumed his most wanton smile and said: 'I say, Dickie darling, are you going to be on duty this evening?'

'Yes,' I said coldly, 'probably in every room but this.'

'Oh, I didn't mean that,' he said, delighted that I should have thought that he did. 'No, that'll have to be another time. I wondered if you'd do a chap a good turn to-night.'

'Depends. Sit forward and let me do your pillows. Not that I care if you're comfortable or not, but it looks better when Matron comes round.' He loved to be talked to like this.

'I say, you are a vixen, aren't you?' he laughed, giving my arm an absent-minded caress. 'Perhaps you'll be jealous of what I'm going to ask you. I know women.'

'Get on with it,' I said. 'I've got three more rooms to do before I bring your breakfast.'

'Well, the fact is, there's a very lovely little lady coming to see me to-night. Wait till you see her, Dickie, she's—' He kissed his fingers to the air and rolled up his eyes.

'Why should I care?' I said, thumping a pillow.

'I want you to make sure that nobody comes in here. I've asked Sister if the Lovely can have a spot of supper in here, and she was dubious at first but succumbed to my charm. So if you'll be the darling that you are and see that the *tête-à-tête* is not interrupted – *voilà, parfait!*' He had been several times to Monte. He spoke the lingo.

'I'll do my best,' I said, 'but mind your gout.' I was awfully pleased; I thought it was so nice for him. I did not for a moment see how I could prevent anyone going into No. 4 if they wanted to, but I didn't think it would matter if they did. Every time I went into Mr Faversham's room during the day, he made some conspiratorial remark or smacked his lips or otherwise indicated his anticipation of a delicious evening. I felt quite like a procuress.

I had told the other nurses about it. He had told me not to tell them, hoping that I would, to enhance his reputation, and we were looking forward to a good listen outside the door.

As seven o'clock approached, he had me into his room again and again, to rearrange the flowers, or push the armchair nearer the bed, or shade the light more enticingly. I opened a bottle of sherry for him, and had some myself out of his tooth glass. He had on his best green silk pyjamas with the frogging, and had shaved after tea. It was bad luck that his gout was especially painful that evening. When I told him he was crazy to drink sherry in defiance of orders, he said: 'My body's got to obey my desires; I've no use for it otherwise.'

It was too sad. It was too heart-breakingly sad. The Lovely arrived, and although she was no raving beauty, she was passable. I mean, she had the right number of legs and arms and you could tell which way she was going, but Mrs Faversham came with her. Not as a jealous wife determined to see what was going on – that would have been all right – but as a matter of course, because they were friends, because they were all friends, the three of them. The two women talked to each other most of the time, earnestly, about clothes.

When the suppers came down from the kitchen, I told Horrocks that the extra one was not needed after all, and she retired avidly with it into the pantry. Lady Mundsley's nurse came along in a frightful state of affront to know what had become of the yellow roses that the Honourable Mrs Fluke-Fulkers had sent that afternoon, and I told her I was arranging them and would bring them in later. I could not very well go and remove them from No. 4 just yet. It would be too poignant.

He carried it off the next day by saying: 'Devilish luck, wasn't it? The Encumbrance didn't play fair last night, but still, you can't blame a woman for being jealous, it's in the blood. We had to be careful, I can tell you. The old girl was watching us like a hawk.'

The girl friend did once come alone. Unfortunately, it was the day of Mr Faversham's first attempts at walking and she turned the corner into the passage just as he was rocking down it with two sticks and a space between his legs the size of the Marble Arch. Even he could not pretend that the situation had glamour.

Outside the hospital, spring was waxing, as one realised with surprise whenever one went outside the gates. Changing seasons made no difference to the life within, except that one was either too hot or too cold and that there were fewer or more chest conditions. People wrote letters to the papers noting that not even Hitler could stop the daffodils from flowering, although it would have been far more noteworthy if he could.

As I walked down Redwood High Street, tenderly conscious of the pavement through my shoes, the blue sky and embryo clouds gave me a few pangs of pre-war nostalgia. Incredible to think that there had once been a time when one could go out of doors when one felt inclined, and stay out all day if the weather was like this. When the sun was shining, I always had a passing desire to throw up nursing and be a Land Girl and had to deliberately remind myself of pigswill and dirty chicken houses and sleeping in a loft with nine other girls in bottle green jumpers and shapeless breeches. On a day like this, one is always haunted by the thought that it might never happen again. Germans apart, something might go wrong with the Cosmos and there might never be any more springs, never any more radiant Mays and basking Julys. One ought to grab at them now, in case.

That morning, while I was blanket-bathing that crashing bore, Miss Pennefeather, I had kept looking out of the window in an agony of frustration and Miss Pennefeather, sensing my restiveness, had said humbly: 'What a nuisance I must be to you, Nurse; so silly and helpless. You really shouldn't bother about me when you're busy.'

It had been one of those slack mornings, when you had time to keep looking at your watch, which you could not imagine ever showing two o'clock. Yet here it was half-past two, with the dragging morning obliterated, and I was out of my uniform and the sun was still shining. I was on my way to Redwood Court, on an errand for Miss Anstruther, the Headmistress of St Cecilia's School for Girls, late of Blackheath. One of the mistresses had brought some papers up to the hospital for her approval and I was returning them with strict instructions to give them to nobody but the Assistant Head. I gathered that they were examination questions and it would be a major disaster if they should fall into the wrong hands and give someone the opportunity to cheat.

At the bottom of the High Street there were cross roads, with traffic lights and a policeman, who had once been a customer with us for hammer toes. To the left, the road led to the station and the factory estate, and to the right it wound its way back and up through the purlieus. I went straight ahead, on the road that quickly shed its houses and led to the country. Turning off through lodge gates on the right, I started off up the long drive which followed the ambling contours of the park, passing self-consciously a crocodile of schoolgirls in short green tunics and red blazers. Breasting a gentle slope, I saw the house below me, and in front of it, more green tunics were playing cricket on a shaved flat piece of the park, which had obviously been all too recently a hockey field.

The Rowan family, who had originally lived there, had left the place more than two centuries ago, and a succession of owners had added bizarre improvements until the place was a hotch-potch of architectural styles. The original Redwood Court, a smallish red brick house with irregular chimneys and casement windows sunk into thick walls, was practically eclipsed by the additions that had been stuck on to it. Shrouded in creeper, it huddled between the wing of a French château on one side and on the other a Victorian excrescence, hung with balconies and sunblinds and sprouting a domed conservatory of coloured glass. The front door was still in the old part, and I made for it, increasing my pace as a hard ball came hurtling in my direction accompanied by cries of 'Shot! Good Shot! Yes! No! And again! Can you? Oh, *fielded*, Mavis!' as a spidery girl hurled herself passionately on the ball just where the long grass would have stopped it anyway.

I wiped my shoes on an Italian wrought-iron scraper and rang the bell. 'To see Miss Saunders?' said the maid who was old and battered with years of service. 'Who shall I say?'

'It's from the hospital,' I said. 'Miss Anstruther sent me.'

The maid asked me to follow her, turning as we went to ask me how the Headmistress was. 'I hear she's very poorly. Miss Collis said you hardly know her.' This didn't quite fit in with the deep-voiced figure in No. 10, who radiated unconsumed energy, bullied the doctors about letting her up, ate heartily and made frequent trips to the X-Ray department in a wheel-chair, robed in a purple quilted dressing-gown and overtaxing my strength. I always felt that she should be doing the pushing and I the riding.

I hastened to reassure the maid, but she didn't want to be re-assured. 'They pull you down, see, kidneys do,' she said. 'Wicked things, kidneys. My sister had 'em for years, see, only they never suspected it till they cut her open after she died. She'd been a wicked colour all her life and always had trouble with her— *you* know. I always said it was kidneys. "You know what's the matter with you?" I used to say. "You got kidneys." But would she go to the doctor? And it was just the same with Miss Anstruther, see. "I don't like the look of her," I used to say. If I said it once, I said it a hundred times. And when they took her away, I said to myself: "I wonder when we shall see you back?" I said.'

'I believe she's coming out quite soon,' I said, walking gingerly on the mats that slid on the highly polished floor.

'She'll never be 'erself, though. Don't talk to me about kidneys. In here, dear.' She opened a door and showed me into what had probably been the room in which the master of the house escaped from his women. It was comfortable and shabby, with leather fur-niture, a lot of books, and pictures of horses with short tails ridden by men in billy-cock hats. The inside of the house through which we had made our way had been as inconsistent as the outside. The floor was all on different levels, and we had walked over red bricks, wide, uneven oak boards, modern parquet, and even a cold marble corridor, where sightless busts occupied niches in the walls, except where the drawing mistress had removed them for the studio. The miscellanea of education looked very out of place. Notice boards hung next to dark oil paintings of far-off Rowans, all with that long thin nose and little ferrets' eyes; a cardboard box on the refectory table in the old hall was marked 'PUT YOUR HISTORY ESSAYS HERE'. Red blazers and gas-masks lined the walls of a long empty room with beautiful chandeliers, and through an open door I had glimpsed a room with red wallpaper and a dark brown dado, from which all the desks and blackboards in the world could not obliterate the atmosphere of heavy Sunday luncheons.

I had not waited long in the study before the door was opened briskly by a leathery woman in a short tussore tunic, black tights and a snood. 'Good afternoon,' she said, flinging out a hand. 'You're from Queen Ad's, aren't you?'

'Yes,' I said. 'I wanted to see Miss Saunders.'

That's me. Oh, ha-ha! Of course.' She glanced down at herself. 'You must excuse my rig. I've just been taking a Greek Dancing class. This war, you know – the usual instructress doesn't come any more. Tell me, how's the Head? Do sit down.' She flung a string-coloured woolly over her bony shoulders, and I perched on the arm of a big leather chair.

'She's very satisfactory,' I said. 'She's coming out soon. She—'

'Grand, grand! Jolly good!' Miss Saunders strode up and down, rubbing her large dry hands. 'No one can afford to be ill nowadays, can they? I always say, if you can't fight for your country, you can jolly well keep fit. Who knows, Englishwomen may have to fight one day, side by side with the men. Look at the Spanish women!' She was obviously all set for the Invasion. 'I tell the girls: "You may feel pipped that you're too young to help the war effort, but there's no need to hinder it by getting flabby!"'

'*Mens sana in corpore*—'

'My hat, yes! That's the school motto. How extraordinary you should say that.' Not so extraordinary, considering I had seen it stencilled in red and green by the Art Class above the marble sepulchre that was the ballroom fireplace.

I held out Miss Anstruther's envelope and stood up. It was time for me to go if I was going to have tea at the Blue Lady before I went back on duty. 'Miss Anstruther asked me to give you these papers.'

'Goodo. The Exam papers, I expect. They're frightfully important, you know. By the way, talking of exams, I've just thought of something. You're a nurse, aren't you?'

'Yes,' I said, though technically speaking I should not be for another two years, if then.

'I wonder if you'd be an absolute brick and have a look at one of our girls? She's come out in a beastly rash, and our Matron's away for the week-end. I say, is it awful cheek of me to ask? D'you mind?'

'Of course not.' I was quite ready to give an opinion, whether I knew anything about the subject or not, although I saw my prospects of tea receding. They always had lemon curd tarts at the Blue Lady on Saturdays. Miss Saunders told me I was a sport, opened the door and collared a small girl who was scuttling by with a load of books. 'Don't run in the corridors, Doreen,' she said. 'Walk briskly. You'll get there just as fast and twice as quietly. Cut along now, and ask Beryl Otway to come here. She's in the Monitresses' Room at the end of Dorm 3 passage. Don't go near her; just call outside the door.

'I've been keeping her isolated,' she explained to me, shutting the door. 'The child doesn't feel ill, but you never know with these skin things. I don't want the whole school coming out in spots.'

Beryl Otway took her time. Miss Saunders and I made desultory conversation, and I had abandoned all hope of lemon curd tarts by the time an irresolute knock sounded on the door.

'Come in, come in!' cried Miss Saunders. 'Gracious, child, what a time you've been.'

'I was undressed, please, Miss Saunders,' mumbled Beryl, which explained her appearance. Her hair was scattered and her tunic bunched up under her girdle, showing green bloomers, a gap of skin and black stockings rolled above the knee. She blinked and peered, because she had forgotten to put on her spectacles. Above the crumpled collar of her blouse, a lumpy red rash crept up her neck and on to her cheeks, making her face puffy.

'Well, we won't say anything about untidiness now,' said Miss Saunders briskly, but with an underlying threat. 'Nurse here is going to have a look at your rash. I hope you haven't been scratching?'

'No, Miss Saunders. It does itch, though.'

'Calamine lotion,' I said knowledgeably.

'Yes, of course, I'll get some,' said Miss Saunders, hanging on my words. 'Let your tunic down, Beryl, and take off your blouse so that Nurse can see.' She switched on the light and drew the curtains across the window, though there was nothing outside but a blank wall and a roof with pigeons on it. Beryl shuffled bashfully out of her clothes and revealed a narrow chest and back flaming with the rash. I had not the slightest idea what it might be, but as Miss Saunders expected me to be a trained nurse, I tried to behave like one. There was an awed silence while I took Beryl's pulse. 'I've taken her temp,' said the mistress. 'Nothing wrong there, and she feels all right, don't you, Beryl?'

Beryl mumbled, crossing her arms over her chest. 'Appetite?' I asked, and this gave me an idea. Perhaps it was food poisoning. I made her tell me everything she had eaten just before the rash appeared, and as it mostly seemed to be stews or shepherd's pies, there was no knowing what she might not have taken into her system.

'Nothing but wholesome stuff,' said Miss Saunders proudly. 'Unless the child's been eating too many sweets or chocolates.' Beryl was heard to mutter that she hadn't tasted chocolate for a year and only wished she could.

'Don't scowl,' said Miss Saunders, and turned to me. 'It can't be food poisoning,' she said triumphantly, 'because some of the others would have got it. They all eat the same.'

'Yes, of course, that's what I was thinking,' I said, glad that she had thought of it for me. I inspected the rash again from every angle, half-remembered words running through my head – Eczema, Erysipelas, Scabies, Urticaria – or was that something else? – Dhobie's Itch. Poor Dhobie, or was it better to be immortalised for your itch than not at all?

'Well?' Miss Saunders was tapping a bronze-slippered foot.

'It's hard to say,' I said, judiciously. 'It might be one of two things. I've seen them both often before, but never quite as virulent as this.' Beryl looked scared.

'The point is,' said Miss Saunders, 'is it catching?' As I didn't want to be responsible for the whole of St Cecilia's dying of the plague, I thought it would be safer to say 'Yes'.

Miss Saunders exchanged a look of horror with Beryl. 'Oh, but that's awful,' she said. The child's taking a scholarship exam the day after to-morrow. She simply must sit it. She's got a very good chance; she's been swotting like mad, haven't you, Beryl?' The girl nodded and blinked and looked as if she were going to cry. 'What do you think? Should we let her go to London? Even if we covered the rash up, it wouldn't be playing the game to let her go about spreading something.' Here was a dilemma for me. On my word, apparently, hung the fate of hundreds of unknown girls, and also the future career of Beryl Otway. Her whole life might be affected if she did not go to this college. On the other hand, the youth of England might be ravaged by Spotted Fever. I sent up a quick prayer to *Sister Fairchild*. If only I had her tucked under my arm!

Miss Saunders was watching me avidly, her eyes passionate under the snood that bound her dust-coloured fringe. I was just taking a deep breath, hoping that words would come of their own accord, when Beryl herself saved me.

'Perhaps I'd better see a doctor,' she suggested, hesitatingly. Of course! It had not occurred to me before. Miss Saunders's acceptance of me as the ultimate oracle had made me forget that I was not. I intimated that Beryl had taken the very words out of my mouth, and suggested that she should come back to the hospital with me and go to Out Patients, where we might just catch the Medical Clinic. This was frightfully sporting of me. Miss Saunders was thrilled to bits, and insisted that we should go back in a taxi at the School's expense. Beryl pulled up her clothes, and the pigeons were allowed to look in at her again. Then Miss Saunders rushed her off to put on her outdoor things, and appeared at the front door with her, muffled like a leper, as the same old Rolls that had first taken me to the Queen Adelaide trickled gently down the drive, past the cricket match that was now giving Three Cheers.

'Who won?' called Miss Saunders, making a trumpet of her hands. 'Tchk,' she said, as the reply came faintly back from the Games Mistress, 'The Fifth Form'll never win a match till they get a bit sharper in the field.' She packed Beryl and me into the car, commanded the driver to wait and bring the girl back, and watched us off, waving cheerily, with her skirt fluttering above her knobby knees.

Beryl was silent, gazing out of the window, and unresponsive to conversational openings. I hoped she would be more expansive with the examiners. I also hoped she wasn't infecting the beige whipcord of the Rolls.

As we passed the Town Hall, halfway up the hill, I saw to my horror that it was already twenty to five. I would never be changed and on duty by five. Sister was off, and I would have to explain it all to Nurse Farren, leaving out the part about being taken for a trained nurse, and she would be righteously understanding and probably moved by her conscience to report me.

'I say,' said Beryl suddenly, in a small voice, 'I think I ought to tell you something.'

'Go ahead,' I said abstractedly, my mind still occupied with the time.

'Well, I did eat some tinned lobster the day before yesterday.' It was difficult to see whether she were blushing or the rash was getting worse.

'You did? Why on earth didn't you say so before?'

'Well,' she looked at me pleadingly through her large tin spectacles, 'how could I, with Miss Saunders there?' I saw that. I couldn't have myself.

'You see,' Beryl went on earnestly. 'She might have given me a Report, and then our class couldn't have won the shield this term.'

'D'you think it was bad, the lobster?'

'It might have been. It tasted a bit funny.'

'Where did you get it? In the town?'

'Oh, no. We're not allowed to go to the shops. I found it in my locker. It had been there ages and I'd forgotten about it.'

'How long?'

'Oh—' Beryl squirmed. 'About two years.'

I was horrified. I told the driver to go even slower than he was going, so that we could have this out. 'I can't understand why you weren't sick,' I said.

'Well I was,' she mumbled. 'Ever so. But nobody knew, 'cos I was in a room by myself. I did it out of the window. I say, you won't tell Miss Saunders, will you?'

'Of course not.'

'Cross your gizzard and hope to die?'

'If you like. Look, there's not much point you going to the hospital now I know what's wrong. They'll only tell you you've got smallpox and put you to bed and observe you.'

With an effort, I pushed back the unwilling glass panel between us and the driver, and told him to turn round and drive back to a chemist. I was going to be late anyway, so a little later wouldn't make much difference.

'I'll get you a Dose,' I told Beryl, 'and you'll have a ghastly time to-night and probably all day to-morrow, and serve you right, but you'll be able to take the exam.'

'What'll I tell Miss Saunders?'

'Tell her you saw the doctor and he said it was – let's see, something harmless – Nettlerash. That'll do. I expect it looks quite like what you've got.' To help the illusion, I also bought her some lotion which said: 'For heat rash, nettlerash, stings, bites and all skin irritations', got the Rolls to drive me back to the top of the hill, and sent Beryl off, well primed with what the doctor had said to her, looking small and scared and holding her medicine as if it were a Time Bomb.

I was so late by now that there was no point in rushing my dressing and appearing on the ward with studs gaping, stockings wrinkled and cap awry. While I was doing my hair, it occurred to me that if Beryl had ptomaine poisoning and became sick unto death, the doctor would be blamed for not having spotted it, it would all come out that he had never seen her and I should probably be charged with taking his name in vain, if not with Manslaughter.

I concocted my excuse for Farren on the way up to the ward. The trouble that I expected for being late seemed negligible compared with what might be coming to me. I climbed the stairs at a comfortable pace and found, on arrival, that everyone was waiting for me to take a case to Theatre as there was no one else to go. The porter was there with his trolley, the Theatre telephone ringing every two minutes, the patient drugged – Private Patients were never taken conscious to the horrors of the Anaesthetic Room – and Nurse Farren taking up an attitude that surely was not Loving her Neighbour as Herself.

When we got to the Theatre, the Surgeon was pacing with gloved hands clasped in front of him, all ready scrubbed up, and Theatre Sister's thick black eyebrows were beetling at me over her mask. The porter, who disliked all nurses on principle, was only too pleased to explain why we had kept them waiting, and as well as the floor being wiped with me on the spot, I was ordered to leave my card on Sarah P. next morning.

I lived in a state of great anxiety for the next few days. I was longing to ask Miss Anstruther whether she had heard anything about Beryl, but I thought that the less I said about it, the less was likely to come out. Even if everything was all right, I didn't want anyone to know that I had posed as an authority. However, the next time Miss Saunders came to visit her Headmistress, she romped out with the whole of her side of the story, praising me to the skies in her delight that Beryl had been able to take the exam, and had been understood to say that she had done all right, she supposed, which probably meant that she had sailed through the papers. The fact that she had continually to leave the room, under vigilance, in case she was making an excuse to crib, was attributed to the nervous strain of the occasion.

I had to go and have my hand wrung by Miss Saunders and be told how jolly I looked in my uniform and be thanked for my help by Miss Anstruther. She knew that the House Surgeon who took the Medical Clinic was the same one who attended on her, and, to my dismay, said that she would ask him about the cause of the rash next time he looked in. I hastily told her that Beryl had not been to his Clinic, as she had been lucky enough to catch one of the occasional visits of an outside skin specialist.

'It was so sensible of Nurse to consult another opinion,' said Miss Saunders, sitting bolt upright in the chair, with her thin legs planted well apart, showing beige Directoire knickers. 'So many trained nurses are so jolly conceited that they'll say anything rather than admit that they're not sure.'

Miss Anstruther agreed, but I could see she was laughing at me. She knew perfectly well that I was nothing like a trained nurse, knew, in fact, exactly how unlike, for she had experienced my ineptitude in various ways. But she never let on. I blessed her for that, and hoped fervently that, for the honour of St Cecilia's alone, Beryl would get the Scholarship.

The old man in No. 11 died quietly and unobtrusively in his sleep one afternoon and Sister told me to ring up his people. I spoke to his daughter and she forgot about it being a merciful release and began to cry over the telephone because she had not been there when it happened. 'Shall I come up there?' she said. 'I could come straightaway.'

'If you wouldn't mind bringing a suitcase,' I said. 'His things . . . ' I hated this part of hospital deaths; it always seemed so callous to ask grief-stricken people to attend to practicalities. Especially on the General wards, where a new patient was into the bed as soon as a clean mattress could be brought. You had to intrude on people's sorrow with a brown paper parcel of pathetic trifles and unforgivable inquiries about rings and false teeth. It was a necessary routine, but hatefully inhuman.

When Horrocks had finished with the old man, Sister sent me to tidy the room and make a list of his belongings. While I was in there, the daughter came in, her fur wet from the rain and her eyes leaping at once to the sheeted bed. She was a tall, immature woman of about thirty-five, with uncertain, clumsy movements.

She was the sort of woman who tries quite hard with her appearance, but always just misses, because she can't bring herself to risk a new fashion until it's going out, and never manages to be dressed completely suitably for any occasion. She wore black now, with a hat whose inappropriateness was somehow pathetic.

I made a movement to go, but she said breathlessly: 'Don't go. I don't want to be alone.'

'Would you like to see your father?'

She laughed nervously. 'It sounds awfully silly, but – I'm a bit afraid. I've never seen anybody dead before.' I lifted the sheet from the old man's face, because I knew she would find her fear unjustified, as mine had been the first time.

'Oh,' she whispered, and came up to the bed. 'Why, how funny, he isn't there at all. It's his face, but it – it just isn't him.'

That's why one doesn't mind. When you read in books about dead people looking happy, or agonised, or malevolent, it isn't true at all. Their faces may be fixed in a certain fashion, but they have no actual expression. Expression comes from within and what was within has gone, fled instantly on the moment of death. Nor do they look as if they might at any moment speak, any more than their garments might, or the house in which they had lived. I never can understand how anyone who has seen a person after death can make a fetish of their grave. Reverencing it as a memorial is one thing, clinging to it for what lies below is a sham. The person simply isn't there.

We were to have a patient transferred from Jane English Ward. She was a woman who had been in a motor accident and was brought into hospital unconscious. When she woke up and found herself surrounded by thirty other women, there was Hell to pay. She demanded to be put in a private room immediately and on being told that there were none vacant, clamoured to be removed to a Nursing Home. When she was told she could not be moved, as apart from other injuries she might have a fractured skull, she laid herself out to be impossible. The nurse who brought her down to us as soon as No. 11 was vacant, wiped imaginary sweat off her brow and made a long nose at the closed door behind which Mrs Gordelier was recovering from the ardours of the journey and considering the defects of her new abode.

Her bell rang, not once, but as if she were giving the Victory sign in Morse.

'Bitch,' said the Jane English nurse and went thankfully back to her ward.

Mrs Gordelier's face was covered with very white powder, in case she should not look wan enough.

'I simply must have another pillow, Nurse,' she said, 'the discomfort is excruciating.'

'I'm sorry,' I said. 'I'm afraid you're not allowed to be any higher, because of your head.' She must have been told this on the ward upstairs; she was simply trying it on. She moaned. 'I shall have to ask you to do *every*thing for me. I'm too weak to do a thing, you know.'

'Of course,' I said pompously. 'That's what we're here for.' However we were not there to be treated as that woman treated us. She rang and moaned and requested and complained and demanded all day long and the night nurses said that if it wasn't for the invention of Barbiturates, they would have gone raving mad.

When it was discovered that her skull was not fractured, and she was allowed to sit up, she immediately rang to be laid down again: 'Or I shall faint, Nurse,' she said threateningly, though I would have preferred that she did, so that I could get on with the teas. Ten minutes later, she had to be sat up again, and all that day she was like a Jack-in-the-box; up and down, up and down, with two nurses needed to move her every time, until Sister finally got Mr Ridley to say that she must sit up and stay up, or she would never mend.

'I shall never get better anyway,' she told me with a face of tragedy. 'I've been a hospital nurse and I know.' If this was true, she should have known better how to behave as a patient. She would allow nobody to touch her except Sister and the Staff Nurse, and when Summers went in once to dress the cut on her leg, she said: 'Don't touch me. Are you trained?' Me, of course, she treated like a moron slave and alternately chivvied, patronised and corrected. One day, when I was bathing her, I saw that the Elastoplast on her leg was coming unstuck, so I fetched some more and prepared to strap on a new piece.

'My child,' said Mrs Gordelier. 'Are you doing this of your own initiative, or did someone tell you to? Surely you are not experienced enough yet to touch dressings. At my hospital the Juniors never did anything like this except under supervision.' I intimated tersely that I thought I was old enough to apply a piece of sticking plaster and she watched me anxiously, ready to scream at the first suspicion of pain. Of course, the Elastoplast would have to behave like a demon, sticking to itself and getting twisted, and my scissors would choose to have a screw loose, and merely collapse on themselves instead of cutting. Mrs Gordelier's triumph grew as she watched the mess into which I was getting. The plaster kept snapping back and folding itself together so that I had to cut the end off and start afresh. In the end, the gauze and wool dressing slipped off Mrs Gordelier's leg, exposing a small healing wound, and with a short sharp scream, she rang the bell and demanded of the nurse who came that she should not be used as a practice dummy by incompetent novices.

She treated Mr Ridley like a dog, summoning him at all hours of the day and night and detaining him in her room with endless stories of her ego, as if he had been a psychoanalyst. He suffered it all urbanely, because he was cultivating a bedside manner, with a view to inheriting his father's wealthy practice.

Mrs Gordelier's injuries were not serious, but they were multiple, and the fracture of her wrist was an uncommon one. Sir Curtis Rowntree, being not entirely satisfied with its progress, called a bone specialist into consultation. This was a big day for Mrs Gordelier. When I took in her X-Rays, she was lying back wanly with a grey chiffon scarf wrapped round her head, looking from one to the other of the men with big eyes while they discussed her. Sister was standing in a corner, fiddling with her fingers, darting forward to turn back a sheet or hand a towel, trying to anticipate their wishes. The Osteopath was a smug, dapper little man with shiny pointed shoes, who called her 'Dear Lady' and Sir Curtis looked as scornful and unassailable as ever, which of course made it heaven for Mrs Gordelier that he should be obliged to concentrate on her. Before I left the room, she whimpered a little and asked for her smelling salts. Across the corridor a thumping began. 'Oh,' said Mrs Gordelier, 'I hope I'm not going to faint.' Sir Curtis, I was pleased to see, pretended not to hear, but the Osteopath spoiled it by telling her how brave she was and she looked at him out of the grey chiffon with swimming eyes.

I went to see what the mad woman in No. 3 was making such a noise about and to remind her for the hundredth time that there was a bell pinned to the front of her cambric nightgown. She had to have everything pinned on her: handkerchief, spectacles – even her book was attached to her by a string through the back of the binding. Otherwise she either dropped things on the floor or lost them in the bed and sat on them. I was getting tired of posting broken glasses to the oculist. It always took quite a time to get out of her what she wanted. When you answered her bell or her thumping stick, she would pretend that she had not summoned you. A secret look would come over her face and you had to question her patiently or guess. If you lost patience and went away before you had discovered what she wanted, she would set up an infernal commotion with bell and stick, and when you came back would scold at you under her breath like an angry cat. This morning, it transpired eventually that the splint on her arm was uncomfortable. No wonder. She had been fiddling with it until she had managed to skew it sideways, so that the edge cut into her arm. While I was undoing the bandage, I taxed her with this and she looked sly and began to mutter at me.

Her friend came in with an umbrella twice the size of herself and a cracked leather shopping bag trailing on the ground. 'Here I am, Nurse,' she said brightly, 'turned up again like a bad penny, you see!' As the majority of her conversation was on a par with this remark, she had got so used to not getting an answer that she automatically repeated everything.

'Showery weather for June – I say, showery weather for June,' she chatted, putting her shopping bag on the bed and beginning to fish out various crumpled parcels and torn paper bags.

'Are you rolling up that bandage – I say, are you rolling up that bandage?' she said, producing a vest like a long woollen tube and holding it against her for her friend's approval. 'Bandaging up Lottie's arm – I say, you're bandaging up Lottie's arm.' I was tempted to say: 'No, playing the piano,' but she wouldn't have seen it. So I went on bandaging Lottie's arm as tightly as I could with her jerking it at critical moments. I would be glad when she had some more plaster of paris put on. They had had to take off the last lot, because she had picked at it so much that it was falling into the bed in lumps, which she sat on and gave herself a sore bottom.

'Where's the biscuits, Ellie?' she snapped, trying to bend up her thumb so that the bandage would loosen when she straightened it.

'Hey presto, here we are – I say, hey presto!' said Ellie triumphantly producing a brown paper bag with no corners. 'I couldn't get your favourite Petty Bewers, so I got you Nice and Mahree. What a terrible thing a war is when you can't get what you want isn't it, Nurse – I say, what a terrible thing a war is.' Lottie stretched out her sound hand greedily for a biscuit and mumbled away at it while Ellie and I discussed rationing and the iniquities of shopkeepers. Lottie wouldn't wear her teeth, so she had to suck the biscuit into a pulpy mess, which she then swallowed and usually choked herself.

'Choke up, chicken – I say, choke up, chicken,' piped Ellie cheerfully. 'Raise your left arm,' this being the broken one. A bell rang and I left them pecking over the contents of the shopping bag with ejaculations from Ellie and grunts from Lottie. Ellie gave me a packet of blancmange powder to make up. 'She always had a sweet tooth – I say, she always had a sweet tooth.'

Mrs Gordelier was ringing, ostensibly to have the window pulled up and down until it was right to the fraction of an inch, but really to impress me with what the Doctors had said. 'Being a nurse, of course I can understand what they tell me,' she said, 'but Mr Fennimore said that if it had been anyone else, he wouldn't have risked telling them, with their nerves in such a state.' It looked to me as if she had mauve powder on to-day. What with that and the chiffon scarf shrouding her face like ectoplasm, she looked like a banshee.

'Of course, no one knows what I've suffered,' she said complacently. 'Just lower the blind a fraction, child. My eyes ... Yes, the Doctors say, with what I've been through, it's a miracle that I've kept my sanity.' I refrained from the obvious retort and let the blind down with a rush that made her call for her smelling salts again.

She kept me standing by the door, itching to get away, while she gave me some more verbatim extracts. That was the worst of private patients. You had to waste such a lot of time listening to them. I opened the door and began to edge out. Her parting shot was: 'In a way, I'm thankful for my pain. I'm offering up my suffering as a prayer to the Almighty.'

She and Nurse Farren got on splendidly. They both knew the Bible slickly and sycophantly, and could make the most shaming remarks without turning a hair. When I first came on to this Wing, I wondered what it was that Farren was always singing under her breath. Then I made beds with her, and found that it was the Psalms. She intoned them as she worked in the quavering, back-of-the-throat voice with which vicars' wives encourage a sheepish congregation. Once, when we were making Mrs Yule's bed, we got on to the subject of holiday clothes. Mrs Yule was telling us about a bathing dress with which her youngest daughter intended to startle the inhabitants of Bigbury-on-Sea, so I told her about the new shorts that I had just got for tennis. Nurse Farren suddenly stopped in the act of pulling through the drawsheet and seemed to stiffen all over. She leaned towards me, her nostrils quivering and her muddy eyes intense. 'The Woman who putteth on Man's clothing,' she hissed, 'is an abomination before the Lord. Isaiah 70. 19.' I drew back, startled. 'And I'll tell you another thing,' she continued, fixing her gaze on my head. 'The Woman who cutteth off her hair is also an abomination before the Lord. Job 53. 8.' Mrs Yule broke the tense silence. 'Could you pull the drawsheet, please,' she said plaintively. 'I can't hold myself up much longer.' As soon as we had finished, and Farren had gone out, lifting her eyes to the hills whence cometh, Mrs Yule said: 'Quick, give me my writing case. I must write to Angela before I forget it.'

Mrs Yule enjoyed everything, from her food onwards. She always appreciated a good story about one of her fellow patients, and would retail it to the Home Guard when he came in the evening, and get it wrong, and have me in to tell it again, and he would take out his cigarette case and scoop all the cigarettes into my hand. After she left the hospital, she had Summers and me to dinner and filled us with food and drink, and Summers, who turned out to be called Yvonne, quite blossomed forth in a green silk dress with her hair tonged up, and revealed an unsuspected talent for the piano. She played, and we sat in deep chairs on a sort of loggia and watched twilight deepen into dusk until the midges drove us indoors. There was a son on leave from the Army, who was clever and shy, and after a bit he sang one or two of the things that Yvonne played, and her hair looked clean and fluffy with the light on it, and her strong nurse's hands moving over the keys were full of grace.

She never would admit it, but I believe he was going to take her out. She kept her hair in its curls and suffered the personal remarks which always abounded if anyone changed their appearance, but in a few days we heard that he had suddenly been sent out to the East, and Summers let her hair go straight again.

Bibi Preston left about the same time as Mrs Yule and their rooms were taken by a scarecrow of a woman with pernicious anaemia and a diabetic Professor of Mathematics, who was a constant worry to me, because he would not eat the food that I weighed out so meticulously, under strict instructions to see that he took it all. We used to have terrible tussles, while I got hotter and the food got colder and the Professor retired under the blankets and put a pillow over his long grey head and snarled like a hibernating animal.

Miss Pennefeather got duller, Lottie madder and Mrs Gordelier more exasperating than ever, and to crown everything, Lady Mundsley, who was recovering in spite of herself, sent away her private nurse and announced that she would get her money's worth out of us.

It had now been diagnosed, for want of anything else, that her trouble might be gastric, so she was accordingly put on hourly feeds of milk and harmless puddings, for which I had to be responsible. Sometimes, even now, when I see the clock pointing to the hour, my mind automatically registers a curse. I could never start doing anything without having to leave it in the middle to take a feed to No. 12. No sooner had she drunk that milk, with delicate sips and a lot of fuss if there was skin, than it seemed it was time to take along the baked custard. I used to spend nearly an hour in the morning concocting the little nonsenses with which the private nurse had always been so tediously occupied. But she had only that to do, whereas I had the maiding of eleven other rooms besides. Also, invalid cooking is not my speciality and many is the rasher of bacon that has owed its richness to curdled custard or a watery junket or lumpy blancmange. Matron came round once in a nosey mood, and with Sister Graham twittering nervously at her heels, went into the kitchen and fired a salvo of complaints in every direction. With her face set in a censorious sniff, she snatched the lid off the pig bucket and poked at the contents with a long-handled spoon. Unfortunately, that was the day that I had burned both the porridge and the milk pudding, and she had also found a decomposing blancmange which had been there for days, sticking to the bottom every time the bucket was emptied.

Once I forgot the hourly feeds. Lady Mundsley would give me exactly two minutes and then reach for the bell. Nurse Jones, who was much too superior to answer bells as a rule, used to make a practice of answering on these occasions, so that when I panted up with something slopping over on to a tray, she could be standing there with her mouth pursed like a snapdragon, receiving complaints about me and promising to see that I was suitably reprimanded. I beat her up once in the bathroom with a back brush and she fought back meanly with nails and feet and eventually pushed me out into the passage into the arms of Mr Morris Evans, who merely set me aside, removed a speck of dust from his trouser leg, cleared his throat and walked on.

When Lady Mundsley was allowed to get up, it was ordained

that she should be wheeled into the garden to take the sun in an invalid chair. This involved as much preparation as a Continental journey. Eiderdowns, pillows, handkerchiefs, scarves, rugs, sunshades, sunglasses, book, magazines, Gastric Barley Sugar, Eau-de-Cologne and a foot-stool, all had to go out as well, which meant several journeys up and down stairs and round three sides of the garden to the spot which Lady Mundsley had selected as not ideal, but good enough until she saw somewhere she liked better. Then she would ting-a-ling her bell, for which I always had to keep one ear open, and I would have to leave someone in the middle of a blanket bath and go and push her all over the grounds until her restless spirit found somewhere in which it could settle and by that time the sun would probably have gone in and she would want to go back to bed. By the time I got back to my blanket bath, the patient would either be resigned but shivering, impatient, or ringing bells according to temperament.

Lady Mundsley didn't like me much, because I was always knocking things over. I was clumsy enough in the other rooms, but in hers, it seemed I could never touch a vase without spilling the water or tipping the flowers out on to their heads. If I had to break a medicine glass, I would always break it in No. 12 and Lady Mundsley would draw in her breath and say: 'Such a *noise!*' The list of her idiosyncrasies was far longer than any other in Sister's room, even than Mrs Gordelier's, which might have been condensed into: 'Whatever you do, it's wrong.' Lady Mundsley apparently had some influence with the Governors of the Hospital and even Matron had to kowtow to her. Sister Graham was in and out of the room all day, with creased forehead and fluttering hands. She always had to have the best vases and the newest linen, and clean pillowcases far more often than anyone else. It was a good thing she was not on a normal diet, or she would have got all the best food.

At night, Sister would never go off duty until she had paid

Lady Mundsley the ten minutes' social visit which she thought was due to her status. Neither of them enjoyed this session. Sister Graham never knew what to say and if Lady Mundsley knew, she couldn't be bothered to say it. Sister would come out of the room flushed, shut the door with noiseless care, and go off down the corridor, her shoulders straightening with relief at being free from the cares of the Ward, but her mind already busy with to-morrow's worries.

It was about this time that Horrocks began to circulate the rumour that Sister was engaged to be married, but nobody paid much attention. She had no real evidence to offer, but merely tried to look like Mona Lisa and said: 'I *know* certain things,' which always meant she knew nothing.

I don't know who it was who suggested that Lady Mundsley should be taken on a tour of the hospital for her diversion. It was most embarrassing. I had to push the wheel-chair, while Sister walked by the side, pointing out features of interest. Lady Mundsley had on her best velvet dressing-gown and a soft Angora rug over her knees. Her high-nosed face was carefully made up and her blue-grey hair, which her coiffeur came every week to keep blue, carefully set. Thus she was wheeled round the wards like a district visitor, being wheeled up to one bed or another to exchange a few gracious words. In Herbert Waterlow, some of the men began to mutter and scowl, but most of the patients got the impression that she was Royalty and took it quite well. I don't know whether Lady Mundsley enjoyed it. She said afterwards that she was worn out, and when I went to settle her that night, she said: 'I feel, Nurse, that I'm going to be difficult.' She was always difficult on the nights when I was going to a dance. To-night, I was going with Delphine Lorrimer to a soldiers' dance in a hall on the Factory Estate. I didn't really want to go but she assured me that we were going to have 'a hot time with some cracking fellows'.

While I was just finishing the alcohol rub without which Lady Mundsley swore she could not sleep, the Junior Night Nurse came in and winked at me as I was rubbing the wavy white back. She was a friend of mine, a girl called Lister, who would sit on my bed for hours in a gaudy silk dressing-gown with feathered slippers tucked underneath her, talking, talking about anything that came into her head, from religion to the life history of her Aunt's cat at Thorpe-le-Soken. Sometimes I would drift off, waking again to the weight on my legs and the voice still going on. When we heard Sweet Fanny Adams's rubber soles squeaking along the passage to see who was up to what, we would turn out the light, and a quarter of an hour later, when they came squeaking back, having done the round of the hostel, we turned it on again and continued the session. Round about eleven, we would make coffee with the milk that one of us had sneaked off the Ward. I missed Lister now that she was on Night Duty, but I got a great deal more sleep.

'No. 7 wants you before you go off,' she said, and Lady Mundsley, looking over her shoulder to tell me not to rub so hard, caught another wink and thought it was meant for her.

'Are you being rude, Nurse?' she asked distantly.

'I don't know,' said Lister. 'Am I?' Some nights, she met her boy friend at the pub across the road before she came on duty. This was one of the nights.

'Your upbringing should tell you that,' said Lady Mundsley. 'Rub the back of my neck, please Nurse. I think I got into a draught along those corridors.'

I hoped Oliver Carew didn't want me to go to the fish-and-chip shop and get him fourpennorth of fish with batter and twopennorth of chips, which he sometimes did when the supper had been fiddling little messes in tiny dishes. Not that I minded going in the least; I usually bought some for myself and ate them with him, but to-night I had promised Delphine to be ready for the dance at half-past nine. She had an evil temper, and if put out at the beginning of the evening, could wreck any party. However, when I went into No. 7, there she was, sitting in the armchair and showing a great deal of sheer black stocking. It was Oliver's birthday and Lister had brought him up some champagne. At a quarter-past nine, we turned out the lights and crouched behind the bed, and he grunted sleepily as Sister put her head round the door to say good night on her way off duty. Lister came in and had a quick drink in between answering bells, but the Senior Night Nurse, who was a joyless flat-chested girl, only came in with a few impersonally professional remarks. She couldn't say anything to us, because she set too much store on riding my bicycle which was her greatest, if not her only passion.

After the second toothglass of champagne, Delphine became very society and put on her special voice and took off her cap and kept pinching up her shiny auburn hair. After a while, Mr Sickert came in, which was what she had been waiting for, and it transpired that they were on Christian name terms. Horrocks, who had been off for the evening, came sneaking back in a striped dress which made her look endless, and Oliver lay back and smiled happily and enjoyed his party. Delphine didn't know which to sparkle at, him or Mr Sickert, so after a while she solved the problem by saying: 'Well, I suppose we'd better go on to this party. Felix gets *raving* if I'm more than an hour late,' and we left, she glancing back at the door, as if almost expecting to see it bulge with the seething atmosphere of jealousy which she felt sure she had created within.

The only way of getting to the dance was on our bicycles, and when I went to draw the inadequate blackout of my room, I saw that it was raining. Chaps have got to be very cracking indeed to be worth bicycling through the rain for, even downhill. Also, the champagne had made me delightfully sleepy. I saw my bed, and thought I would make myself some coffee and go to bed with a pile of magazines that Mr Levine had given me. I kicked off my shoes, undid my stiff dogcollar which had branded me with a permanent mark on each side of my neck, and went along to Delphine's room. She was sitting on the bed in black chiffon knickers and an uplift brassière, putting orange varnish on her nails. Her friend Peterson was in there too, in a grubby cotton dressing-gown, washing her hair in the basin. She was also sexy, but without attraction. No amount of hair washing could ever make her anything but intrinsically dirty.

'Delphine,' I said, 'I don't think I'll come.' She looked at me with blazing eyes, jerking her head back aggressively.

'Well, of all the bitches—' she said. 'Of course you must come. I'm not going alone.'

Peterson raised her head from the basin. 'Of course you must go,' she said thickly, through a curtain of seaweedy hair. 'I think it was damn nice of Delphine to ask you.'

'Why don't you go yourself, then?'

'Haven't got anything to wear. Besides, my hair's wet.'

'You could put it in a snood. You might go. I'm much too tired.' I didn't want to go a bit. Delphine was now at the dressing-table, larding on orange lipstick. 'I don't care which of you comes,' she said crossly, hunting among the litter of smeared pots, broken combs and crumpled face tissues for her powder puff, 'but I'm not going alone.' She found a moulting puff and proceeded to dab white powder carefully all over her face and neck.

'I'll go,' said Peterson to me, 'if you'll lend me that green hair net and that dress with the pleats. Oh – and a pair of stockings.'

That settled it. I had to go. Delphine and I, furious with each other, bicycled down the hill a short distance apart with scarves over our heads. When we arrived, after riding up a muddy lane with potholes which she managed to avoid and I did not, she flung her bicycle against a fence and stalked in. A ladder zipped down my stocking as I dismounted and my bicycle fell down twice before it would stand up. I followed her, barking my shins on a small blast wall, which I didn't expect to find outside the entrance, and came into a narrow dark space like the place where you leave your coats outside a squash court. Two military policemen and an ordinary one were chatting in the gloom, and a couple of Tommies pushed past me with a noisy blur of song. Beyond the wooden partition came the sound of a band with too much saxophone.

Tickets, please,' said a man sitting at a table by the door. 'Oh – I think my friend inside—'

'One-and-six, please,' he said pityingly, as if he had seen many more efficient gate-crashers than me. I certainly wasn't going to pay; that would be the last straw. I was sure Delphine would not let the cracking fellows get away with that. They had probably taken our tickets. 'I think my friend bought my ticket,' I said. 'It's probably inside.'

'No one's bought no tickets for nobody,' he droned, holding out his hand for my money. Curse Delphine! She might have waited.

'I'll go in and see,' I said haughtily, and stepped forward to find my way barred by one policeman of each sort. I was furious. It might have been eighteen pounds at issue instead of eighteen pence. I flung the money at the man at the table and flounced into the hall, which rose up and hit me with heat, smell, noise and unshaded electric light. I pushed my way through a crowd of soldiers gaping on the edge of the floor and saw Delphine dancing with a hairdresser in khaki. They were evidently having a row. She saw me and pulled him out to the edge of the floor.

'Where the hell have you been?' she asked, scowling. This is Felix.' She indicated the hairdresser contemptuously, and he smiled with rabbit's teeth beneath a thin black moustache and said: 'Pleased to meet you.'

The other chaps haven't turned up,' said Delphine casually, 'but you'll find someone to dance with if you stand around a bit. You've got a ghastly ladder in your stocking, did you know?' Felix, who had been tapping his feet rhythmically, suddenly pulled her close to him and whirled her into the crowd of dancers. I watched them dance out of sight, with a great deal of hip-swaying and Palais-de-Dance footwork.

At the far end of the hall was a stage on which the four members of the band sat playing a bit of uninspired strict tempo. Down the sides of the room were chairs on which girls sat, trying to look as if dancing were the last thing for which they were here. Soldiers and airmen stood about in groups, staring at the dancers and at the girls but not doing anything about it. In a corner on my left the crowd was thick. There were trestle tables here, behind which two or three havocked-looking women were wiping glasses and dispensing drink, a lot of which seemed to be on the floor. I wished I were a man. I would then have had a drink and gone home. As it was, I would just have to go home. I was turning away, preparing a dignified face to wear going past the man with the tickets, when my eye was caught by a couple on the floor and I stood transfixed. They had disappeared into the crowd before I could see them properly. Perhaps it was my imagination – but no, through a gap in the dancers, stepping sedately and slightly out of time to the music, were a stooping, spectacled officer in khaki, and – Sister Graham. It was always a shock to see a Sister out of uniform. Somehow, one didn't imagine them ever wearing anything else; it seemed so much a part of their character. She was wearing a nondescript brown dress, with a suspicion of petticoat showing at the back, and she looked quite human – soft and plump. Just as she looked wrong out of uniform, the man looked wrong in it. He was in early middle age, an indoor type, with a kind, tired face.

As I was staring at this phenomenon, a throaty voice beside me said: 'Excuse me, but might I have this dance?' and before I could think whether I wanted to, I was out on the floor in the arms of a sturdy, ginger-haired man in battle-dress, the top of whose bullet head came on a level with my shoulder. He breathed heavily and didn't want to talk. He was too busy trying to see his way over or around me. I kept trying to steer away so that Sister should not see me. He tried to steer me the way he wanted to go, and we battled silently, while the drummer, looking anxious, sang *Johnny Pedlar* into the microphone.

When it was over, my partner wiped his forehead and said: 'Coom and have a drink,' and there at the bar was Sister Graham, sipping beer with a wrinkled nose, while her spectacled man talked to another officer.

We smiled at each other. I don't know which of us was the most sheepish. Farther down the bar, Delphine had three men round her, none of which was Felix. She was making a lot of noise and tossing her hair about.

'Don't worry,' said Sister, 'I won't say anything about either of you. I should, of course – oh dear, I wish I hadn't seen you—' Her partner turned round to see to whom she was talking. 'This is one of the nurses, Godfrey,' she said. I saw that he was a doctor. He asked me to have a drink, and as I could see no sign of bullet-head, I accepted. Soon after, my partner came pushing through the crowd with the tumbler of grapefruit squash which he evidently thought met my case. I couldn't do any introducing, as I didn't know anybody's name. He was furious at finding me in an officer's party, and stuck out his jaw and went pink about the ears. Sister did nothing to help the situation, and Godfrey was vaguely at a loss as to who we were. Bullet-head drank the grapefruit himself, looking at his boots, then mumbled something and disappeared. I felt like a blackleg and wanted to go after him, but I think he was glad to be rid of me. He had not bargained on being quite so much shorter than I was.

Godfrey went on talking to the other officer, while Sister and I searched desperately for something to say to each other, and I was thankful when he took her away to dance. I felt happier after my drink, and thought that perhaps I would stay and have another dance before I went home. I went and sat down in the row of girls, but nobody came near me. I got up and looked for the ugliest girl in the row and sat down next to her. Presently, quite a nice-looking soldier came towards me and I smiled politely and half rose.

'Will you dance?' he said to the ugly girl, and waltzed her away with a large hand in the small of her back hitching up her skirt behind. I got up and then wandered about and then stood in a conspicuous place, fixing likely looking men with my eye, but I might have been a leper. Delphine was dancing now in a rather abandoned way with a red-haired Sergeant-Major. Sister was dancing with Godfrey, his face solemn with the concentration necessary for reversing. I *would* dance. Delphine had seen me, and I wasn't going to please her by ringing up 'No Sale' and slinking defeatedly away. I felt uncomfortably exposed standing about in the open space in which I had chosen to display myself. I went and mingled by the bar, and presently a man who saw at least three of me swept me on to the floor just as the band finished the tune. 'Never mind,' he said, 'Time for a little drink.' We had a little one, and another little one. Delphine came up with her Sergeant-Major and hailed me like her dearest friend. She put her arm round my shoulders and nearly wept over me, then in a moment was roaring with laughter at something perfectly ordinary that I said, and shrieking: 'You are a scream, Dickens, honestly you are! My dear, I think it's the funniest thing I ever heard!'

'Listen to this, then,' I said, and told her about Sister. She laughed herself nearly sick, but not because she took it in properly. She was just laughing. 'Sargie,' she said, pouting up at him and nestling against his sleeve, 'ickle Delphie wants a drink.'

For a girl who aspired to sophistication, ickle Delphie held her liquor worse than anyone I have ever seen. About an hour later, when I was just beginning to enjoy myself with a blond AC2 whom I had picked up in the Paul Jones, the red-haired Sergeant tapped me on the shoulder and said: 'You'd better go and see about your friend. She's not quite the thing.'

I found Delphine outside, being sick over a wire fence, which she thought was the rail of a ship. She was quite happy after-wards – too happy. She was long past bicycling, and I didn't see how I was going to get her home, much less get her through the bathroom window and into bed without waking the whole hostel. As we stumbled back into the Social Hall, we collided with two people coming out.

'Whoops!' said Delphine, and pinched me. It was Sister Graham and Godfrey. He flashed his torch on us and grasped the situation.

'Could we give you a lift if you're going back to the hospital?' He glanced at Sister for agreement, and she made a few nervous beginnings of sentences. I was very relieved. I was only too thank-ful to leave our bicycles and hope that they would still be there to-morrow.

Delphine and I sat in the back of the car, and I tried to sit on her when she burst into song.

'Have you got late passes?' asked Sister.

'Well – not exactly,' I said.

'How are you going to get in?' I didn't like to mention the bathroom window; it might spoil it for future occasions. I hedged a bit, and she said: 'You'd better come in through the front with me, then you'll be all right.' Delphine looked like being sick again, and Godfrey, turning round to look at her, drove on faster. He stopped outside the railings, and I lugged her out of the car and into the geranium bed. The Night Porter looked at us in sur-prise as we walked through the front entrance, with Sister looking the guiltiest of the lot. She rushed us along the corridors, terrified of meeting Fanny Adams.

I had a trying time getting Delphine to bed. She made such a noise that she woke Richardson, who slept next door and came in looking very square in pink cotton pyjamas to see what was going on. Between us, we got her on to the bed and left her, fully dressed and moaning weakly that she wanted Sarge.

'I'll get her up in the morning,' said Richardson grimly. 'It'll be a pleasure.'

Delphine at breakfast, combined with over-ripe kippers, was a sight to put you off for the day. She and I made beds together, communicating only in grunts, and she nearly bit poor Oliver's head off when he asked her if she had had a good party. She got more and more ravaged-looking as the morning wore on, and finally retired to bed at twelve o'clock and lay inanimate for several hours. Sister let her go without a word. She had not said anything to me about the night before and had avoided being alone with me in case I might talk about it, which would embarrass her exceedingly.

A few days later, she came up to me in a great state of confusion after lunch, hemming and hawing and finally coming out with: 'I've got someone coming up to tea with me this afternoon, Nurse. Perhaps you could make some sandwiches – or something – or toast.' She was more uncertain than ever these days. She seemed to have no control over her hands, started nervously at the slightest sound and dithered over any decision. She appeared to have something on her mind, and I wondered if it could still be the dance.

I was in the kitchen, washing up the plates that Maggie had left as a protest against their being brought out of the rooms five minutes late on her afternoon off. Having told me about the tea, Sister seemed reluctant to go. She stood twiddling the doorknob, obviously wanting to say something. I went on scraping off mustard, hoping that she would either come in and say it, or else go away and shut the door, because there was a draught.

'As a matter of fact,' she ventured at last, 'it's Captain Hope – the friend who was with me at the dance, you know.'

'Oh, good,' I said. 'I mean – is it?'

'Yes. He's coming to say good-bye, you see. He goes up to Scotland to-morrow – oh dear,' she put her hand to her mouth, 'perhaps I shouldn't say that.' There was silence after that, and I thought she had gone, but when I turned round to get the dish-cloth, there she was, still twiddling the doorknob, still trying to make up her mind to say something.

Actually, I don't suppose she was so very much older than me, but the gulf that etiquette had put between us was greater than any disparity of age. She wasn't very friendly with any of the other Sisters. She was obviously dying for a confidante, but she was a Sister and I was a Nurse, and East is East and West is West.

I was still in a draught. I tried to get her started. 'I expect you'll miss Captain Hope,' I hazarded. And then, suddenly, out it all came in a rush. She fell over her words, trying to get them out before she lost courage. She didn't look at me and I didn't look at her, just went on drying dishes with my auricular timpani, as Sister Tutor would say, popping with surprise.

He had asked her to marry him. He had been asking her repeatedly for several weeks. He had actually asked her the last time while Delphine was in the geranium bed.

I congratulated her delightedly. I supposed she had said 'No' at first, because that was how she reacted to any proposition, coming round to it afterwards if you gave her time.

'But I haven't said I would,' she said in an anguished voice. She had shut the door by now, and was standing by the stove wringing the oven cloth into a rag.

'Oh, but Sister, you *must*.' He would be perfect for her, so stable. Even if he had not been so nice, there seemed to me to be no question between getting married and withering away your womanhood in a hospital.

'I simply can't make up my mind.' How she must madden him with her inability to make a decision. But I expect he thought of her as a helpless little woman-thing. If he had any sense, he would just sweep her off to church before she could get her breath.

'You see,' she pursued, turning the gas-taps on and off with little roars, 'I love this work so much, I don't know that I should be happy without it. If I could marry him and still stay on here – but I couldn't. It would mean going away with him, you see.' I had no idea her work meant so much to her. It always worried her so much, I should have thought she would be only too thankful to shake off responsibility, but I suppose that was part of the fascination.

It wasn't my place to tell her that I thought she was daft as a brush, and anyway, she suddenly recollected who she was and who I was and where we were.

She drew herself up, patted her apron and settled the belt round her cosy waist. 'Two o'clock,' she said, putting on an unnatural voice. 'I must go and check the laundry.' The laundry had come back yesterday and long ago been checked and put away, but it got her out of the room and out of the situation. She would be more embarrassed than ever with me now. Perhaps she would have me moved to another ward. I opened the window and door to let out the smell of gas that her fiddling with the taps had created, and went to tell Mrs Gordelier that no, I was not deaf: I had heard her bell, but had been giving an intra-muscular injection, in the middle of which one could not calmly walk away, as she, as a hospital nurse, must know. We brought this allusion up now on every possible occasion, ever since we had discovered from her husband, who had come to try and persuade us to keep her a bit longer, that the sum of her hospital experience came from two half-days a week as a VAD at the Red Cross Convalescent Home.

Captain Hope arrived, walking purposefully down the corridor like a man who has come for his final answer. When I took in the tea, he acknowledged me vaguely, not sure if he had met me, and if so, where.

I know it was unforgivable of me to listen outside the door, but I couldn't help it. I had caught the habit when I was a cook-general, and I couldn't miss a drama like this. Jones and I had taken in all the patients' teas and she had gone off to her own. I applied my ear to the door and had just heard him say: 'Now, Edith, once and for all—' when Horrocks came out of the sterilising-room and said: 'What on earth—'

I flapped a hand at her. Her eyes lit up and her nostrils quivered at the scent of scandal. She would have to know now, though she was the last person who should have, if Sister was going to stay on. She crouched beside me and we listened, shivering with excitement, when Godfrey, fortified, perhaps, by the strength of my Bovril sandwiches, said: 'Once and for all, Edith, you can choose between me and the hospital. I won't stand being fooled about like this.' There was an awful hush, and all we could hear were the basket chairs creaking. I thought I heard Sister begin to cry, and then she gave a little gasp, and just at that moment, Lady Mundsley's bell exploded above our heads, shattering our taut nerves and drowning every other sound for miles. She kept us both in the room fixing her bed, so that we missed the exit, triumphal or frustrated, of Godfrey.

I went into the sitting-room to get the tea things, hoping that Sister would disclose what had happened, but the minute I went in, she rushed out of the room in a panic. She had been crying.

It was gratifying the next morning, when it was all over the hospital that Fanny Graham – of all people, my dear – was going to be married, to be able to say: 'Of course, I've known about it for ages.' Not that anyone believed me, any more than they believed Horrocks, who said it too, or Delphine, who gave minute descriptions of the man, although, until I told her, she had no recollection of ever having met him.

CHAPTER EIGHT

For some time after Sister Graham had left, we were without a Sister. Nurse Farren was in charge, and being a girl with a mania for cleanliness, got down at once to repairing the results of Sister's *laisser-faire* policy. We were not busy, as two or three of the rooms were empty, and I spent several days doing practically nothing but spring cleaning. Nurse Farren had been a Staff Nurse for over a year and fancied her chances of being made a Sister. When it was observed what a good job she made of this temporary responsibility, she saw herself in the near future as Sister Farren of the Private Wards.

So I had to scrub and polish and tidy, and take down from the top of the splint cupboard antique apparatuses that had been there so long they had grown on to the shelves. She tried to rope Maggie into this holocaust, telling her she must turn the kitchen and the larder upside down and scrub every available inch of both. Maggie had no intention of obeying, but she said nothing. She never answered anything she didn't like. She was a sour, knotted woman, dispirited by years of service as a Ward Maid, with degenerate feet that had no thickness through the instep and turned out at right angles to her legs, so that she looked as if she were on a stand. It was one of the sights of Redwood to see Maggie waddling down the corridor between the private rooms, with her toes pointing straight at the walls, her cap on the back of her head and a great rusty hairpin hanging down her back on a loose tail of hair. She was anti-everything, except such of the patients who were good for a gossip while she was sweeping their room. If you lost her in the morning, you could track her down by the brush and dustpan lying askew outside a door, and inside you would find Maggie, leaning on the broom handle expounding some Crying Shame.

While I was turning out the medicine cupboard as ordered, she came shuffling into the room for her cough medicine. Sister Graham had allowed her to have it last winter when she had slight bronchial trouble, but although it had cleared up months ago, she refused to give up the syrup. She adored taking medicine. She was not allowed to take anything out of the medicine cupboard, but she was always on at one of the nurses to give her some senna, or Epsom salts, or iron tonic. I once caught her fishing about in the dispensary basket, looking for dregs in the empty bottles which were waiting to be taken down for refilling. She had just uncorked a small dark bottle and was about to dose herself with a drachm of nitric acid.

I got down off the chair from which I was exploring the top corners of the cupboard, uncorked the bottle of Mist. Expect. and poured her dose into the handleless cup which she always carried about with her. She brought it on and off the ward every day, saying that she was not going to risk her death by drinking out of something that somebody with the Dear-knows-what had used. As she did the washing up, perhaps she was right.

'I think you're cracked,' she said, smacking her lips over the syrup. 'I wouldn't break my neck for that stuck-up, 'ymn-singing young Madam. "Scrub out the larder," she says, if you please.

"Wash the paint, Maggie. Put all the saucepans and bowls on to boil with soda."'

'Aren't you going to do it?'

'That I'm not. No one's going to put upon me. What was good enough for Sister Gray-ham is good enough for any la-di-da, even if she is gone on God. I don't hold with churchiness and such. I'd like to see Nurse Farring bury a husband and two kids, and see whether she's still got a mind to praise the Lord.' Her voice was funereal, every vowel a wail and every consonant drawn out.

'You'll go to Hell,' I said, scraping at an encrusted lump of something on the top shelf.

'I dare say. The company might be an improvement on some I could mention. Got a taste of bismuth there, Nurse? I haven't had any all day.'

Nurse Farren fussed and fretted about the state of the kitchen, and in the end, I had to do it with one of the VADs on Maggie's afternoon off. The VAD was a pert, pop-eyed girl, who worked all week in the Habby Department at Hooper's and gave up her Sundays to what she had thought, in common with many others, was vital work, but turned out to be either doing any dirty job that could be thought up or feeling very much in the way. Although they exploited them, most of the Sisters disliked the VADs. They made dirty digs about them being untrained and irresponsible, but would never give them a chance to be anything else by letting them see what was going on. I have often heard Sister Lewis say about some job like sewing on pillow covers or scraping and oiling trolley wheels: 'We'll leave that for the VAD to do tomorrow, it will keep her out of the ward, at any rate.'

The nurses welcomed the VADs. Apart from being a help they brought with them a breath from outside and relieved the tedium of knowing the conversational repertoire of one's colleagues by heart.

Nurse Farren was off that afternoon, so the VAD and I only

tidied the kitchen perfunctorily and wiped over one or two shelves with a wet cloth to look as though they had been scrubbed. The rest of the time we spent having tea and toast, and Horrocks came in and polished off half a cold rice pudding and a jelly that wouldn't set.

Farren came on at half-past five to the tune of 'Jerusalem the Golden' and seemed quite satisfied with the effect we had created. The VAD wanted to give a blanket bath for practice, so Farren found her a nice little job sitting in one of the empty rooms and marking the bundle of new linen that came from the proceeds of the Linen Guild's American Tea.

Nurse Farren was thrilled with her achievements on the Private Wing, and was smug enough and rash enough to point out the improvements to Matron on her morning round.

'I should hope you *are* keeping it clean,' said Matron, through rigid lips. 'That's what you're here for.' I laughed inwardly, remembering how she had once said the same thing to me. I laughed again, but not quite so inwardly, because everyone on 'Privates' was laughing, when it was announced that Staff Nurse Beaver was to be Sister of the Private Wards. Poor Farren was sent to be Staff Nurse on the Maternity Wards, whose Sister was the hospital terror, and was later reported to be going about crooning darkly to the babies about the Lord confounding his enemies.

It seemed strange to see old Beaver in a dark blue dress instead of a striped one and the pointed Sister's cap, which she had not yet quite mastered. The square, strapless apron bib was an improvement. There was not so much strain. It jutted straight forward and was fastened at the salient point with vast safety-pins where the other Sisters wore gilt tiepins.

The ward gradually settled back into the comfortable disorder from which Nurse Farren had roused it. Sister Beaver was earnest and competent, but she was also short-sighted and too eager to be jolly girls together to command any discipline. The Private Wards were heaven to her, because she could indulge her sociability to the full. Lady Mundsley, who had chosen to have a relapse and looked like being with us for ever, discharged herself within a week because she could not stand any more of Beaver's conversation.

Mrs Gordelier was still with us, however. Her husband kept persuading her to stay on. Not that she needed much persuading, although her injuries were sufficiently healed. She was quite annoyed when the plaster cast was removed from her wrist and she was told to exercise it. The most she would do was to waggle her fingers feebly, and that not without much groaning and a nurse in the room in case she fainted.

It was July, the month when one ought to be planning holidays. We were supposed to get three weeks' holiday in the year, which meant that I ought to get mine at least by the end of September. People told me, however, that there was not a hope. I would be sure to have to wait. Often one went for a year and a half without the smell of a holiday, and it was said that Fanny Churchman tried to wangle it so that you caught up with your next year's holiday, and at the end of your three years you found you had only had six weeks off. I had several reasons for wanting a holiday in August. One morning, I was foolish enough to go and tell Matron so. It needed a lot of courage to bring myself to it, but I did want that holiday, and in any case, she couldn't kill me. Or could she, I wondered, seeing my turn approach outside the door and wishing I had not come.

She only said: 'I suppose you think you're the only nurse in the hospital, Nurse,' but it was the way she said these things.

It was much too hot to work. The rooms filled up, Nurse Summers went off sick and was not replaced, and we toiled on, with the starch melting in our high collars. At the end of the day, one was too limp and tired to go out and enjoy the lovely pastel evenings. I sweated up and down after the bells, with a cross red face and a molten area round my waist under my stiff belt. We had a patient in with Shingles, and when my waist got hot, I used to think I had got them, too. She had them all round her back and under her ribs, and Maggie said that when they met in front she would die.

One morning, I suddenly felt very dizzy and reeled against the Professor's wash basin. I put it down to blowing up his rubber air-cushion and thought no more about it until I felt dizzy again in the sluice, without having blown up anything. Perhaps I was going to have a heat stroke; my head felt very muzzy. We were very busy and I didn't have much time to feel ill, but I had a vague sensation while I worked that it was all a dream and that I was using somebody else's legs. When I got a moment to think about it, I hoped that I was going to be ill. It would be a rest if nothing else. Presently, I hoped more fervently; I didn't want to feel like this for nothing. My head was swimming, but I put off taking my temperature in case I should be disappointed. By tea-time, I couldn't take in properly what was said to me. Surely now I was ill. But as I went to the medicine cupboard to get a ther-mometer, I remembered. To-morrow was my day off. My father was fetching me at half-past eight to-night and driving me up to London. I couldn't be ill yet, otherwise they would keep me here in my black iron bed. If I could stave it off, I could be ill at home, which would be lovely.

I sneaked off with a thermometer and locked myself in some-where to see whether I was dying. I was over a hundred and two, and my pulse was trotting along like a pony trying to keep up with a horse. Joy and a faint sense of pride mingled with alarm at the prospect of bearing up for four hours more. I felt worse now that I knew there was something wrong.

A merciful haze lies over those hours. Only the passionate longing for home, which is one of the symptoms of illness, kept me going. I kept taking my temperature, and watched it creep beyond a hundred and three with morbid satisfaction. The others were too busy to notice if I looked peculiar or talked at random, and when Beaver said once: 'Are you all right, old thing? You look a bit flushed,' I was able to pass it off as the heat. By half-past eight, I felt so ghastly I didn't care if I stayed on all night, I couldn't feel any worse. Beaver – now, of course, known as Fanny Beaver – sent me off punctually, saying that I looked tired which, I thought resentfully, was underestimation considering that my temperature was nearly a hundred and four.

I found that by going about it very slowly and deliberately, I could just manage to get changed, though I couldn't get as far as packing a case. My ordeal was not yet over, because if I told my father about it before we got home, he might refuse to take me and put me straight back to bed at the hospital. I would have to keep up the pretence for another hour. I would lie back and pretend to be asleep, so that I didn't have to talk.

Luckily, it was dusk when I got out to the car and his sight wasn't good enough to see what I looked like.

I had forgotten about his sight. 'You can drive,' he said casually. 'I can't see a thing in this light.'

We got home somehow. My performance merely confirmed his previous opinion of my driving, but how we missed that island at the junction of Hendon Way and the Finchley Road, I shall never know.

A few days later I felt strong enough to open *Sister Fairchild* to see what she had to say on the subject of chicken-pox. She showed me a terrifying photograph – no, that was smallpox. Chicken-pox was on the other side, almost as bad, but in different places. I couldn't think how I had caught it. There had not been a whisper of it in Redwood.

'May be contracted,' I read, 'through contact with a case of

Herpes Zoster.' I was sure we hadn't got any of that – wouldn't be seen dead with it. I looked it up in the index: '*Herpes Zoster, or Shingles.*' I felt like writing to the *Lancet.* It is always so surprising when the written word is proved by experience.

When I returned to Redwood, I learned that I had started quite a run on chicken-pox. Nurse Donavan, in fact, had made a palindrome of *Sister Fairchild's* theory by subsequently getting shingles.

Whenever you had been away, you had to report to Matron's office that you were back. What did one say? 'I'm back,' was so obvious and was liable to elicit the retort: 'Where from?' for Matron could not be expected to have the comings and goings of some hundred odd nurses at her finger-tips. Labouring up the hill in the bus, I considered: 'Here I am,' 'Please, Ma'am, I'm better,' or just walking into the room and presenting myself for inspection like a child in a new dress, with feet planted and stomach well out. Sarah P. was one of those people for whom one always rehearsed beforehand. Not that it ever got me anywhere. I never went into that room, with its misleading homey chintzes, without saying the wrong thing.

I was lucky to-day. Matron was out, and I had only to report to Sister Harriman. I found her in her narrow office, which abutted on Matron's like a junior clerk's, putting a lot of art work into a notice which I read upside down across the desk:

LOST!!

Nurse Jepson has lost a small gold watch. Any nurse possessing information likely to lead to its whereabouts to report same
IMMEDIATELY
to   E. Harriman, Ass. Mat.

Unless nurses can exercise more care over personal property, valuables must be deposited in the office.

This was not so much a dig at Jepson as a mild allusion to the number of petty thefts that had occurred recently. Nobody was ever caught at it, and everyone suspected everyone else. You could not leave a pair of stockings drying in the bathroom if you wanted to see them again. If you laid down a pair of scissors in the ward, they were gone in an instant, almost from under your nose. Before I bought a padlock for my bicycle, it was always disappearing, sometimes for two or three days at a time. Although it found its way home, it was not the girl it had been when it started out. First, it was raped of its pump, then the lamp and basket, then the bell. When there was nothing else to take, it used to come home with a puncture. We had no keys to our bedrooms, and pens, underclothing, aprons, books – not money, because we never had any – were constantly disappearing. Once, I came off duty to find my drawers half open and the contents obviously disturbed. Not that I had anything worth stealing, but the fact that someone had been poking about was infuriating enough. In a towering rage, I checked up on my belongings, but the only thing that seemed to be missing were two cups that I had brought off the Private Wards for evening coffee.

Next morning, I burst upon Matron to protest, but my righteous indignation was somewhat damped to find that I had let myself in for a row about the cups, because it was she herself who had discovered them on her periodical round of the nurses' rooms.

I could never get used to this absence of privacy. You were given a room of your own, but it was not your own. The authorities considered themselves responsible for us and made that an excuse for snooping. It was probably even their duty to read any letters we might leave lying around if they looked interesting enough. You did not belong to yourself any more; you were a cog in community life. It was a wonder we did not have to throw all our clothes into a common wardrobe at night and draw at random in the morning, like nuns.

I had arrived back just in time for one of Sister Tutor's Question Papers, with which she periodically tested our chance of passing the Prelim Exam, now only three months away. Although I had missed three weeks of lectures, I had to take the paper, and Toots pursed her sorbo lips over the result and had fears for my future. I could not see why being able to trace the passage of waste from the lavatory pan to the main sewer, or write notes on (a) upland surface water, (b) shallow water, (c) artesian wells, should make me a better nurse. Nurse Jones, who had got top marks and had her answers read out for our edification, was, as far as I could tell, one of the worst nurses on the wards. She was lazy, disobliging, unsympathetic and heavy-handed, but she could write a short essay on 'The Ethics of Nursing' and knew the difference between ventilation with Tobin's tube, Cooper's disc and Galton's grate, all of which had been out of date when Sister Fairchild was a probationer. I pinned my faith in her tripping up over the practical exam.

When I first came back, I was sent to the Theatre for a few weeks. I thought this would be exciting, but I was not there long enough to get much farther than sluicing out the gowns and towels which piled up round me all day as I toiled with sodden hands in the sluice. Things that had been taken out of people used to be brought out here in bowls until they were sent down to the Laboratory, and though at first they made my hair rise, I soon got blasé and could pass an appendix or a kidney or even a finger without having to peep with horrified fascination. Some people liked to have their bits and pieces pickled as a memento. A private patient once insisted on having her spleen bottled for her treasure cupboard. They tried to dissuade her, for the thing was abnormal, the size of a football, but she made as much fuss as if she were being robbed, and eventually took it proudly home, where I believe it reposes in a kind of goldfish bowl among the Wedgwood and Ming.

Theatre Sister was trying. She had a wicked temper, which had to be watched like a barometer, and prided herself on being unable to suffer fools. I was quite glad to be obliged to spend most of my time in the sluice, because in the operating theatre it was possible to do more things wrong to the minute than anywhere else. Even the Surgeons were susceptible to Sister's moods. If she were feeling jocular, the operation might be performed with something of the party spirit, but if those eyebrows were drawn down like bars of iron and that foot was tapping, the atmosphere became so thick you could hardly get in at the door. The Surgeon was irritable, the House Surgeon nervous, the Anaesthetist monosyllabic and we Nurses sweating with anxiety.

Sister would snap a demand for something from behind her mask, and I never knew which was the most dangerous: to ask her to repeat it, or to run briskly off and return with what I thought she had said. If she did not fell you verbally on the spot, you knew it was only a pleasure deferred. If she happened to be feeling sunny that day, she would save her castigation until such time as her temper was bad enough to do it justice. It wasn't really safe for her to be loose among all those razor-sharp scissors and scalpels. Once, when I had been particularly silly, she brandished a villainous instrument at me, declaring that she would love to use it on me. I discovered afterwards that it was an instrument used for crushing a baby's skull.

Theatre Sister had once left nursing to be married, returning on the death of her husband. Consequently, she was either called the black widow spider or the Praying Mantis, the female of which, according to Sister Tutor, was given to killing the male.

Apart from the Praying Mantis, I loved working on the

Theatre. Operations were enthralling, each one a scientific drama, and daily I marvelled at the things a body will stand. When I saw Sir Curtis Rowntree removing clots from a femoral artery as easily as he would clean his pipe, I thought that nothing could be more miraculous until I saw Mr Vavasour do a Caesarean.

I was quite prepared to come over queer. I had read stories of nurses and students thudding to the ground right and left and being left to lie there while the white-robed, inhuman figures with their shining knives bent over the still, shrouded figure on the table, oblivious to all save their glorious task of saving life. I found, however, that if you are near enough to see anything, interest overcomes nausea. Sometimes, especially in summer, the heat, combined with the fumes of ether and the necessity of standing motionless for two hours or more, makes you feel slightly dizzy. You dare not lean against a wall, so you stand on, feeling noble, a swaying figure in the shadows outside the cone of light which throws up the dramatic grouping of the concentrated figures. All light, all eyes, all minds, are magnetised to that one point, the small uncovered area which for that hour is the centripetal focus of existence.

Although I was disappointed when Sister Gilbert announced one morning that I was to go to Martin Callaghan, the Men's Medical Ward, I was relieved to have escaped what was coming to me for letting the sterilisers boil dry the day before. I underestimated Theatre Sister. She made a special trip down to Martin Callaghan and took care to let Sister Tarling know what kind of vermin I was.

Not that Sister Tarling paid much attention. She was a kindly old body, who steered her own unhurried course oblivious of distractions. She had been nursing for more than thirty years and knew exactly what she was at, and if she sometimes favoured the Fairchild rather than the modern idea, she seemed to get just as good results as people who were always talking about psychotherapy. She called all the patients 'Dear', from little boys with infantile paralysis to cracked old men with disseminated sclerosis. She moved about the ward slowly, because her legs hurt her. She would have been retired if it had not been for the war.

There were two nurses on this ward junior to me, so after having been only a bad smell on the Theatre, I felt quite important. The humble Weekes was the Senior Pro, and an insolent girl with a tight shiny skin and a bouncing figure was the Junior. I was Relief Nurse, which meant that I did the work of whoever was off and brought a welcome variety to life. One day I would be bustling importantly about with dressings and forceps, and the next I would be back at my old game of scouring the sluice. The First Nurse was Dawlish, still talking about leaving, but with even less intention of doing so now that she had passed her Prelim, and felt herself eminent. The Staff Nurse was a girl called Jackman, who had been at the hospital as long as anyone could remember, waiting to be married. She was engaged all right, with a ring that she wore round her neck on a piece of wool, but her fiancé could never actually bring himself to come within touching distance of the altar. Jackman went on patiently getting her bottom drawer together. She had the nature and appearance of a trusting dog. Her long face drooped like a bloodhound's from triangular, weepy-looking eyes, and brown loops of hair flopped on either side like ears. All she needed was studs and a name-plate on her high starched collar.

We had a nice lot of men on the ward. They were a gentler, quieter lot than on Herbert Waterlow, and being a medical ward the whole tempo was slower. We had fewer emergencies and casualties and more chronics. Patients were admitted at respectable hours into beds that were ready for them. There were no stretchers constantly arriving in the middle of dinner, with mangled men on them who had to be given a blood transfusion immediately by a House Surgeon who could not be found. Some of the men who were only in for observation needed hardly any nursing. Many of them were allowed up and did a lot of our housework for us. They seemed quite pleased with any job that broke the monotony of a day that began at five o'clock.

There was one particular man, a Gastric called Siddons, who had been in for weeks and weeks to see whether an operation could be avoided by treatment. He was short and stocky, with hair like a carpet brush, and all the hospital dressing-gowns were too long for him. He flip-flapped about in a pair of carpet slippers, pouncing on any job that was going and looking after the other patients like a mother. The men called him 'Auntie'. He would do anything for anybody, but he kept them in order. He had been there so long that he regarded the ward as his own, and was determined to see that it was properly conducted.

He was solicitous with the old men and tender with the ill ones. Each new arrival would soon find Siddons at his bedside, jollying him along in case he felt homesick, and if anyone was in pain, he would be along to comfort him and to hurry Nurse Jackman up with the dope. When anyone was coming round from an anaesthetic, Auntie, who had been hovering close by, peering anxiously at the mottled face for the first signs of returning consciousness, would be up to the bed in a flash, growling: 'All right, Chum. Take it easy, you ain't dead yet,' and muffling the half-insensible oaths with the palm of his hand.

There were a lot of Gastrics on this ward. I had been harassed enough over Lady Mundsley's feeds, but these would have driven me demented if it had not been for Siddons. Some were on milk only, some on pre-digested milk, some hourly and some two-hourly. There was a list up in the kitchen, but Sister had taken the paper shortage too seriously, and whenever the diets were changed would cross and recross out and overwrite rather than start a fresh piece of paper. The result, in her illegible handwriting, was chaos, but Auntie had it all at his fingertips. He knew when a patient's diet was changed, either from hovering about listening to the doctors, or from studying their charts, which he was strictly forbidden to do. He took a deep interest in everything that went on and loved nothing better than to settle down to a medical discussion, propounding a mixture of the old wives' stuff on which he had been reared, and technicalities that he had picked up during his long sojourn in hospital.

'Poor old Forbes,' he would say, coming into the kitchen and seating himself on the table while I was cooking up the milk for yet another round of feeds. 'Occult blood, I see on the Path Lab report.'

'Auntie, you're not allowed to look at people's charts. Who's on milk only?'

'Smithers, Gold and Forrest. Forrest is starting a three days' test. Oh – and that new boy'll be on milk only for the first few days, won't he?'

I peered at the list and scratched my head, but it was simpler to trust Siddons. 'D'you have milk or custard this feed?' I asked him.

'Milk. I've had a bit of a nagging pain all to-day, nurse. You know, I think that ulcer's travelling.'

'Don't be silly, it couldn't possibly.'

'Couldn't it? What about my uncle, then? He had the Barium meal and Hex-ray, and they diagnosed an ulcer in the duoddenum. Month later, they opened him up and there it was, right up at the top of the stomach. Travelled, you see – they do.'

'You tell that to Sister Tarling,' I said, setting out cups on a tray.

'Bless her heart,' said Siddons. 'She'd say "Yes, dear," and get me a bottle of barley sugar out of her cupboard. I reckon she's got Oedema in the legs, don't you, Nurse?'

'How on earth d'you know that?'

'Oh, I get around.' He hopped off the table, tripping over the hem of his dressing-gown. 'Carry that tray in for you? Better let me. You'll only go and give 'em out wrong else.'

Siddons was subjected to all the indignities and discomforts of gastric investigation. Tubes were forced down his throat and the contents of his stomach sucked up for inspection. X-ray after X-ray was taken and various different diets tried, from the insipid to the nauseating. He was sustained by his absorption in everything that was done to him, and used to ask pertinent questions which sometimes left even Mr Morris Evans stumped. One day, turning his cocky little snub face up to the Surgeon's, he said: 'Come on now, sir. Out with it. I seen on me chart "Query Operation". When you going to carve me up?'

He had a week in which to get used to the idea of being carved. He spent this time coaching a young Diabetic to take on his duties when he should be bedridden. His wife was inclined to be tearful when she came to visit him the day before. 'Cut it out, Norah,' I heard him say. 'This what they're going to do to me is one of the miracles of the age.' He proceeded to give her a detailed description of the operation which he had got from a medical book, concluding with: 'And if I konks out, I wants me body given to the hospital for research.' Mrs Siddons, an anaemic woman who had worked too hard all her life, came over faint on the way out and had to be revived with cups of tea and a sit-down in Sister's room.

When I took him to the Theatre the next day, he was furious because he was going to be anaesthetised outside. 'I been looking forward to seeing the Theatre,' he grumbled, lying on the trolley looking clean and innocent in the high-necked operating gown. 'Fancy not letting a chap see the slaughter-house. It's a bit rough.'

'Good morning,' said the Anaesthetist, breezing in, followed by the porter wheeling the gas and oxygen apparatus. 'Now, old man, you're not going to mind this a bit.'

'Course I'm not – I don't mind,' Siddons waved that aside. 'What you going to give me, though? Ether, gas, general anaesthetic?'

'Now just *breathe* in,' said the doctor, taking no notice and clapping the gauze mask over Siddons's enquiring face.

'Yes, but what you—' He raised a hand to push it aside.

'All right, all right, old chap – nothing to be afraid of. Just breathe in and see what you can smell.'

'I want to know—' came thickly from under the mask.

'Better watch out he doesn't struggle, Nurse,' said the Anaesthetist. 'Nervy type.' He did struggle. He had told me he was going to take the anaesthetic slowly and calmly, so as to notice his reactions, but he was so infuriated at not being in the know that he tried to resist the gas, and went under choking, and finally turned dark blue and stopped breathing. 'The damned ignorance of these people,' said the Anaesthetist, after we had got him going again with artificial respiration and a gale of oxygen, 'If they knew a bit more about it, they wouldn't panic so.' Mr Morris Evans poked his head through from the Theatre. 'What the devil are you doing?' he asked. 'We're all scrubbed up and I've got a nephrectomy to do after this and an old woman to see in Cambridge by three o'clock.'

The operation started badly and everyone was in a temper throughout. The Surgeon cursed the Anaesthetist because Siddons was heaving, and the Anaesthetist cursed Siddons. Sister cursed Miss Llewellyn, who was assisting, and Miss Llewellyn cursed me. I cursed the heat and my feet.

The operation took longer than they expected. The nephrectomy was waiting in the anaesthetic room, getting more hysterical every minute, and Mr Morris Evans sent me telephoning all over the place: to his wife, to say that he would not be home for lunch, to Cambridge, to tell the old woman he would be late, to Callaghan Ward to tell them to prepare for a blood transfusion, and to the porter to tell his chauffeur to go and buy some sand-wiches – ham, if possible – if not, beef, but for God's sake no mustard – and a bottle of beer.

When he was coming round, Siddons gabbled about Oxygen and CO_2 and Ethyl Chloride sprays. When he woke up, he was thrilled to find his leg splinted and to see the blood dripping in through the glass connexion in the tube. He was very disap-pointed that he had been asleep while they cut into the vein. He had his morphia, watching the syringe critically, and presently began to mumble restlessly.

'All right, dear,' Sister said. 'You'll be all right. Just sleep now, quietly,' and the well-trained Diabetic approached as near as he dared and said: 'Everything's OK, Mr Siddons.' Still he mumbled and complained. It was quite a time before I discovered that he would not settle until somebody told him what his blood group was.

The next day I had to tell him everything, leaving out about the atmosphere. 'Took three hours, eh?' he said proudly. 'I must have been an interesting case. Something a bit out of the ordi-nary. They like that. Reckon they had a rare old time playing about with me up there, eh, Nurse?'

'Rather,' I lied.

Every pain he had, he studied and mentally charted. 'The stitches in the abdominal wall tweaking now,' he would say, or 'That's me peritonitis. Reckon I got a bit of wind lodged in the hole where the ulcer was. You can, you know.'

'You can't,' I said, but he produced his uncle again as proof. I gave him *Sister Fairchild* to read, and he followed the nursing treatment with grave concern, always holding the medicine glass of citrated milk that was all he was allowed at first up to the light to see whether the amount was correct. He kept a strict eye on the Diabetic, and from his regal position, propped up on pillows, would direct him up and down the ward, wherever his sharp eye noticed something that wanted doing.

'You taking your diet right, son?' he would enquire. 'You swear you got no sweets in your locker? What was that I saw your girl bring you in a paper bag last visitors' day?'

'Water biscuits, Mr Siddons.'

'Where'd she get 'em? You can't get 'em in Redwood. If you been eating sweets – how was his sugar this morning, Nurse?'

'My girl comes from St Albans. She got 'em there,' said the boy, peevishly kicking the wheel of the bed.

'Don't kick my bed, you'll burst all me stitches else. Then there'll be trouble, and I'll tell you for why. All me organs'll fall out into the bed. Won't they, Nurse?'

'If you say so.'

'It's time for me feed. One and a half ounce milk and one and a half ounce water this time. I go up half an ounce at twelve o'clock. Here, son, you go with Nurse and bring it back. She's got plenty of other things to do, without you hang around like a sick headache.'

I felt sorry for the Diabetic, whose main object in life was to get back to his earphones as soon as possible in case he should miss a moment of 'Hi Gang' or Sandy Macpherson. He was a tall, drooping boy, with a small face and long eyelashes, and he knew the words of all the dance tunes, especially the ones about rain in a lane and the sun smiling through, which were his favourites. He had been admitted to the ward late one night, in charge of a policeman, who had mistaken an Insulin coma for a drunken stupor. As he had been officially charged with this, it took weeks of form filling and consultation of sects, and paras, before the idea could be uprooted. Even the doctor's evidence left them unconvinced, and the wretched boy was always receiving visits from ponderous blue figures, looking undressed without their helmets, come to question him just once more, with almost wistful hope. There was so little doing in Redwood.

Life trickled gently along. Sister started knitting a pilch for her niece's baby and frequently had to have the stitches counted or picked up for her. When Sister was off duty, Jackman stitched away at the nightgown that she was embroidering for the problematical bridal night, for we were not at all busy. Dawlish went about her work in a dignified way and added another layer of curls to the pile on which her cap reposed. Weekes seemed as busy as ever and scuttered about with a puckered face even when there was nothing to do, and the Junior flounced about yawning and saying: 'Am I bored? Gosh, what a deadly hole this is. Gosh, I'm fed up. Oh, ask somebody else for your feed, Saunders. I can't be bothered.' We wanted to write to her mother and ask if she didn't think it was time the girl was put into corsets.

Like someone who has lain too long in bed, it was almost more than we could do to rouse ourselves when it suddenly became necessary. One morning, we were fiddling away the time between cleaning the ward and going off in relays to have coffee and change our aprons. Twenty minutes was allowed for this, but Sister didn't treat you like a criminal if you took half an hour. As long as the work was done, she didn't mind occasional petty infringements. The years had given her a more balanced idea of these things. I was off duty that morning, and was doing the flowers in the bathroom, spinning them out until it should be half-past nine. The telephone rang and after allowing a decent interval for someone else to answer it, I went through the ward and picked up the receiver. It was Sister Harriman. When she had rung off, I felt almost like ringing her back again to ask if she had really said that. It was too fantastic. It was impossible. Where's Sister? I must find her at once. Quickly! Not a moment to lose! I was in a fluster. I didn't see how we were ever going to be able to cope.

'Nurse, Nurse, whatever are you rushing about like that for?' said Sister placidly, as I cannoned into her coming out of the kitchen. She accepted the news rather like a cook being told there will be two extra for dinner: it's a nuisance, but we'll manage.

'But *twelve*, Sister! We haven't got half those beds – and air-raid casualties – most of them'll probably have to be operated on. It must have been last night's blitz. The wireless said London had got it badly. I suppose they daren't leave them there another night. But *twelve*, Sister – and two hours' time! You'd have thought—'

'Poor dears,' said Sister tranquilly, 'we must try and make them as comfortable as possible. Let me see, now.' She stood with one fat finger to her lip, deliberating, refusing to be hurried. The thought of the swarm about to descend on her at eleven o'clock left her unmoved. 'You and Nurse Lawson had better start getting the extra bedsteads out of the cupboard, while I go and see which of the men we can move. Poor things, it does seem a shame to upset them. Nurse Jackman—' I heard her call, as she went into the ward, 'there are one or two things I want you to do.'

One or two things! The Junior and I toiled away in the cupboard, heaving out the folding iron beds that the Government had provided at the beginning of the war, presumably for just such an occasion. Who says England is never prepared before the event? When they were not pinching your fingers, they were barking your shins or biting your ankles. Lawson kept saying: 'Why should we have to do this? It's not fair. I didn't come here to do this. They ought to have men to do it.' I told her to go away and join something with a Trade Union. 'I may tell you I needn't stay here if I don't want to,' she said, kicking a bed which had just kicked her. 'I can get a commission in the WAAFs any time I like. My uncle's in the Air Ministry.' One of her favourite patients, a Guardsman with ear trouble, came along to ask if he could help, and I left her to unload her grievances into the sound ear while I went to see if we had enough pyjamas for the new patients, for we had been warned that they would come with no belongings.

Sister Harriman came along, red in the face and all of a dither, to say that no one was to go off duty. 'Government order,' she said impressively, as if she visualised Churchill himself dictating it. She and Sister Tarling talked for a while in the corridor, looking, through the glass doors, like two comfortable countrywomen gossiping on a doorstep. The ward was in an uproar. It was almost as bad as the night the burns came, though it had not the same nightmare quality. A lot of the men were helping – too many of them. In spite of Siddons sitting bolt upright with his hair on end, giving directions, there was no sort of organisation. Beds were being pushed up and down without purpose, sometimes travelling all round the ward and ending up where they had started from, with the patient inside crying 'Nice day for a sail,' and 'Thanks for the buggy ride' – anything to add to the uproar.

Dawlish had the day off that day. She would. Jackman was paddling up and down, the loose skin of her forehead corrugated with worry. Weekes was pushing lockers about with a hideous squeaking of wheels, trying to trace the beds to which they belonged. Lawson and her boy friend came staggering in with the end of a bed under each arm, her face shining like a polished apple and his bandage cock-eyed. Sister went on calmly chatting. When I went past on my way to the linen cupboard, I heard her insisting on having an extra ration of tea sent down. 'It will be the one thing they want after the journey, poor dears.'

There'll be all sorts of things they want,' said Sister Harriman. 'but I don't know about tea. All the House Surgeons are standing by, and Mr Harvey Watkins and Sir Curtis are coming at eleven. There'll be a terrible lot to do, I'm afraid, a terrible— do you allow Nurse to use hospital sheets on government beds, Sister?' she asked, as I staggered by under a bundle of linen. 'Surely you were issued with government sheets?' Sister had never bothered about this before. So long as the patients had plenty of clean sheets, that was all she cared about, but she had to send me back to the linen cupboard now, with an apologetic look to show me that she thought it was as silly as I did. Sister Harriman checked up my new bundle as I passed her leaving the ward. 'Even in an emergency like this, Nurse,' she said, 'these little things are so important. It's just the difference between a good nurse and a bad one.' There would obviously soon be another notice up about which sheets to put where, and why.

Miraculously, and without agitating anybody, Sister managed to create order on the ward. By eleven o'clock, we were ready, and we looked at our handiwork proudly and mentally rolled up our sleeves, thinking: 'Let 'em come!' I was exhausted already, but I supposed I should somehow last out the day.

The twelve empty beds were ready at the top of the ward, hot bottles in, bedclothes turned back so that a patient could be slid in from a stretcher. A pair of pyjamas, a towel, soap and face flannel were in each locker, and clean charts hung in the holders on the wall, ready to be filled in. The sterilisers were boiling like cauldrons, the blood transfusion instruments were laid out on the trolley under a sterile towel, gauze, wool and bandages were heaped on the low cupboard in the middle of the ward and the hypodermic syringes lay ready in a dish of sterile water. All the men had been got into bed, rather cramped together at the far end of the ward, but they seemed to like it: it made card-playing easier. Nurse Lawson had been sent to the hostel for clean aprons for all of us, and Jackman had even cleaned her shoes.

All we needed now was the patients.

At half-past eleven, I asked Sister if I might dash away and telephone to Mrs Yule to explain why I could not come to lunch.

'Don't be a moment longer than necessary,' said Sister, 'they may come any minute now.' On my way to the telephone box, I passed the doctors' sitting-room and saw an impressive display of white coats sprawled in chairs or standing about, waiting for the casualties. I was glad I was not on Theatre now. They would have a terrible day. Sister Harriman and the Out-Patients Sister, porters, nurses, the Dispenser and various hangers-on, were milling round the entrance hall like a reception committee waiting for a film star. Even the enormous, apoplectic head porter had levered himself out of his glass hutch and was filling the front door, doing a Sister Ann act. As I came out of the telephone box, someone said: 'Hurry back to your ward, Nurse, I can hear the ambulances coming up the hill now.' I fled like Mercury and created a gratifying stir on the ward with my announcement. Everyone ran about doing some little last-minute job, and then we all stood ready again watching the corridor expectantly. It was just like a music-hall act, when the orchestra keeps working up a terrific roll of drums to announce some stupendous entrance, and nobody comes, so they start the crescendo again and still nobody comes, and they roll again even louder, and just when you know your head will burst if they don't stop, the noise ceases, suspended in mid-air. The stage is still empty, people laugh uneasily, and then, suddenly, Nobby Navarino turns anti-climax into climax by crawling meekly out from under the back curtain or climbing out of the french horn, or being spot-lighted hanging by his hands from the stage box. The only difference with us was that the protagonists never appeared at all, even after the fourth and fifth roll of drums. At half-past twelve, Sister got so tired of hearing that the ambulances were in sight, that the stretchers were being lifted out, and other alarums that came to nothing, that she sent us off to dinner. She was getting tired. 'If they come now, they'll have to wait till my nurses have had their lunch,' she said quite testily to a porter who had only come innocently down to borrow a piece of string.

I had missed a good feed at Mrs Yule's for nothing. Chris was at lunch, and she told me that Johnny Briant had told her that the no off-duty order had nothing to do with the Government but was entirely Matron's idea.

Something did happen after lunch. It was visitors' day, but Matron had decreed, naturally enough, that with all the commotion of casualties arriving – at least fifty were expected altogether – it would not do to have visitors thronging the wards. The men understood that and had not grumbled above an undertone when they were told, but when two o'clock came and there were neither casualties nor visitors, the undertone was an ugly rumour of war. The rumour rose on all the wards and grew to a clamour that was answered by another, shriller clamour from without. When I went along to the porter's desk with a message from Sister, I saw a remarkable sight. Sister Harriman was standing on the step of the front door, arms folded, feet planted, keeping at bay a rabble of relations. They were mostly women – at least it was the women who were making the most noise. The men were tweaking at their coats and obviously trying to persuade them to come away and leave the thing alone, but the wives and mothers and sweethearts were not going to be cheated of their rights. It was visitors' day and they intended to visit. Equally, Sister Harriman intended to keep them out and the result was deadlock – institutional authority versus outraged possessive instinct. Black coats and best hats dipped and surged in argument on the gravel. Umbrellas and paper parcels waved. Those behind kept pushing, so that those in front had their noses almost touching the enemy's skirt. An untidy, hysterical woman with a jumping face kept waving a paper carrier and shouting: 'What about my Fred's clean pyjamas? What about that, I say?' For one moment, I thought they were going to storm the hospital. A common impulse suddenly swept through them like the wind through corn, and as they all pressed forward, Sister Harriman made a sort of defensive movement with her hands and took a step backwards. And then suddenly the forward movement stopped, the noise stopped, the mob instinctively fell back a pace, as Sarah Churchman appeared silently on the step above them and quelled them by the mere expression on her face. It was most dramatic. I expected her to say: 'Down, you rabble, you gutter curs – back to the sewers where you belong and rid us of your stench!'

They listened quite reasonably to her explanation of why they could not come in, and such was her power that some of the syco-phants actually started to back her up and to turn to their neighbours and say that the Matron was quite right, and didn't they know there was a war on.

One nurse was to be sent from each ward to collect the things that the visitors had brought for the patients, and as I was on the spot, I was loaded with flowers, books, food, clean vests, and per-sonal messages of every sort, from Sid having written at last to say he'd got there and it's stifling hot and lots of sand and where might that be, to Em and Baby sending their fond love and when are you coming out?

I had to make several trips before I had collected all the parcels and given out the dirty washing and messages from the patients. The entrance hall by now was like a madhouse, with nurses and relations yelling at each other across the crowd, paper bags burst-ing, apples rolling over the floor, and two women fighting for a dirty pair of pyjamas that each claimed came off her husband.

And still the casualties did not come.

We took the ward teas round early, so as to get that done while we could, and soon afterwards Sister said that we could go off in relays for an hour's rest. I trailed off at about six. I had been excited at first about the casualties, feeling that at last we were in more tangible contact with the war, were taking part in it in a second-hand way. But now I hoped they wouldn't come at all. Perhaps they were already dead. I was too tired to take any inter-est in them, far too tired to cope with the many hours' work that their arrival would entail. They would probably arrive in the middle of the night and we would have to get up.

I kicked off my shoes and lay down on my bed with a cigarette. After having got up twice for my book and an ashtray, I had just got comfortable when Janet's thump nearly stove in the door: 'All Naa-assis got to go buck to the wards!'

Before I went through the door and up the stairs to the hospital, I turned the other way and looked out of the hostel door on to the gravel to see what was doing. As I looked, a khaki woman on a motor-cycle skidded in through the iron gates as if a whole Panzer division were after her. She hurled herself off at the front door and plunged into the hospital, a canvas bag swinging on her hip. A despatch rider, hoping to be mentioned in despatches. Then I turned and ran, for I had seen the nose of the first converted bus sliding past the porter's cottage. Everyone was alert again now. The atmosphere had sprung back to eleven o'clock that morning, and we were on our toes, ready to do our best for them, forgetting how we had cursed them all day, now that they were actually here.

When the first stretcher came in with a very old man on it, we all thought 'Poor old man to be blitzed,' but when another one came in only a fraction younger, and then another and another, all old dotards and all, as far as one could see, without a scratch on them, realisation began to dawn. Some of them began to get up as soon as they were put to bed and start to prowl tremulously about. 'Been out of bed for months,' they said, when we remonstrated, 'we was never in bed at the other 'orspital.'

They were dear old infirmary chronics, who had been evacuated to make room in London for the real casualties. The only arrangements that we had made that still stood were the cups of tea, although one old man threatened to walk back to London if he couldn't have cocoa. He was destined to be a nuisance; one could see that. He had a long, curly grey beard, and looked just like Judas, with small glittering eyes. Nobody could find out what was wrong with him, because all he would say was: 'You mind your business, gel. Ask me no questions, I tells yer no lies.'

The Surgeons went home, and the House Surgeons either went or sent out for beer. We turned off the sterilisers, put away the bandages and instruments, and took down the six beds that were not needed. By the time we had got the ward straight and tucked in the old men, who, incidentally, had a suitcaseful of belongings apiece, it was nearly nine o'clock and the sirens were going. All the old men sat up, and you could see by their eyes what they had been through last night. Sister went round explaining to them that the siren was a mere formality and probably praying inwardly that the Germans would not choose to-night to have a go at Redwood aerodrome. 'It's all right, dear, you're safe now,' she said, just like a mother whose child had woken up with night terrors. It seemed to work. Even Judas lay down and consented to go to sleep, though not until he had made someone get him another cup of cocoa.

None of the Old Daddys, as Sister Tarling called them, seemed to have any address other than the hospital from which they had been evacuated, or the one they had been in before that, or the one before that. Hospitals to them were like South Coast hotels to Colonels' widows – the only home they knew, and, like Colonels' widows, they dug themselves in almost immediately and managed to establish prior claims to the best chairs and least draughty corners. From the cardboard suitcases and canvas bags that they had brought with them, they produced photographs and china ornaments and other knick-knacks, which they arranged on their locker tops to make themselves at home. They were nearly all allowed up, as there was nothing much wrong with them except senility, and they used to sit round the fire in the ward, for it was a chilly October, smoking foul blackened pipes and conversing in monosyllabic grunts. They gave a homey atmosphere to the place which orderly rows of spotless beds and the smell of antiseptic normally failed to provide, but we were after all supposed to be a hospital ward, not a Home of Rest.

They had been in hospital so long that they had almost forgotten any other life, and most of them had been likewise forgotten by their relations. They hardly ever had any visitors, but they didn't seem to mind; they were perfectly self-contained between the four walls of the ward. The oldest of them all was Daddy Johnson, who was nearly ninety. He had a cherubic face with faded blue eyes, a scarlet button nose and a fringe of grey beard that went right round his face to where baldness suddenly started above his ears. When he had the wireless headphones on, he looked exactly like a baby in a bonnet. He was the goodest old man, and made far less trouble than some of the others who were not confined to bed as he was. He used to crack very feeble jokes with the younger patients, at which Siddons always laughed, even if nobody else did, and the old man would cackle delightedly at the back of his nose. As he had nobody to bring him extras, Sister used to buy him chocolate cakes, which he ate so slowly that the chocolate used to melt and run into his beard. She called him 'the Bladder Daddy', because of his complaint.

When I asked him the name of his next-of-kin, to fill in on his chart that first evening, he only stared at me innocently with his china eyes. He had no idea. He had once had a daughter, it transpired, but she was in Australy now.

Much as she loved the old men, except Judas Iscariot, whom nobody could stand, Sister spent her time urging Mr Sickert to arrange for their disposal elsewhere. We were not supposed to keep people who required no nursing and the beds were wanted for other patients who were waiting to come in. The Infirmary eventually took most of them, and Mr Sickert managed to get the Bladder Daddy into a very superior convalescent home that was chiefly staffed by voluntary ladies who wore the Red Cross uniform as fancy dress and made up to it accordingly. Nobody would take Judas Iscariot; it seemed we were stuck with him for life. He had the most irritating, as well as the dirtiest habits. His locker was an offensive glory hole which nobody could bring themselves to turn out, even if he had allowed it. He was an inveterate hoarder, and the night nurses said he used to be opening and shutting the drawer and cupboard all night long, gloating over his scraps and oddments under cover of the dark. Every evening, we had to collect the newspapers and put them by the dustbin for the porter to clear away, but Judas would never give his up. Even after three or four days he would insist that he was still reading it and would curse you venomously if you removed one while he was out of bed. He used to fold them up meticulously with his crooked, bony fingers, so that there were only about four square inches of print showing. This he would pass up and down in front of his avid, glittering eyes, folding it again as carefully to the next section when he had got his money's worth out of every word. He only had to buy a paper once a week; the Sunday paper lasted him for seven days. When he had finished it, he would tear it into squares and line things with it: his locker shelves, the soles of his slippers, his dinner tray, anything so as to get every ounce of value for his twopence.

We had got the ward straight again, government beds stacked away, and the other beds returned to their proper places, when the old Bladder Daddy suddenly turned up again in a wheel-chair. There appeared to have been some mistake. The convalescent home was only for the military. They had been expecting some handsome young lieutenant with curly eyelashes, and who should turn up but old Daddy Johnson with his cherry nose that Siddons insisted was due to drinking bad beer. He was glad to be back. The convalescent home, he said, had been too fiddle-faddle. He settled down gratefully into his old corner near the fire, and spread out his spotted china dog and his turnip watch and his ashtray with the Broadstairs Arms on it.

Not all the other wards had been able to dispose of so many of their evacuees. Herbert Waterlow was still overcrowded with them, and the consequence was that when Sweetie's Anti-Aircraft unit brought down a German plane in a ploughed field five miles outside the town, we were the only ward that had beds to spare for the two survivors. Sister Tarling, who was so patriotic that she cried when the wireless played 'There'll Always Be an England', hated the idea, and had to summon all her professional sense of duty and innate compassion to conquer her racial instincts.

'After all, Nurses, a case is a case,' she told us, all gathered in her sitting-room before the arrival of the Germans. 'I want you to look on it like this. To us has been given the privilege of healing the sick. It's a responsibility that transcends all other issues. The science of medicine is universal; it's far greater than any political upheaval or any war that was ever fought. These men are sick men. That's all you've got to think about – don't think about their nationality, and if you can't stomach their language, don't talk to them.' She paused. She had come to the end of the piece which she had prepared as much to convince herself as, us.

We had not given much thought to the matter before. The mental apathy engendered by hospital routine had dulled the patriotic fervour which was responsible for half of our presences here. War news could no longer get us worked up; in fact, we seldom studied it, and as for discussing it – there were far more absorbing topics much nearer home. So the idea of two German patients had not moved us to murderous frenzy. It would be something new; you could say that for it. Now that Sister was making a Thing of it, however, we began to feel those very reactions which she had called us in here to eradicate. We saw how strongly she objected. Her usually smooth, untroubled face showed traces of the struggle between her obligations and her instincts.

'After all,' said Dawlish, in her slow, resentful voice, 'they did come here to drop bombs on us. I don't see how we can be expected to forget that. I think it's awful cheek myself to expect us to nurse them,' she added, twizzling up a curl. 'I shall give in my notice to-morrow. I didn't come here to toady to a lot of Nazis. I shall tell Matron so.' Sister made a shocked, hushing face. 'I know it's difficult,' she said, 'but it isn't easy for me, either, and I look to you to back me up, as I know you will.' We all made *esprit de corps* noises. 'They'll be nursed behind screens, of course,' she went on, 'and there's no reason why the men should know who they are. You are strictly forbidden to mention them to the other patients. Is that clear?' she added, with a burst of severity, which she hoped might stop Dawlish humming and cleaning her nails with the nails of the other hand.

It didn't make any difference. The men found out within a day. Trust Siddons not to be kept in the dark about anything that was going on in his ward. He was allowed up by now, and one had to keep constant watch on him to prevent his sneaking behind the screens to 'see what the bleeders looked like'. It was all rather embarrassing. The Germans were quite pleasant, well-mannered boys, not too badly injured to be perfectly aware of the effect of their presence on their unseen fellow-patients. Naturally, they hated being here as much as we hated to have them. They both had fractures and were difficult to move, and anything one had to do for them, like bathing them or making their bed, took a long time. I suppose if I had been a good nurse I should not have grudged this time, but I did. Even if there was nothing particular to do on the ward, I felt I would have been better employed talking to Daddy Johnson about the Crimea. Whenever the men saw one going behind the screens, they would yell out: 'Cut 'is bleeding throat, Nurse'; and other suggestions unprintable. Sister used to come into the ward and flap her hands at them, and although they stopped out of regard for her, they broke out again as soon as she had gone. The night nurse said that it was dreadful at night when there was an air raid. The men had never taken much notice before except to curse sleepily, but now they would all wake up to hurl abuse over the screens, and the Germans would lie blushing and silent, contemplating the irony of having a bomb dropped on them by their own side.

Judas Iscariot, of course, nursed as big a grievance as anybody. He would lie with his glinting eyes trained on the screens, muttering Hebraic imprecations and complaining to the nurses that there was a bad smell in the ward. If anyone smelt, it was he himself. We told him so. It didn't matter what you said to him; he was uninsultable. That was the creepy part about him.

Dawlish had been to Matron and complained. 'So I said to her: "Matron," I said, "I don't see why I should be expected to surrender my patriotism for the convenience of your hospital. You can get some other nurse to do it. I feel too strongly for my country." And Matron said: "But you must stay, Nurse," she said, "I count on you for the smooth running of that ward."' Jackman, of course, believed this and was in a torment of worry for days at the thought of the aspersion cast on her.

When she had exhausted the limelight of rebellion, Dawlish thought there might be a certain piquancy in discovering the good qualities of the Germans. Everyone else was too bigoted to appreciate them. She alone had the discernment to realise their intellect. She became more boring than ever with endless verbatim reports of conversations she had held with them, usually ending up with: 'Of course, you think it's appalling of me to treat them like human beings, but I'm afraid I've never been able to develop this unthinking, automatic patriotism that everybody goes in for in wartime. I can't help seeing them as people, you see. I'm funny like that.' She would take up any attitude which she thought would disassociate her from the common herd in thought or deed. I told her she'd better marry one of them and see how far individualism got her in Germany.

We used to tease Dawlish about being keen on them, but the joke turned to ashes on our lips when Lawson announced one day in all seriousness that she was in love with Oberleutnant Himmelheber. She came and cried into the diabetic specimen that I was testing and told me all about it. Now that I came to think of it, I realised that she had got thinner in the last few weeks and was not so frequently to be found in the kitchen filling up the corners left by steak pudding and hot jam roll. To quote Godfrey Winn when he saw an egg being boiled: I turned away, sick with disgust. I suppose she was attracted by the novelty. There were plenty of perfectly good Tommies in the ward on whom she could have sublimated her adolescent desires, but no, she had to go and pick on a German who, by the time he was discharged from the ward, was strong enough to 'Heil Hitler' at Sister as he was being wheeled past her on the trolley.

She went scarlet in the face as if someone had hit her, and a perfect fusillade of oaths was hurled from all sides at the glass doors as the trolley went through. Siddons leaped out of bed and ran down the corridor in pyjamas and bare feet before anyone could stop him. He lost the trolley after it had gone into the lift, and, haring about the hospital, found himself at the front door and was brought back by the fat porter, like a policeman bringing home a stray. He then retired to bed with indigestion. And all this time, Nurse Lawson was leaning her soft bosom on the draining-board in the sluice, crying her eyes out and swearing she would never smile again.

She may not have, for all I know, because the next day I was moved to another ward, and became so oppressed by the unparalleled afflictions of my new existence that, as far as I was concerned, everyone wore a face like a boot.

CHAPTER NINE

I was on Grace Annie Sprock, the maternity ward into which I had blundered when I first came to the hospital for my interview. My brief, informal meeting with the female cataclysm who ran this ward had left me reeling, and whole days of her now were devastating. She ran that ward as if it were a totalitarian state, and although the result was full-tilt efficiency, I could not help thinking that a little less commotion might have been better for the mothers and babies.

'You on Midwiff?' Barney asked me at supper. I nodded, with my mouth full of toad-in-the-hole that was all hole and no toad. 'Oh, yes,' she said, 'your apron's all over babies. How's mad Maria Ramsbotham?' I shrugged my shoulders dejectedly.

'You'll get used to her,' said Barney. 'You mustn't take her seriously. She's mad, of course – quite starkers.'

It was the energy of the woman that was so shattering. She never stopped going from morning till night, and even when there was nothing much doing, she would frequently miss her off-duty and even her meals because of her mania that we did not work properly without supervision. When babies were born, she was a dynamo of activity. She was here, there and everywhere –

admonishing the doctor, exhorting the mother, slanging the nurses, telling you to do something and then snatching it away to do it herself, and altogether raising such Cain in the Labour Ward that when the baby arrived, his first breath was a gasp of astonishment.

The only time when she was unenthusiastic about the arrival of a baby was when it looked like being born between nine and ten at night. It was a moot point whether this was her responsibility or Night Sister's, and although she would have overridden anyone else and if necessary stayed up all night, she and Fanny Adams were such sworn enemies that she was only too pleased to present her with a little bit of extra work to start off the night and upset her routine.

The work on this ward was confusing at first and arduous compared with Martin Callaghan and his well-behaved Gastrics. Apart from the fact that many of the women were in a nervous and difficult state, the babies required endless attention. There were usually about five or six of them sleeping or yelling or threatening to choke in the white cots that hung over the end of their mothers' beds. There was bathing them and changing them and feeding those that were on bottles, and 'putting up' and 'taking down', which involved much shifting of screens and frequent visits to the mother to prevent her and the baby falling into a bucolic stupor of contentment at the mere fact of each other's existence. Each baby wore its name on a piece of tape round its wrist, but when two were born close together, the fracas was such that one was never sure that Sister had not labelled them wrong in her excitement. Well may Mrs Finnucane say to her son as she clips him over the head in a few years' time: 'You unnatural child!' I always had a suspicion that he belonged to Mrs Duff. He looked much more like her, and the baby that crowed and squeaked in the cot at the foot of her bed was so markedly unlike Mr Duff that one seemed to detect a slight coldness in his manner towards Mrs Duff on visitors' day.

Even when I began to get accustomed to the work of the ward, Sister still followed me about admonishing me. She would always tell you to do a thing just when you were about to do it, so that you got no credit for initiative. Even if you managed to forestall her and got on with a job of your own accord, you would see her making for you, her whole being itching to interfere. 'That's right, Nurse. Change Mrs Larkin's sheets.' She could let nothing pass without comment. Before she had even had time to notice whether you were doing it wrong, she would embark on a voluble exposition of the correct method, which she had already told you ten times, while you listened without being able to concentrate on anything but those amazing false teeth. There was a legend that once, when she was upbraiding a nurse with particular vehemency, the teeth had slipped their moorings and shot into the kitchen sink and down the waste pipe, whence they had to be retrieved with long Cheatle's forceps.

Lawson, who was First Nurse on the ward, prayed that if it happened again she might be there to see it. She said that Sister Ramsbotham was a Hyperthyroid, and certainly she had the characteristic popping eyes, the fine, dry hair, the nervous excitability and restlessness. Perhaps she was taking herself as the norm when she accused me of having Myxoedema, which *Sister Fairchild* translated as thyroid deficiency, characterised by slowness of mind and speech, a defective memory, excess of adipose tissue and abnormally large hands and feet.

It seemed incredible to think that I had been in hospital for more than a year. I had never worked for so long without a break and was beginning to think that here was a concrete example of eternity, but when I was summoned to Matron's office one morning, I thought it must be my holidays at last.

'Well, Nurse,' she said, not looking up as I came in, 'you've been here a year now, haven't you?'

'Thirteen months, Ma'am,' I corrected her respectfully. She ignored this. 'So do you think you're entitled to a red star?' she pursued, looking up. I made modest noises, but she ignored these, too. She was evidently going through a formula. 'A red star is a sign of responsibility, a sign of increased authority,' she went on. 'You should by now be a trustworthy person to have on a ward; you should be able to carry out nursing treatments without supervision, and you should realise your duties in regard to upholding hospital discipline. A red star will give you a certain amount of influence over the Juniors, you know. As you gradually become more Senior, you are expected to help the Juniors and to assist in their training. Do you think I should give you a red star?'

Put like that, an answer obviously was 'No', but I said 'Yes', and smiled obsequiously. The whole thing was a farce, because she had obviously had reports on my work and knew perfectly well whether or not I was worthy to decorate my bosom with the scrap of red felt which she then handed to me with as much condescension as if it were the DSO.

'You can sew this on to your apron for to-morrow,' she said, 'but you must buy some red felt and make the stars for your other aprons.'

Mean old devil, I thought, while verbally licking her boots.

'I trust you to be worthy of it, Nurse,' she said in her thin, unresonant voice. 'Don't let me down.' It was just like being presented with one's hockey colours by the headmistress. I went out, clutching my bit of felt proudly, but sceptical about its ability to transform me suddenly into a miracle of efficiency, on whose every word the respectful Juniors hung.

The trouble was that most of them seemed to know more than I did. The Junior on Grace Annie Sprock had been at a Maternity Home in Bedford, and I was always having to ask her how to do things like putting on a nappy, about which I couldn't very well admit my ignorance to anyone else. It looked so uneducated. It was as bad as not knowing how to herring-bone when I had to pad splints on night duty.

Sissons was always telling long stories about the Maternity Home, where she had had a crush on the Matron. I got sick of hearing what a Saint she was and how she had made the place a home from home, with everyone mealing together to the accompaniment of bright conversation, and afterwards bringing their sewing to her sitting-room to listen to the wireless. Often, on her day off, she would dash back to Bedford for twenty-four soggy hours of bliss. I wondered whether she would come rushing back to Redwood all the time after she left the Queen Adelaide. She would not be put up if she did, that was certain. Matron had once allowed the mother of a very ill nurse to stay in the Nurses' Hostel for a night, as she had travelled from Cumberland and could not find a room. The next day, she informed her crisply that she must find lodgings, and when the mother mentioned the difficulty of finding accommodation, Matron said: 'I shall have to get the Lady Almoner to fix you up.'

'Thank you,' said the offended mother, drawing quite a good mink-marmot coat around her, 'but I don't think I need fall back just yet on Charity.' She spent a whole day tramping the town in search of a room, and was so tired when she visited her daughter in the evening that she cried over her, and the daughter cried too, and worked her temperature up two points.

When I started on the Maternity Ward, there were six babies, varying from cherubs to wizened old men. Besides their mothers, there were half a dozen or so other patients who would either soon fill a cot or were else in for some essentially female complaint. I felt sorry for the latter. It must have been awful to be kept awake at night by the crying of babies, none of which were your own, especially if, like one or two of them, you had just had an operation which ensured that now you never could have a baby.

I was particularly sorry for little Irene Hicks, who had been brought in on the point of death and even now, with nearly a gallon of somebody else's blood in her, was waxy-pale. I remember the afternoon she came in: it was visitors' day, and the ward was full of staring women, their sense of drama deliciously titillated by the livid figure being wheeled into the ward. Outside, stood Irene's mother, bearing something in a pudding basin covered with a bath towel.

Poor Irene had wanted that baby, but had allowed herself to be persuaded by her young man to visit someone that a pal of a fellow he knew swore by. Before I was a nurse, I was not in favour of legal abortion. Now I think that anything would be preferable to some of the ghastly things that are perpetrated outside the law. If women could see what some of their sex have to go through in consequence, nightmare old women in basement flats would lose their trade.

Irene would lie turning her peaky little face from side to side, watching the women with their babies. She wouldn't be able to have one now.

Quite a different proposition was Bella, a Streatham girl, whose only thought was to get back into circulation as soon as possible. 'Me for some fun, as soon as I get out of this dump,' she said, sitting up in bed in a bright yellow jacket that clashed with her hair. 'Little Bella was not quite so clever this time as she thought she was.' She had a deep, rich, unashamed laugh. I once heard her say to Chubby: 'I bet you think I'm an awful naughty girl, you naughty boy.' His ears went magenta; he was highly embarrassed. Mrs Dewey in the next bed listened open-mouthed. She was unable to shut her mouth, because as she only had half a set of false teeth, she wore the one plate halfway between her upper and lower gums. She was eccentric before her baby was born and more so afterwards. One rather trembled for the child. She told me that she had three others – 'and one I buried last March, dear, lovely little coffin, 'e 'ad' – and that one day, when her husband had thrown a cup of tea at her, saucer and all, her eldest son had hurled a fork which had made three holes in his father's chest.

'So what did you do?'

'Well, I picked up the first thing that came to hand to stop Dad going for young Ern. It was an OK Sauce bottle; luckily it was nearly empty, else we should have had a mess.'

I hoped that next time they had a row the first thing that came to hand would not be the baby.

Farren was still Staff Nurse on the ward, somewhat chastened by Sister's constantly-voiced opinion of her but still keeping her end up with canticles. If you asked her a question, she would always finish the phrase before answering, which was maddening if you were in a hurry, which you always were with Fanny Ramsbotham chasing you about like Simon Legree. We all used to look forward to Sister's week-ends off. The ward, though perhaps not so smartly run, took on quite a different, friendly atmosphere, and you had time to chat to the women, without hearing: 'Come along now, Nurse Dickens: if you've got time to gossip, I certainly haven't. Come along now, Nurse, you've got two hours' work to do in one!' We paid for our freedom when she came back, however. She went through the ward and the sluice and bathroom and specimen rooms like a devouring flame, flinging a finger towards neglected corners, banging the lid of the dustbin, picking up an imperfectly cleaned bowl and hurling it into the sink so that enamel chips flew, routing in the cupboard for dirty dusters and flinging them in my face with a savage cry. If any patient in the ward was worse, or a baby had been born dead, Farren was in for trouble, even though the baby might have been dead long before it was born. I once heard Sister say to the Night Nurse: 'Now, Sister, if that woman dies in the night, I shall hold you entirely responsible.' A nice comforting thought for poor Rogers, who was as nervy as a squirrel, to start the night with. After she had finished with us, and sworn as usual that never again would she take a week-end off while such imbecile nurses were on her ward, Sister would roar into the kitchen to have a go at Dora, the stunted little Ward Maid, who didn't care a hang and showed it, which incensed Sister still more. There would be a cacophony of spoons and forks being counted and hurled into drawers. 'Prison's the place for a waster like you in wartime,' she once said to Dora. 'All those crusts are to be buttered and sent into the ward at teatime.'

'Can't do that,' returned Dora stolidly. 'They're hard as old boots. I wouldn't give 'em to me own grandmother, let alone anyone that's not quite the thing.'

'Some of them are quite well enough to eat them,' said Sister. 'I will not have perfectly good food wasted.'

'Eat 'em yourself, then,' said Dora, turning with a shrug to her sink and beginning to run the taps noisily. Sister pretended not to hear. She couldn't treat Dora quite as she treated us. Ward Maids were not so easily come by.

'If you was to give me out a bit of jam now, to put on them crusts,' said Dora, who was fond of anything sweet.

'I have exactly one pot in my cupboard to last two weeks,' said Sister, picking eggcups off the dresser to see if there was dust underneath. 'You people don't seem to have heard of rationing. Sometimes I wonder whether you even know there's a war on – all these drawers want fresh paper, and you'll have to wash the walls down one day this week. A nice surprise you'll get, when the Germans walk in and you find yourself in a concentration camp, which is the place where they put people like you.'

'Wouldn't be much change from this,' said Dora, as Sister swung out to see what she could find wrong with the linen cupboard.

'What d'you think of that?' said Dora, as she and I were click-ing our teeth over the crusts while we prepared the teas. 'Wouldn't give 'em as much as a spoonful of jam. Mean? She wouldn't give you the drippings from 'er nose.'

'I can't think how you answer her back like you do,' I said. 'I wouldn't dare.'

'Oh, well,' said Dora, flinging a mildewy crust into the pig pail, 'I never was one to mince my bones.'

Nurse Lawson was in love. Or thought she was, because when you're in love for the first time, how can you tell whether you are in love? You have nothing to compare it with except a furtive romance with a stable boy when you were fourteen, and it is cer-tainly an advance on that. You have not yet realised that because a man has a sports car and knows what to say to waiters, it does not necessarily mean that he is your soul mate. To Lawson, whose idea of a night out was three ports at the station hotel and a giggly walk back up the hill in the dark with the dispenser's assistant, a man who took her up to London – first class and a taxi at the other end – was heaven indeed. He had been a patient on the pri-vate wards, while she was on night duty there. He came in two days before I got my chicken-pox, a glib man, with eyes like those green marbles that used to come out of the neck of ginger-beer bottles. He was an astute business man and had a finger in many pies: a chain of grocery shops, canteens in some of the factories, one or two small hotels, and even an interest in a local film unit. This enabled him to talk with authority on many subjects, as indeed, he talked about everything, whether he knew anything about it or not. He was not unpresentable, and probably did pos-sess some of the qualities that Lawson saw in him. If he had been born dumb, he might have been quite a nice person.

The first time I met him and Lawson in the bar of the Rowan Arms, I thought I should scream if he said once more: 'I know for a fact.' There was an older man there, the manager of a cigarette factory, who kept producing packets of ten out of concealed pockets, and a friend of his, a soldier who had been out in France. However, this John Davenant evidently knew more about the army and commerce than either of them, and everything that was said he capped with a story which centred round the word 'I'. He aborted any discussion by being unable to keep it impersonal, and the only heed he paid to anyone else's opinion was occasionally to wait without listening until they had finished talking and he could go on undisturbed. The story of the BEF was embodied in the experiences of a boring friend of his at GHQ, and when somebody mentioned Dunkirk, he knew the skipper of what one might have thought to be the only vessel of that conglomerate fry. He also knew a great deal about armament factories, but as there was a large picture of Hitler dressed as an eavesdropping ancestral portrait above his head, he was able to convey a sealed-lips omniscience, without necessarily having any knowledge to back it.

Lawson watched him round-eyed over the top of her glass, and when we went to the 'Ladies', pounced on me with: 'What d'you think of him? Isn't he marvellous? He's awfully good in company, don't you think? He makes me feel terribly ignorant, I hardly dare say a word.' She circled a powder puff over her smooth, freckled face that never succeeded in looking made-up whatever she did to it. 'Oh dear, my hair! D'you like it taken up at the sides like this? John's used to going about with such sophisticated girls, it's really rather a strain. The other day, when we were in Town, we met a girl he told me he once had an affair with. He's had lots, you know, he told me, but I don't mind; I think a man ought to be experienced. Well, this girl – I had been feeling quite smart up to then, I had that blue suit of Barnett's and some decent stockings – but as soon as she came and sat with us, I felt a mess. She was fearfully sophisticated. Red hair and green eyes and a marvellous fox cape – oh dear, my *hair*!' She wrestled to make a bang on top of her head *à la* women's fashion magazines. 'I think I shall go and have a platinum rinse next payday.'

Long after I was in bed and asleep that night, I woke to see the door opening cautiously and to hear the floorboards creaking like mad with Lawson's efforts to be silent.

'Oh, were you asleep? I didn't mean to wake you. I just thought I'd look in in case you were awake. D'you mind if I come in for a moment?' She flopped on to my feet. 'Had a good time?' I asked, yawning and fishing for my hot bottle and finding it cold.

'Marvellous!' She breathed an ecstatic sigh. They had been up to Town – first class. They had been 'up West'. John had taken her to a club – 'Everyone knew him there, I was awfully proud' – and there had been fruit machines and Lawson had had several gin and tonics. They had come back again – still first class – and John had half a bottle of whisky in his coat pocket and had tipped the guard to lock their carriage. What possible answer could there be to his proposal?

'I'm so happy,' she purred, picking feathers out of my eiderdown. 'Don't you think I'm terribly lucky? You do like him, don't you?'

I tried to conceal my dismay with suitable enthusiasm. Lawson was sweet and naïve and clean. She would have made somebody a marvellous wife. She could have been deeply and faithfully in love.

'When are you going to be married?'

'As soon as we can. John's got to go up North and he wants me to go with him. He's going to get a special licence. It's awfully difficult to get nowadays, I believe, but he knows a man who'll wangle it for him. He knows lots of people. Gosh, to think of getting out of this foul hole! I can't think how I've stuck it for two years.'

'Still, in a way, it seems a waste—'

'Oh, no, I'd never have passed my Finals in any case – not that I really wanted to. It would be ghastly to be a Staff Nurse, and think of being a Sister! I was always terrified of becoming like these frightful women – think, one might even turn out like Fanny Ramsbotham. Oh, no, apart from John being so marvellous, it's a merciful escape!'

Escape. So many nurses marry the first men who ask them, because they have had neither the time nor the opportunity to meet anyone else or to realise that life holds other alternatives besides hospital and marriage. They are thrilled to escape from a monotony which they know only too well into something of which they know nothing and therefore expect a great deal.

Lawson had a grand time telling everybody and giving in her notice to Matron, and buying clothes and showing people her ring and introducing John to people as 'My Fiancé', and talking, talking about him in a boastful but legitimate way. After all, he was a man, and quite a personable one at that, even if he was a crashing bore. People swanked about the runtiest of boy friends so that anyone who landed a real man was entitled to boast.

Lawson lived in a whirl of excitement that left her no time for doubts and eventually got married at St Anne's Church, in a pale blue dress and coat and a small round hat, to John in a brown pin stripe suit with a double-breasted waistcoat, making the responses very loudly, while hers were barely a murmur. Afterwards, I went to the reception with five or six other nurses who had managed to get the morning off, and we all trooped in, branded as nurses by our awkward hands, red from the early morning's scrubbing, our air of having borrowed bits and pieces of clothes, which we had, and the alacrity with which we attacked the buffet, as if we hadn't tasted decent food for weeks, which we had not. Lawson's mother and father were there, looking rather baffled, Lawson was stammering with pride, and John took the halfhearted cries of 'Speech!' to mean that people really wanted him to speak and held forth pompously for several minutes, while everyone stood round interjecting polite 'Ha-has' and 'Hear-hears' and wishing that he would stop so that they could get on with the drinking.

I seemed to be dogged by spouters. To replace Lawson on the ward, we had a wide-hipped girl called Jobling, who called every one 'Kid' and babbled on like a moorland stream about anything except what she happened to be doing at the moment. I wondered that Sister did not treat Jobling to her: 'If you've got time to gossip, I certainly haven't' line, but apparently Jobling was popular because she was good with the babies, which none of the rest of us were, except Sissons, who didn't count, because she was the Junior and mere. I suppose the babies appreciated Jobling's maternal shape, anyway, they behaved much better with her than with us, and we were constantly treated to: 'Look at little Nurse Jobling there. There's a girl who knows how to bring up a baby's wind.' Anyone whom she liked was always 'little'. I dare say a psychoanalyst would explain this as some sort of inhibition about her own size. Mountainous Mrs West, who had fulfilled Sister's prophecy by producing twins, was always 'little Mrs West', and a tall VAD who came three times a week and bathed the babies with the skill of manifold personal experience and had a brother who was a Baronet, was 'the little VAD'. I liked the days when Mrs Finney came. It was refreshing to work with someone who had other things to talk about except shop and boy friends and uninteresting family histories. As she was not on the payroll, she was in a position to stand up to Sister. If she did not agree with something she was told to do, she would argue it, and while at first we stood with bated breath expecting to see her crushed like a beetle, I soon realised that Sister responded better to being answered back than to having her boots licked. However, while appreciating that the best way to deal with a bully is to bully back, I never quite had the nerve.

Looking back, I could remember a time when I might have

been more rebellious and less blindly acquiescent. Hospital life does alter your character. It dims any personality you might have once possessed. Through working to routine and never to initiative, your brain becomes like a car with a bad pick-up. It ticks over fast enough to cope with what is required of it, but its acceleration deteriorates until it is almost impossible to rev it up sufficiently to keep pace with anyone not similarly affected. One did not notice this in the hospital, where the conversation was unambitious and the humour unsubtle and chiefly lavatorial, but the moment you went among outside people, you felt dull and inadequate. I had never been to the Fellowes' house again for this reason. The nearest I got to them was occasional meetings with the down-trodden relation, with whom, as she told me that the 'Four Winds' set gave her an inferiority complex, I felt a certain bond.

It was a different matter going to Mrs Finney's. She had a dear little slice of a house in the arty corner of the slums, with a red door and window boxes and half a dozen small dogs to whom she was a slave. If I was fed up, I could always go there and get the hospital out of my system by talking about it, and if she was bored, she never showed it. She understood what it was like to be always tired, and sometimes, when I arrived yawning to dinner, she would put me to bed for an hour or two and then wake me with drink and food, and we would sit over the fire on a sofa that was almost as big as the entire drawing-room, and pick everyone at the hospital to pieces, an occupation of which it took a long time to tire.

Once, at her house, I met Sir Curtis Rowntree and his wife. They were charming, and it seemed funny to think that only that morning I had been calling him 'Sir' and scuttling out of his way, and that he had thrown a pair of rubber gloves at me because I had put them away wet and he couldn't get his hand into them. I reminded him of this, and as it seemed to go down well, I told him what a to-do his coming always created and how Sister always careered round practically measuring the set of his patients' counterpanes with a micrometer – 'Because Sir Curtis is so particular about these things. He always notices whether a bed is correctly made.' He promised that he would try and remember to notice next time.

The following morning, he came along to see a new patient, and Sister, standing by the bed like a duenna, snapped her fingers at me to bring screens.

When I brought them, Sir Curtis smiled the beautiful curved smile that relaxed the sardonic lines of his face and said: 'Good morning, Nurse. How are you?' – just, as old Sow would say, as if I had been anybody. Sister's eyebrows shot into her hair, I went red and mumbled, and Sir Curtis said: 'I've brought you that book we were talking about,' and fished it out of his bag. Sister's teeth were flashing at me like a heliograph and I mumbled again and slunk away, tripping over a tear in the screen and enabling Sister to say: 'Why wasn't this screen cover changed this morning? You see, Sir Curtis, what a dirty lazy lot of nurses I have to put up with. Don't you think it's a disgrace the way the modern girl goes about her work? Work! They don't know the meaning of the word. Get away and get on with your babies, Nurse. They should have been put up ages ago. You don't seem to—' But I had gone, so that if Sir Curtis wanted to agree with her for the sake of peace and quiet, he could.

Later, when I went into the medicine room for Sister to give me Mrs James's post-operation morphia, she paused, with the bottle in her hand, and said incredulously: 'Do you *know* Sir Curtis, Nurse? I mean, do you know him *socially?*'

'Yes, I do, as a matter of fact.' I handed her the syringe.

'*How* do you know him?' The idea seemed fantastic to her. A scullery maid might as well have claimed acquaintance with a duke.

'Well, I met him out at dinner,' I said sullenly. 'I'm going to a cocktail party at his house next week,' I added, knowing that this would infuriate her.

'Oh!' She jabbed the hypodermic needle viciously into the rubber top of the bottle. 'There, six minims – one sixth. Check this, please.' I checked the level of the liquid in the syringe. Her eyebrows were in her hair again; she was looking at me unbelievingly. 'Do you know the Rowntrees *well?*' she persisted. She couldn't get over it.

'Yes, quite well,' I lied.

'How strange,' she said rudely, and turned to lock the morphia in the drug cupboard.

When one of the first remarks of a new patient is: 'Now, I don't want to be any trouble,' you can bet your shirt they are going to be more trouble than anyone else in the ward. Mrs Drucker said it when she was brought in, pale but brave, to have her second baby. She had had her first in a nursing home, but this time, patriotically, she had decided for economy's sake to face the horrors of a general ward. She took great care to let us know that she was used to better things. How different it had all been when she had her Rosemary – but we were to make no difference for her – absolutely no difference at all. She wanted to be treated just the same as all these brave women, she said, and then proceeded to take umbrage because she was.

It wasn't that she complained or objected or made a fuss outright. She annoyed in a much more subtle way. If she wanted anything, she would not ask for it until she could say, with a brave little deprecating laugh: 'I wanted so-and-so two hours ago, but you looked so busy, I didn't like to ask.' Perhaps I forgot that she didn't take sugar in her tea, and instead of asking for another cup, she would drink it, so that she could say, preferably within earshot of Sister: 'I managed to get it down, Nurse. I know how easy it is to forget all our little fancies when you've got so much to think about, but it does seem a waste with sugar rationed, doesn't it?' If she could put you in the wrong in front of Sister, her day was made.

Her baby was not expected for another two days. 'It'll probably be late,' she said, with that irritating little laugh. 'Anyway, whenever it comes, I know I shall have a dreadful time; I went through torture with my Rosemary. I'm sure I don't know how many stitches I had. I dare say I shall cry out, Nurse, but you mustn't take any notice. I shall try not to, but sometimes these things are bigger than oneself, aren't they?' To hear her talk, you would think that nobody had ever had a difficult birth before, and after the baby came – a disgruntled, alcoholic-looking old man – nobody, as far as she was concerned, had ever had a baby before. This sentiment is common to all mothers, but whereas with others it is due to glorious pride, with her it was self-pity.

As she had a very easy time, she did not have to have any anaesthetic until the last moment, so that this gave her a great opportunity to gasp, in between pains, how wonderful they had been at the nursing home and had given her a very special sort of dope right at the beginning, but, of course, she realised that when one was in hospital one naturally couldn't expect any sort of extras, and she wanted to be treated exactly the same as the other mothers. 'Oh, dear – oh, Nurse – oh, the pain's starting again. I'm trying to bear it, but I've always been more susceptible to pain than other people. Oh, Nurse, I can't – I shan't scream – Oh!' – a piercing yell – 'Oh, d'you think Mr Vavasour will come soon? I'm sure he knows best, but he does seem to be leaving it rather late, doesn't he?'

'Don't worry,' I said, hating myself for not being able to feel sympathetic, 'you're not going to have it for hours yet.'

'Oh, Nurse, I'm sure you're wrong. Not that I question you for one moment, but if you could just go and ask Sister – no, no, don't leave me. I think the pain is going to start again at any minute. Let me hold your hand. I don't want to make any noise or disturb anybody. I don't want to be any bother to you, Nurse.'

Her screams were the most piercing ever heard in that Labour Ward, even from Mrs Morgan, who never lived to tell the tale of her terrible suffering. Rogers said that she kept everyone awake all night and then got one of the House Surgeons out of bed because she declared she was starting a haemorrhage. 'But don't worry about me. I knew something like this would happen.'

Her soldier husband came a few days later to see the baby and tell her what a brave little woman she was. He looked fresh and healthy, and was probably benefiting by his life away from her. I heard her say to him: 'Now, whatever you do, you're not to worry. I dare say it's silly of me to be nervous, but you know I can't help it. I seem to sense these things. I dare say I shall be quite all right, after all, and as for Baby's little squint, perhaps I *am* imagining it. Anyway, don't worry, and don't feel you've got to write to me if you don't feel like it. I shall understand perfectly that you've got so many other things to think about. After all, Baby and I can't expect to come first with you all the time, can we?' I was glad to see that Sister collared him as he was leaving and told him that his wife was the healthiest mother in the ward and would be out as soon as we could get rid of her.

Nearly all babies have some charm, but Master Drucker managed to avoid it. He would not cry in chorus with the others, but would wait until they had quietened down, so that he could raise his voice and start them all off again. No one would have minded his mother thinking him beautiful if she had kept her opinion a bit more to herself. When you went to fetch him from his feed, in a hurry, probably, to get him back to his cot and get on with something which Sister said you should have done hours ago, Mrs Drucker would keep you hanging about while she pointed out the monstrosity's attributes, and the only way to make her give him up was to say: 'Oh, *let* me hold him, the darling,' as if it were the world's greatest treat. Although it was hard on the mothers, it was an understandable rule of the ward that, for both their sakes, they could only have the babies with them at feed times. Mrs Drucker was always pleading to have baby Philip in bed with her. 'I like to feel him near me,' she said, adding 'I'm funny like that,' which was a remark she was fond of appending to the most ordinary inclinations. She was what the Germans call '*Ich bin so*'. She was the sort of person who says: 'Of course, I'm frightfully interested in people. I find them fascinating' – which usually means that the speaker's interest is confined almost wholly to the fascination of herself. 'Of course,' Mrs Drucker once said to me, 'I have a horror of war.' Everyone else loved it, of course.

Mrs Drucker's conviction that she was the only woman ever to give birth was belied by the spate of maternity work that flooded our ward that autumn. They say that war always increases the birth-rate – it's a form of compensation. They say that, for the same reason, more boys than girls are born in wartime. I don't know. They say a lot of things. They also say that a baby cries for exercise. They evidently have never been on a maternity ward. It cries to annoy, like the Duchess's baby. Otherwise, why should it stop when you pick it up and start again when you put it back in its cot? It could exercise itself just as well in your arms.

We were so busy that Sister kept going to Matron's office and insisting that she should be given another nurse. She was always having rows with the authorities, chiefly as a vent for her energy, and would be quite capable of storming a board meeting if it was the only way of getting a new clothes-line for the nappies. As she was promised an extra nurse, she thought she had won this fight, and then she was not so sure, because all she got was Gunter.

When I first came to the hospital, Gunter had seemed to know a lot in a silent way, but having worked with her, I saw that she was incapable of putting it to practical use. What she had learned at her Northern hospital was about as far as she could go. After more than a year at the Queen Adelaide, she was as awkward as if it were her first week. It may have been because she was slightly deaf. She was always hearing things wrong, and, with a bland smile, doing what she thought she had been told to do and causing Sister Ramsbotham to speak of her without lowering her voice as 'that fool'. She took a passionate dislike to Gunter from the moment that she set foot in the ward, trod on some spilt liquid paraffin and trod it all over the floor, which made her contempt for me affectionate esteem by comparison.

Perhaps the east wind got on her liver. I was often tempted to send her anonymously a box of Beecham's pills, for she was absolutely impossible these days – to the patients as well as to us. She was even occasionally rude to Jobling, who was so surprised that she talked endlessly about it, as if it had never happened to anyone else. 'Listen, kid, she said to me, she said: "I don't know why you go on, Nurse. You'll never be a nurse."'

'That's nothing,' I said, 'I get that every day.'

'Yes, but listen, kid, she said it to *me*. So I said to her, I said . . . and she said to me, she said . . . I was absolutely frosted, I can tell you – Oh, and what d'you think, kid? Who d'you think asked me to go out to tea with him on Saturday? Well, I was surprised, I said "Whatever next?" I said, and listen, kid, I must tell you what he said—'

'Who?' I and the woman whose bed we were making yawned simultaneously.

'Who d'you think, kid? Chubby, of all people! I'd no idea – well, I mean he used to come down and yarn when I was on night duty' – I could imagine who had done most of the yarning – 'You know, kid, I really do believe he's quite keen. Tee-hee-hee—' Her giggle really did sound like that. Poor little Chubby. He would be rather overlaid.

I was so tired these days. The increase of work and Sister's incessant and noisy nagging were enough to damp the most selfless enthusiasm, which mine certainly was not. I used to snap at any patient who asked me to do something which would delay me for a moment, and I never had the energy to go out at night. I tried to work for the pending exam, but I so constantly fell asleep over the book, and even in lectures, that I saw little hope of passing.

Gunter had become more fumble-fisted than ever under Sister's scorn, Sissons was monosyllabic and couldn't be bothered these days to tell me things I wanted to know, Farren behaved as if she were a candidate for canonisation and bore any adversity with a lift of her eyes to heaven, as if to say: 'Don't miss this, God. Chalk me up another pip on martyrdom.'

Even the patients that Sister liked felt the repercussions of her autocracy in our work. A hospital ward can be such a friendly, cheerful place, but this was a place of nervous, scudding feet, of jumps and starts and whispers, and conversation that broke out with a pent-up rush when Sister went to dinner and ceased as suddenly at the sound of her feet on the corridor linoleum. Even the babies were subdued when the east wind blew.

We began to have fears for her sanity when the appalling news came that an inventory was to be taken. Every single movable thing on the ward was to be counted by Matron; every bit of linen, every bowl, every kitchen utensil, every last hot-water bottle had got to be collected together so that Matron could view it all with the least possible inconvenience to herself and the greatest to us. I cannot convey the work that this implied, but anyone who has moved from a twelve-room house in which they have lived for twenty years into a bungalow with no cupboards will have a faint idea if they double that and add twelve women and eight babies who normally made overtime work.

It was over at last. Matron had checked everything with a list as long as her arm, and we had been on the ward until after ten, putting everything back.

At last we went to ask if we might go off duty. 'Quite finished?' said Sister, who was writing the report, which most Sisters wrote three hours earlier so as to get out of the Night Nurses' way, but with Sister Ramsbotham the opposite desire prevailed.

'Everything's done,' we said, with tired pride, but instead of commendation, all we got was a tirade about the condition of the mackintosh sheets which Matron had said were a disgrace both to the hospital and the nursing profession, and how Sister was expected to run the ward with a lot of vicious imbeciles – 'And Nurse,' exposing her orange gums at me, 'You've let me down. Oh, how could you let me down like that? Matron was disgusted.'

'But, Sister, I – what have I—?'

She pointed to my wrist. 'How could you do it, Nurse, I simply don't know. Wearing a watch in uniform. No!' She held up her hand. 'There's simply no excuse. If you have been too stupid to learn the hospital rules in the time you have been here, there's not much hope for you. I can't see why you go on, really I can't.'

Nor could I. I was too tired to think it funny, but there I was, back on the job at seven the next morning, disliking more than ever the cheesey shine of Gunter's face and the equine back view of Jobling. It was visitors' day, which Sister always hated, except that it gave her a few more people on whom to sublimate her dictatorial instincts. Mrs James's mother was foolish enough to take down Mrs James's chart and study it in full view of Sister, sitting at the desk writing out medical 'Cerstificates'.

When Sister went to tea, murmurs broke out from all sides. 'It's not right' ... 'The way she spoke to her. I wouldn't speak like that to a dog' ... 'Talk about old man 'Itler' ... 'Streuth, you can't call your soul your own.' Even Dora came in from the kitchen and egged the women on. Mrs James was in tears. Of course, we had to stand up for Sister and try to appease them by telling them what a marvellous nurse she was. She was, technically; it was her manner, as governesses say. 'She may have pulled me through me operation,' said Mrs Fisher, 'but streuth! I'm not sure I wouldn't be better off pushing up the daisies, after all. It sours the food in me when I see how she treats you girls. I 'eave, honest I do.'

Farren told Mrs James that these things were sent to try us, and Mrs James cried harder than ever. When Sister came back, she told her that if she didn't stop she would harm her milk and probably make baby James gastric for life. The murmurs faded, of course, as soon as she was back in the ward, but there was still an uneasy, resentful atmosphere. I wished Sister would say or do just one thing that would destroy the antagonism. The women could be so easily swung round to friendliness. They had no real conviction of antipathy, any more than workers would have if it wasn't for Trade Unions.

It was Gunter who achieved it in the end, through sheer puerility. She had the methylated spirit lamp alight in the test room, and because she wanted to fill it up with methylated, she uncorked the bottle and tried to pour it in without blowing out the flame. I was in the sluice opposite, having a lecture from Sister about the glycothymoline stains on the toothmugs, when we suddenly heard a kind of aboriginal yelp and, turning with one accord, saw that what had been Gunter was now a sheet of blue flame. For a split second, Sister's eyes met mine, and I saw my horror mirrored in them. Intimacy leaped between us, and then, before I had time to think, she had hurled herself across the passage and borne Gunter heavily to the ground.

Gunter somehow escaped with only superficial burns and a wordless dread of fire that made her incapable of lighting the gas stove, but Sister was not so lucky. She had bad face and hand burns and had to go into one of the private rooms for two weeks. She was the heroine of the hour. Everyone was talking about her and either withdrawing their previous opinion or saying that they had known her true worth all along. There was even a small paragraph about her in the local paper: 'SISTER RISKS LIFE TO SAVE NURSE.' The women on Grace Annie Sprock were wild with excitement and could not wait until she came back so that they could show her what they thought of her. All their animosity was forgotten. They classed her with people like the Queen and Gracie Fields, and never tired of talking about what they had said to themselves when they smelt burning and heard a crash, or how they saw the heroine borne from the ward by two House Surgeons. They would talk about it for years.

On the day that she was due to come back, we laboured to make the ward spruce. All the women had clean nightdresses and the babies clean shawls and cot covers. She was a different person in our eyes. I felt that in that one instantaneous flash in intimacy in the sluice, I had seen what sort of a person she really was. I was looking forward to working with her now, and hoped I would not be moved off the ward.

It was eight o'clock. From round the corner of the corridor we heard the familiar speeding footsteps, so different now that we were waiting for them with a welcome instead of anathema. As she turned the corner and Sissons pulled open the glass swing doors, the women struck up *For she's a jolly good fellow* and Mrs James stepped forward with a large bunch of flowers.

Sister swept into the ward. There was a large piece of sticking-plaster on one cheek and she had no eyebrows. 'Stop that noise this instant,' she said. 'I will not have my ward turned into Bedlam. Mrs James – back into bed at once.'

The song withered and died. From the unseeing patients beyond the balcony doors came the ghost of the refrain: 'And so say all of us.'

With malevolent inevitability, the exam drew near, and with it came the news that as Matron was tired of people failing, anyone who did not pass would be thrown out. We were in too much of a state to realise that she would be unlikely to do this in wartime, and our 'What is a cell?' took on a feverish note. 'What *is* a cell?' One had known once, but had ousted the knowledge with so many other fragments since.

Sister Tutor was not much help. She despaired of us, she said, and spent most of our valuable revision time telling us that we were paying now for the slackness earlier on about which she had warned us. Before she came to Redwood, she had been teaching in a hospital in Wales, and such time as she did not take up in disparaging us was spent in eulogising the Welsh nurses. 'My girls could roll up a bandage twice as quick as you,' or 'My girls wouldn't have asked a question like that,' when Kelly, with her brain in a whirl, announced that the sternum was the bone on which you sat.

I prepared my parents for my probable return home and almost ordered myself a pair of landgirl breeches. Two days before the exam, I felt like ordering the jersey as well, because I was told that while Rogers was on holiday I had got to go on night duty on Grace Annie Sprock.

Being on day duty there, one would have thought that the babies exhausted their lung power in the daytime. Being on night duty, one didn't see how they had the energy to carry on during the day. Their crying and my futile efforts to quiet them was the background pattern of all my nights, whatever else was going on. Sometimes, when a baby was being born and I was rushing round in stricken circles, I would not hear them for hours on end, and when it was all over and one more potential taxpayer lay mouthing in its cot and the mother was having her cup of tea, I would suddenly realise that the other babies had been crying solidly all the time. Presently, Sweet Fanny Adams would come down and tell me that I was the only night nurse on Maternity so signally lacking in lullaby qualities.

The women would not have slept well anyway, because we had

233

several nights of air raids. I felt that I did not much care if a bomb did come through the roof. It would at least stop the babies crying, and it might silence Miss Carmichael. At first, I couldn't fathom the clanking and jangling that always followed hard upon the last dying wail of the 'Alert'. Then I traced it to Miss Carmichael and found that she was sitting bolt upright, with a hairnet well down over her forehead, telling her beads. She had some sort of idea that the whole hospital might collapse round her bed and it be left intact, so long as she was at this pious occupation. It reminded me of my father's story of how when he was a little boy he used to clutch the bedrail while he was saying his prayers in case he should be transported to heaven.

There was no question of doing any more swotting. I slept like the dead all day and although I took a text-book to the ward with me at night, I never had a chance to open it. It was all I could do to wangle a quarter of an hour in which to sit down and write my report.

The exam was at eleven o'clock, so that there was no time to snatch a little sleep beforehand. I had to go to it with all the hours of the night piled on top of my brain. Everyone had on their starchiest aprons and had done their hair as uncompromisingly as possible, which apparently was what went down well with the examiner. Mine was done in the unsuccessful bun to which I had had to resort since Matron had sent for me and told me I must either cut my hair or leave the hospital. We were only having the oral exam to-day. The written paper was a treat in store for to-morrow. We all sat in a row of chairs in the passage outside the room in which the torture was to be enacted. Toots came along and looked us over without enthusiasm and said: 'Good luck' as if she were convinced that only that could get us through. One or two idiots started a last-minute frenzied discussion about cartilage, but for the most part we sat numb and hopeless. Each name called out was like a knell. We went in at half-hourly intervals, and the ones who had finished went out by a different door, so that we had no chance of seeing them. It would have been equally encouraging to hear from a nurse coming out either that the ordeal had been a pleasant surprise, or that she had done so badly that no one could do worse. At last I was sitting next to the door. My brain had no medical knowledge in it. It had nothing in it at all, I discovered when I tried to think about something – anything to shake myself out of this vacancy. When my name was called, I found that my left leg had gone to sleep, and I had to stumble into the room like a cripple and endure agony when it came to during the interview, like the Spartan boy with the fox inside his jacket.

Our lecture room looked strange without the desks and chairs. There were just two tables in opposite corners, behind which sat two terrifying women in navy blue coats and skirts, writing busily and seemingly unaware of my one-legged presence. The fattest one looked up. Surprise! She looked quite kind, like the sort of cook who would open the oven door and give you a red-hot scone.

'Over there first, Nurse,' she said, pointing with a pencil, and I limped over to the corner where sat the thin one, who if she had been a cook would not have given you so much as a potato peeling.

She had a face like granite, unmoving but irregular, as if the sculptor's chisel had slipped here and there. Her mouth opened crookedly half an inch, and she shot a few words at one like pebbles.

'What do you know of Personal Hygiene?' I was entirely unprepared for this. I could have told her about sewers, ventilation, even the endearing habits of the bed-bug, but – What do you know of Personal Hygiene! I could only think of the advertisements.

This was the point when my foot began to come to. I can't

remember what I said; I blurted out a few banalities and managed to save myself from bringing in 'Often a bridesmaid, never a bride.' Her face gave no sign that she either approved or deprecated the secrets of my toilet as embodied in my halting answers. When I stopped, she said: 'Anything more?' so that I wondered whether I had missed something out or whether this was a ruse to get me worried. My foot had reached the pinnacle of its agony and was now subsiding into the ever-increasing bliss of relief. The stone woman wrote something down, and attacked with relish the subject of sewage farms, which I welcomed with equal relish as being one of the few things I knew. Still no sign, however, as to whether my knowledge of sludge impressed her, and I crossed the floor to the kind woman with relief. If the other one had been disconcertingly hard, this one was disconcertingly kind. She was so kind that if you hesitated for a moment she began to prompt before you had a chance to say the stuff. I only hoped that she would confuse her knowledge with mine and get the impression that I had imparted most of it. 'Yes, yes,' she kept purring. 'Now tell me, what would you do in a case of shock?' I took a deep breath. I could answer this; I had had enough practical experience of it. Before I got farther than 'Well, you keep the patient warm' – remembering too late Sister Tutor's injunction not to start every answer with 'Well' – the old cook had started like the prompter in a Chinese play, who says every word half a second before the actors. I followed her along, like someone trying to race the Vicar with the prayers in church, and we both finished level on blood transfusion. 'Very good, dear,' she smiled. I think she thought that she had been following me.

That night I took all my notebooks on to the ward, determined that the mothers and babies could stew in their own juice for an hour or so while I put in some solid revising. Often enough, I had bemoaned my life, had said that I lived only for the end of the war to get me out of this prison, but now that my existence there was threatened, I did not want to leave, although recently I had been turning over the idea. Mr Bevin's continual appeals to women had reminded me uneasily that his need was perhaps the most urgent of all. And how satisfying to feel that one had played a part, however infinitesimal, in the manufacture of a tank or an aeroplane. The Germans whom it killed would be almost a personal bag.

Somebody had to nurse, though. Yes, but somebody had to make munitions – and quickly. Wars go so fast these days. In the Hundred Years' War nobody put in overtime on cannon-balls and crossbows. They probably knocked them up at their leisure, but nowadays a country could be overrun before it had time to turn round. Ought one to do something about it?

My conscience gave a little whistle and said: 'Honestly now, are you restless because you want to kill a German or because you are getting fed up with Redwood?'

'A bit of each, I suppose.' Redwood did irk me occasionally. I loved the work, but not its appurtenances. Nursing was fascinating and in a way fulfilling, but the life which it entailed was unnecessarily tiresome. And yet, when one stripped away all the pettinesses and tyrannies and discomforts and looked at the essence of the hospital and the core of its purpose, one saw that it had power to hold and bonds which it would be hard to break without regrets.

Sister greeted me with: 'Come along now, Nurse. Two minutes late and you've got a busy night in front of you. Mrs Arthur is in labour.' My heart sank and I laid my notebooks on the desk with a gesture of farewell. If only I could get an obstetric question tomorrow, I should be all right.

Mr Ripley and Fanny Adams and I fought all night for that baby. At about two o'clock, when it definitely decided to live, the mother decided to die. We thwarted her, however, and in the morning there they were, grey and unsubstantial both of them, but definitely there and likely to stay. I looked forward to telling Sister Ramsbotham of our achievement. Not that she would believe what a fight we had had. She expected everybody to be immortal, and however ill they were, was far more surprised if they died than if they lived, which I suppose was the right spirit.

'How did you get on yesterday?' she asked surprisingly, when I had given the report. I made some sort of deprecating answer.

'Sister Tutor told me that she thought everyone had passed,' she said. 'Good luck for to-day.' What was wrong with the woman? Everything seemed to be conspiring to show me that it was desirable to pass the exam and stay.

Thinking about this, and feeling increasingly tired as the sustaining excitement of the night evaporated, I decided that it indicated that the paper was going to floor me. If everyone had died in the night and Sister had been so unfair that I had decided to join something with a Union, I should have passed with honours.

Perhaps I tried too hard. I wrote so much that I had not time to read through it and delete the rubbish. The questions looked all right at first sight and one dashed ahead to put down every bit of knowledge connected, however remotely, with the subject, only to find, when it was too late to do anything about it, that the question had a catch or a tricky codicil, obviously intended to test the alertness of the candidates.

When it was over, I did not feel equal to the frenzied comparisons and post-mortems that broke out immediately we got into the corridor, so, as I was too tired to go to bed, I went out alone to have some coffee. Of course, Mrs Fellowes's sister had to be in the Blue Lady in a more irritating hat than ever. It looked as though she had gone to bed in it. I pretended not to see her, but she came over to me, carrying her cup of coffee and spilling most of it over the Blue Lady's coconut matting.

I let her talk. I felt terse and depressed. She was wearing a dreadful gunmetal skirt, a green jacket trimmed with a chewed bit of fur, and the shaming hat. She had a drop on the end of her nose and was very excited because she had read a story which I had written months ago to while away the night on Secker Ward. It had gone the rounds and finally come to rest in a woman's magazine, glamorously illustrated and with the heroine's name changed to Hyacinth.

'Such a lovely little tale,' she maundered, 'the doctor falling for the nurse – I don't know how you thought of it. You ought to write a book about Hospital, dear. It's such wonderful work. I'm sure I would give anything to be able to follow such a noble calling.' In her mind, I could see the etherealised figures, people like Hyacinth, flitting about in spotless aprons, shaking pillows, smoothing brows and doing nothing more familiar to the patient than feeling his pulse. Sadistically, I tried to replace these figures with others, jaded, discouraged and dragooned, sickeningly familiar with dawn and the less attractive functions of the human body.

'But those dear little babies,' she said pleadingly. 'You're still on the Maternity Ward, aren't you? The miracle of childbirth—'

I was thinking about the exam and remembering one thing after another that I had forgotten. Venting my dejection on her, I told her about the miracle of childbirth, as specifically as I could with a woman in a mauve hat sitting at the next table drinking in every word.

Mrs Fellowes's sister clung bravely to her convictions. 'No, no,' she said, shaking her head so that I was terrified the drop was going to fly off into my coffee. 'You mustn't think of it like that. It's so noble ... healing the sick ... Florence Nightingale ... the miracle of birth and death ... Yes, yes. You really should put it all into a book.'

'I don't get the time,' I said, not feeling inclined to tell her about the tentative schemes which I had already sketched at the back of my hygiene book and the notes scribbled on the backs of old charts, Path Lab reports and slips of Litmus paper when an idea struck me in the middle of the day.

'Ah yes, that's the trouble, of course,' she said. 'You know, I always say I would write a book myself if I had the time. I've thought of a very good title for it too: "The Travels of a Civil Engineer's Wife."' As I had no idea that she had been married, nor that her travels had been much more extensive than from Redwood to the Army and Navy Stores this revealed her in a new light, even if it did not promise very enthralling reading.

Until the examination results were announced, I joined in the common worrying and the repeated assurances which answered the same purpose of touching wood: 'My dear, I *know* I haven't passed.' It was the bleak time of year between invigorating winter and freshening spring, when everyone feels below par. Hair will not go right and skins bear witness to too much fugging and too little fresh air. I was thankful to be moved from the maelstrom of Grace Annie Sprock.

I was back on Privates again and now I was increasingly beset by doubts. It seemed so unbearably futile to be pulling curtains backwards and forwards for neurotic women, asking them how they had slept and whether they fancied jelly or tinned peaches for lunch. In the end, it was Sarah P. who decided me.

One morning, with the examination results still unknown, I went to Matron for a sleeping-out pass.

'Oh – Nurse,' she said dryly as I was feeling behind me for the doorhandle, 'I hear that you wrote a magazine story about Hospital.' She stretched her neck with that movement she had, like a chicken swallowing, and jutted her sharp chin: 'Is that true?'

Yes, Ma'am.' Heaven forbid that she had read *Hyacinth*.

'Well, kindly, Nurse, never do such a thing again.'

'Why not?' I asked, red in the face with all the things I wanted to say and didn't dare.

'Apart from being an unforgivable breach of etiquette, you only make yourself extremely ridiculous. So please don't try to write any more foolishness about what you see here. If you do, I shall certainly not keep you. Now you may go back to your work.'

That settled it. I had to write the book now, and if she didn't want me, I would go to someone who did. Having dismissed me, she was busy with the lists on her desk again and I cleared my throat and announced in a voice which came out several keys higher than I intended: 'Please Ma'am, I should like to give in my notice.'

The head shot up, the glasses flashed coldly, and the thin lips ejected an impatient, toneless 'Why?'

'Please, Ma'am,' I said, 'I want to go and make a tank.'

VIRAGO MODERN CLASSICS

The first Virago Modern Classic, *Frost in May* by Antonia White, was published in 1978. It launched a list dedicated to the celebration of women writers and to the rediscovery and reprinting of their works. Its aim was, and is, to demonstrate the existence of a female tradition in literature, and to broaden the sometimes narrow definition of a 'classic'. Published with new introductions by some of today's best writers, the books are chosen for many reasons: they may be great works of literature; they may be wonderful period pieces; they may reveal particular aspects of women's lives; they may be classics of comedy, storytelling, letter-writing or autobiography.

'The Virago Modern Classics list contains some of the greatest fiction and non-fiction of the modern age, by authors whose lives were frequently as significant as their writing. Still captivating, still memorable, still utterly essential reading' **SARAH WATERS**

'The Virago Modern Classics list is wonderful. It's quite simply one of the best and most essential things that has happened in publishing in our time. I hate to think where we'd be without it' **ALI SMITH**

'The Virago Modern Classics have reshaped literary history and enriched the reading of us all. No library is complete without them' **MARGARET DRABBLE**

'The writers are formidable, the production handsome. The whole enterprise is thoroughly grand' **LOUISE ERDRICH**

'Good news for everyone writing and reading today'
HILARY MANTEL